ENCYCLOPAEDIA OF
INDIA, PAKISTAN AND BANGLADESH

ENCYCLOPAEDIA OF INDIA, PAKISTAN AND BANGLADESH

(In 9 Volumes)

(Volume 7)

OM GUPTA

ISHA

ISHA BOOKS

Delhi-110033

Encyclopaedia of India, Pakistan and Bangladesh
(In 9 Volumes)

ISBN : 81-8205-389-7 (Set)
ISBN : 81-8205-396-X (Vol. 7)

Rs. 6300 (Set)

Published in 2006 in India by
Isha Books
D-43, Prithviraj Road,
Adarsh Nagar, Delhi - 110033
e-mail : ishabooks@hotmail.com

Laser Typesetting : Vinayak Printers, Delhi
Printed at : Salasar Imaging Systam, Delhi

Preface

According to Oxford dictionary Encyclopaedia is a book or aset of books that gives information on many subjects or many aspect of one subject. This encyclopaedia does that on India, Pakistan and Bangladesh. It is the first work of its kind. There have been anthologies on India but there is no compendium of information in an alphabetical order. Even Britannica could go as far as four-volume encyclopaedia on Indian history.

Encyclopaedia is an extension of a dictionary. The latter gives you meanings of words while the former gives facts about people, places and events. No one can claim to compile all the facts and that of a sub-continent called India. But then it is the prerogative of the editor to pick up his entries that he considers would be useful to his reader. Generally we soon find our comfort levels in a language. And rarely consults a dictionary and lesser an encyclopaedia. But those who dare, find the experience worth it. It can be easily compared to a human body. In our daily life we tend to be our own quacks and medicate on the basis of common sense. If we refer to a doctor we come to know the actual cause of the symptom and get relieved on knowing the gravity of the situation or the absence of it. One would realize that encyclopaedia reveals the fundamentals of any situation, person or the event and we feel at home with that information.

A dictionary and an encyclopaedia can easily enlarge the process of learning even to an uninitiated person. It is truer in case of humanities. Popular myth about encyclopaedia is that it is meant to be referred to in a library only. The librarians, the world over keep encyclopaedia in such zealously guarded protection that the generally refrain from asking for it. Since the advent of internet in our life, the bulkiness of encyclopaedias has disappeared. That is why we have divided this enterprise in nine volumes. Encyclopaedias are generally global in its expanse. Even subject-related encyclopaedias give the global perspective.That is why country-specific encylopaedias have never been seriousy attempted. We hope that this effort will fill that volume. Traditionally encyclopaedias don't deal with factual data e.g. Indian exports, population figures, GDP. That is the job of annual reference books. They are also different from alamans in as much as that they don't give dated entries. That will become texts on history. Encyclopaedias need to be updated. A country is alive and kicking. People and events continue to play role in various aspects of life. Hence they need to be added. That is why either annual supplements or updation needs to be done in encyclopaedias. We would strive for that.

Regarding its contents only those entries have been included that continue to influence the life of a nation. There are historical figures who might have played a significant role in their times but if those deeds have no relevance to the present they have been excluded. Another example is literary awards. They always create controversies because their selection at times is subjective. Hence only universally accepted meritorious work has found place in these volumes. In this context a debatable point need to be stated. Who is more important book or the author. Conventionally work is an end product and only that is a measure of the author's importance but then a prolic writer might have produced a large body of creations. Hence to save space the author is entered with all his important work.That is also an international practice.

Lastly, why India, Pakistan and Bangladesh have been clubbed together. Before India's independence they were one nation. They share a common heritage and composite culture. Their post-independence history is different but 22their foundation is undivided. In order to appreciate the historical context better it is necessary to cross-refer and that was possible when they are juxtaposed.

Om Gupta

N

Naan : Naan is a round flatbread made of wheat flour. Naans are a staple accompaniment to hot savoury meals in Central and South Asia, including the Punjab and Rajasthan and Gujarat regions in north-west India, Pakistan, Afghanistan, Iran, Uzbekistan and the surrounding region. In Turkic languages (such as Uzbek and Uyghur) the bread is known as nan. In Burmese, naan is known as nanpya. It bears a resemblance to pita bread, but is softer in texture. First recorded history of Naan/ Roti can be found in Amir Khusrau notes (1300 AD) naan-e-tanuk (light bread) and naan-e-tanuri (cooked in a tandoor oven) at the imperial court in Delhi. Naan was in Mughal times a popular breakfast food, accompanied by kheema or kabab, of the royals.

Nabaganga River : Nabaganga river is one of the offshoots of the Mathabhanga river. 'The new form of the Ganges from the Mathabhanga' may be the background of the naming of the river. The river originates near the Chuadanga town. Flowing eastward the river receives the Kumar at Magura and the Chitra at Narail. Then it flows southward to meet the Bhairab river. In the past, the Nabaganga was a distributary of the Ichamati, but later its head was silted up and the river became a tributary of the Bhairab. The course of the Nabaganga was choked up into a beel after flowing a short route towards east from its origin. In 1930 the head of the river was dredged but it brought no satisfactory result. This place is known as Gaznavi Ghat. The river meets the Kumar after crossing the Chuadanga and Jhenaidaha districts and gets new life receiving the water flow from the Kumar. In fact, the Nabaganga after Magura is the extension of the Kumar river.

Nabanna : A widely practiced custom among the tribal as well as non-tribal population of Orissa is the offering of thc first fruits to the deities, especially to the village deities. Paddy is the most important crop which is considered as Goddess Lakshmi. There is a special variety of early paddy which is already ripe by this time. A porridge made of new rice is offered to the ancestral spirits and to the local deities.

Nabha : Nabha is a city in north-western India and lies to the south-east of the state of Punjab. It has a population of 54,079 (1991 census). The town of Nabha was formerly the capital of the eponymous princely state in the British Raj: Its territories were scattered; one section, divided into twelve separate tracts, was intersperced among the territories of Patiala and Jind, in the east and south of the Punjab; the other section was in the extreme southeast of that province. The whole of the territories physically belonged to a plain; however, they varied in character from the great fertility of the Pawadh region to the aridity of the Rajputana desert.

The ruling dynasty of Nabha were Sikhs; the state was founded around 1763 by a member of the Phulkian family. The first relations of the state with the HEIC occurred in 1807-08, when the raja obtained protection against the threatened encroachments of Ranjit Singh. After India's independence, Nabha united with four other Phulkian states to form the Patiala and East Punjab States Union (PEPSU), which later merged into Punjab state.

Nadaswaram : Nadaswaram, also spelt Nadhaswaram, and also called Nagaswaram, is one of the most popular classical instruments of south India and the world's loudest non-brass acoustic instrument. It is a wind instrument similar to the Shehnai but larger with a large flaring bell, sometimes metal. It may be swung through the air while playing, creating a doppler effect.

In India the nadaswaram is considered to be very auspicious, and it is the key instrument which is played in almost all Hindu marriages and temples. The instrument is usually played in pairs, and accompanied by a pair of drums called thavil.

U.S. composers such as Lewis Spratlan and Carl Stone have expressed admiration for the nadaswaram, and the jazz musician Charlie Mariano (b. 1923) is one of the few non-Indians able to play the instrument, having studied it while living in India.

Nadiad : Nadiad is a medium-sized city in the Indian state of Gujarat, with a population of about 0.8 million. It is in the Kheda district. It is famous for a holy town named Dakor in its vicinity. It is also about ten miles away from Anand (milk city), the milk capital of Gujarat and possibly of the whole of India. Nadiad also boasts the Dharamsinh Desai Institute of Technology, which is famous in Gujarat for its quality education in the fields of engineering and technology. The temple, Santaram Mandir, famous for its carvings, is in Nadiad.

Naf River : Naf River is a river marking the border of Bangladesh and Myanmar.

It is an elongated estuary in the extreme southeast of Cox's Bazar district dividing the district from Arakan, Myanmar. It rises in the Arakan hills on the southeastern borders of the district and flows into the Bay of Bengal.

Its width varies from 1.61 km to 3.22 km. The river is influenced by tide. Akyab in Myanmar is on the eastern bank and Teknaf upazila of Cox's Bazar district is on the western bank of the river.

Naf River : Naf river is an elongated estuary in the extreme southeast of Cox's Bazar district dividing the district from Arakan (Myanmar). It rises in the Arakan hills on the southeastern borders of the district and falls into the Bay of Bengal. Its width varies from 1.61 km to 3.22 km. The river is influenced by tide. Akyab in Myanmar is on the leftbank and Teknaf upazila of Cox's Bazar district is on the rightbank of the river.

Nag Panchami : Nag Panchami, the snake festival, in Maharashtra is observed at the village called Battis Shitale in the Sangli district towards the end of August or early September. The devotees collect hundreds of cobras, place them in earthen pots and worship them to the accompaniment of folk dances and song. Later they are carried in processions of bullock carts and chariots. On the following day they are released into the fields from where they were captured.

Nag Panchami : Nag Panchami, the snake festival, is observed at the village called Battis Shitale in the Sangli district towards the end of August or early September. The devotees collect hundreds of cobras, place them in earthen pots and worship them to the accompaniment of folk dances and song. Later they are carried in processions of bullock carts and chariots. On the following day they are released into the fields from where they were captured.

Naga : The Naga people of about two and half million are found in Nagaland, parts of Manipur, Assam, Arunachal Pradesh and Myanmar. Of mixed Yunnanese and Burmese origin, they speak tribal dialects belonging to the Tibeto-Burman family.

The Naga have traditionally practiced their Animistic religion and are known for being a warlike people with an agrarian economy. They are also known for their great friendliness, hospitality, bravery, truthfulness and sense of honour. Fundamentalist Baptist missionaries from the USA first arrived in the 19th century and have since converted the vast majority of the Nagas to Christianity. Today they are engaged in a political negotiation with the Indian Government for a sovereignty they have been demanding for six decades. With India still reluctant to accede to the demands of the Nagas, many feel slow progress in the talks is the detriment for development.

Tattooing and dormitories plays a major role in their traditional culture, although this practice is now in sharp decline. Headhunting, which was once widely practiced, has been banned since 1991.

The Naga are in Manipur and Nagaland are mainly Baptist Christians as a result of British missionaries and the later American intervention, which has led to a tear in their ethnic identity ever since they shed their traditional norms. This has led to forms of Naga fundamentalism and Naga-based militant groups such as those of NSCN. The NSCN had the mission of forcibly converting the animist Naga to Christianity and the formation of a larger Nagaland. As of today, almost all Naga in Nagaland are Christians, notably the pro-US Baptist. There are relatively few Christian Naga who combine tribal animist beliefs and rituals with Christianity, as Baptists condemn all non-Christian beliefs as cults and fundamentally contradictory to Christianity.

The majority of the Naga tribes in Arunachal Pradesh and Myanmar remain loyal to their animistic faith, although militant and missionary intervention in recent years is converting them to Christianity. Some of the Nocte are followers of an animistic form of Hinduism. Theravada

Buddhism is also followed by a small number of people, notably the Tangsa.

Naga Dance : The dancer has a heroic feature and wears a special dress. He dances with a heavy load of weapons to the sound of the battle drums. He has ten main requirements, Viz. 1) A shield of the hide of the rhinoceros, 2) a sword, 3) a Kukri, 4) a gun, 5) a horn used as a whistle, 6) an iron shield, 7) a toilet box, 8) bow and arrows, 9) tiger skin, and 10) a bell. His bow bears the face of a tiger and looks awesome.

Naga Hills : Naga hills, reaching a height of around 3825 meters, lie on the border of India and Myanmar. These hills are part of a complex mountain system, and the parts of the mountain ranges inside the Indian state of Nagaland are called Naga hills. In Undivided India, Naga Hills was also the name of an administrative district of the British Raj.

Naga People : The Naga people of about two and half million are found in Nagaland, parts of Manipur, Assam, Arunachal Pradesh and Myanmar. Of mixed Yunnanese and Burmese origin, they speak tribal dialects belonging to the Tibeto-Burman family.

The Naga have traditionally practiced their Animistic religion and are known for being a warlike people with an agrarian economy. They are also known for their great friendliness, hospitality, bravery, truthfulness and sense of honour. Fundamentalist Baptist missionaries from the USA first arrived in the 19th century and have since converted the vast majority of the Nagas to Christianity. Today they are engaged in a political negotiation with the Indian Government for a sovereignty they have been demanding for six decades.

The Naga are in Manipur and Nagaland are mainly Baptist Christians as a result of British missionaries and the later American intervention, which has led to a tear in their ethnic identity ever since they shed their traditional norms. This has led to forms of Naga fundamentalism and Naga-based militant groups such as those of NSCN. The NSCN had the mission of forcibly converting the animist Naga to Christianity and the formation of a larger Nagaland. As of today, almost all Naga in Nagaland are Christians, notably the pro-US Baptist. There are relatively few Christian Naga who combine tribal animist beliefs and rituals with Christianity, as Baptists condemn all non-Christian beliefs as cults and fundamentally contradictory to Christianity.

The majority of the Naga tribes in Arunachal Pradesh and Myanmar remain loyal to their animistic faith, although militant and missionary intervention in recent years is converting them to Christianity.

Nagaland : Nagaland is a state in northeast India. Nagaland borders the states of Assam, Arunachal Pradesh and Manipur and the country Myanmar. The capital is Kohima. Nagaland is divided into 8 administrative districts. About 84% of the population belongs to 16 Naga tribes, an Indo-Mongoloid ethnic group; minority tribes include the 40,000 Chin. There are some 22,000 Assamese and 14,000 Bengali Muslims. Over 90% of the population is Christian, mostly Baptist. This Christian heritage is shared with a majority in the nearby states of Mizoram and Meghalaya and by a large minority in neighbouring Manipur. The rest of India is overwhelmingly Hindu.

Nagalaphu: Nagalaphu is a Himalayan mountain peak located in the Pithoragarh district of Uttaranchal state in India. It is the part of Himalayan mountain massif that divides Lassar-Darma valley and Ralam-Gori Ganga valley. Its summit reaches an altitude of 6,410 metres above sea level.

Nagananda : Nagananda (Joy of the Serpents) is a Sanskrit play attributed to king Harsha (606 C.E. - 648 C.E.). Nagananda is one of the best Sanskrit dramas in five acts dealing with the popular story of Jimutavahana's self-sacrifice to save the Nagas. The unique characteristic of this drama is the invocation to lord Buddha in the Nandi verse, which is considered as one of the best examples of the dramatic compositions. Nagananda is the story of how prince Jimutavahana gives up his own body to stop a sacrifice of serpents to the divine Garuda.

Nagaon : Nagaon is an administrative district in the state of Assam in India. The district headquarters are located at Nagaon. The district occupies an area of 3831 km^2 and has a population of 2,315,387 (as of 2001). Nagaon presents a fascinating and bewildering mix of cultures, Hindu and Islamic. Batadrowa, gave birth to the famous Vaishnavite reformer Sankardeva, who brought about a Renaissance in Assamese society, at the same time the call of the azzan also blends equally well into the unique mosaic and cultural tapestry of Nagaon.Located in the very heartland of Assam, it falls directly at the center of the entire North-East of India. An old district which dates back to 1833.It is Assam's second most populous district, which probably prompted its old British administrators to jocularly describe Nagaon as a district of 3 c's.. chickens, children and cases. The district also plays host to a sizeable portion of the world renowned Kaziranga National Park. The multi-crore Agar perfume industry whose fragrance wafts all the way to the Middle East, is also processed at Hojai, making Nagaon, in its many undiscovered facets- Assam's best kept secret. Few of the oldest establishments of Nagoan are the Rajasthan Hotel and the Jubilee Field. Football Matches held in Jubilee field still attracts a lot of crowd.

Nagapattinam : Nagapattinam is a city, taluk, and District on the coast of Tamil Nadu, India. The city of

Nagapattinam (formerly known as Negapatam and also as Shiva Rajadhani) has a population of about 100,000. It is located close to many temples, hosting the Soundararajan Perumal Koil, Neelayatakshmi Amman Koil and close to the church at Velankanni and the Nagore Durga at Nagore. Of historical importance, Lord Murugam temple is situated in Sikkal, which is 5 km away from Nagapattinam. The distance from Chennai is about 350 km by road. The city is the administrative centre of both the Nagapattinam taluk and the Nagapattinam district. Nagapattinam was referred by early writers and the Portuguese as "the city of Coromandel" (Imperial Gazetteer of India, XIX, 3). In 1657 the Dutch occupied the town, taking it from the Portuguese to become their chief possession in India. In 1676, when the Maratha prince Venkaji had established himself at Tanjore, the grant of Negapatam to the Dutch was confirmed. It was taken by the English in 1781, and from 1799 to 1845 it was the headquarters of Tanjore district.

The Palk Strait is a 40-85 mi (64-137 km) wide strait that lies between India's Tamil Nadu state and the island nation of Sri Lanka. It connects the Bay of Bengal to the northeast with the Gulf of Mannar to the south. The strait receives several rivers, most notably the Vaigai River of Tamil Nadu. It is named after Robert Palk, governor of Madras Presidency (1755-1763). It is studded at its southern end with a chain of low islands and reef shoals that are collectively called Rama's Bridge or Adam's Bridge. Rama's Bridge extends between Dhanushkodi on Rameswaram Island (also known as Pamban Island) in Tamil Nadu and Talaimannar on the Mannar island in Sri Lanka. The Island of Rameswaram is linked to the Indian mainland by the Pamban Bridge.

Nagar : The State of Nagar is a former princely state in the northernmost part of the Northern Areas of Pakistan, which existed until 1974. The state bordered the Gilgit Agency to the south and west, and the former princely state of Hunza to the north and east. The state capital was the town of Nagar. The area of Nagar now forms two tehsils of Gilgit District.

Nagar River : There are two rivers in Bangladesh named the Nagar. The first one originates from the Karatoya near Shibganj upazila in Bogra district. It flows southwest and then turns south to meet the Atrai river at Singra upazila in Natore district. The Nagar receives a tributary from the north which provide its major flow. The total length of the river is about 105 km. On its course, the river demarcates the boundaries between the upazilas of Dupchanchia-Kahaloo (Bogra district), Adamdighi-Nandigram (Bogra district) and Raninagar (Naogaon district)-Nandigram (Bogra district). The other Nagar river is a Trans-boundary river that enters the country through Panchagarh district. Flowing southwest and then southward, the river again crosses the international boundary near Haripur in the Thakurgaon district. The river defines the boundary between India and Bangladesh in various places on its course. The length of the river in the Bangladesh part is about 125 km. The river causes flash floods at times but does little harm. It becomes dry in the lean period, but the local farmers dam the water of the wet season for irrigation.

Nagarhole National Park : Nagarhole National Park is one among India's best wildlife parks, established in 1955 as a sanctuary and designated as a National park in 1975. Recently it was renamed as Rajiv Gandhi National Park after the late Prime Minister of India. The park is located at Kodagu (Coorg) in Mysore district in the state of Karnataka. The vast area of the park, 572.90 sq km is united with Arikeri, Hatgat, Nalkeri, Mysore reserve forests, streams, waterfalls, Hills and valleys etc.

Nagarjun : Nagarjun (1911-1998), was a major Hindi poet who has also penned a number of novels, short stories, literary biographies and travelogues. The most popular practising Hindi poet in the last decades of the twentieth century, Nagarjun was considered as the only Hindi poet, after Tulsidas, to have an audience ranging from the rural sections of society to the elite. His poems are usually centred around regional topics.

Nagarjuna Sagar Dam : Nagarjunasagar is the world's tallest masonry dam, which irrigates over 10 lakh acres of land. It has also created one of the largest man-made lakes. It is in Andhra Pradesh.

Nagarpanchami : Nagarpanchami falls on the 5th day of the bright half of the lunar month of Shravana in Karnataka. On this day, newly married girls visit their parents. Swings are put up in the village on which both adults and children indulge themselves without any inhabitation, irrespective of caste, creed or sex. The religious part of the festival consist of offering worship to cobras and snakes by pouring milk. In several houses, clay images of snakes are worshipped.

Nagaur Fair : Nagaur awakens to bustling life every year with the thronging of cattle, horses and camels accompanied by their turbaned owners and eager buyers in Rajasthan. This cattle fair held annually is supposed to be one of the largest in the country. The Nagaur bulls are renowned for their fleet-footedness and therefore, attract buyers from all over. The day starts with buyers and sellers engaged in earnest bargains. Once the price of a horse, bullock or probably a camel has been settled, the day draws to a close with fun and festivity. Games, tug of war, camel races and strains of ballads create a joyful atmosphere with the setting sun in the background.

Nagaur Fair : Nagaur awakens to bustling life every year with the thronging of cattle, horses and camels accompanied by their turbaned owners and eager buyers.

This cattle fair held annually is supposed to be one of the largest in the country.

The Nagaur bulls are renowned for their fleet-footedness and therefore, attract buyers from all over. The day starts with buyers and sellers engaged in earnest bargains. Once the price of a horse, bullock or probably a camel has been settled, the day draws to a close with fun and festivity. Games, tug of war, camel races and strains of ballads create a joyful atmosphere with the setting sun in the background.

Nagendranath Basu: Nagendranath Basu(1866-1938) is the author of the first encyclopedia in Bangla, archaeologist, historian and writer, was born in Kolkata on 6 July 1866, though his family was originally from Mahesh in Hughli. Nagendranath was a versatile scholar but he is known mainly for the Bangla Bishwakosh (Bangla encyclopedia), the first volume of which was compiled by Rangalal Mukhopadhyay and edited by his brother, Trailokyanath Mukhopadhyay. Nagendranath worked for 27 years to publish its other 22 volumes. The last volume was published in 1911. Its Hindi version in 24 volumes was published between 1916 and 1931. Nagendranath died in 1938.

Nagercoil : Nagercoil is the southernmost city in South India, situated close to the tip of the Indian peninsula in the state of Tamil Nadu, India. The town is also the administrative headquarters of Kanyakumari district. It was a part of Kerala, the erstwhile Travancore state, till almost a decade after India's Independence from Britain in 1947. In 1956, it was merged with Tamil Nadu. In its earlier days, the town and its surroundings were known as Nanjilnadu. This is one of the Ayyavazhi populated districts of Tamil Nadu.

Nagina : Nagina is a town in Bijnor district, Uttar Pradesh, India. Nagina was the site of a battle between the Nawab of Najibabad and the British April 21, 1858. The British won the battle and established their authority in Bijnor. Nagina is famous for its Wooden handicrafts, esp. ebony work.

Nagod : Nagod or Nagode is a town in Madhya Pradesh state of central India. It is located in Satna District, 17 miles from the town of Satna. It is the administrative headquarters of Nagod Tehsil. Nagod was formerly the capital of a princely state of British India. The state was founded in 1344, and was known as Unchahara after the former capital of the state (until 1720). The state came under British influence in 1802, and became a princely state in the Bagelkhand Agency of what was later to become the Central India Agency. The state was made tributary to Panna from 1807 to 1809. The area of the state was 501 square miles, with a population of 67,092 in 1901. The population of the state decreased 20% in the decade 1891-1901. The rulers, whose title was raja, were Rajputs of the Pratihara clan. Nagod was formerly a British military cantonment, and had an English language school and dispensary.

Nagpur : Nagpur City name is derived from River "Nag" which flows through the city. In the Hindi language 'Nag' means Snake. Nagpur city located near the geographical center of India, in the state of Maharashtra. With a population of 3.5 million (2005 est.), Nagpur is the 13th largest urban conglomeration in India. It is known throughout the country as the "Orange City", as it is a major trading centre for oranges and because the entire region has a climate favourable for large-scale cultivation of oranges. Recently Nagpur celebrated 300 years of its establishment. It is the Winter Capital of the state of Maharashtra and is also headquarters of Nagpur District and Nagpur Division administration. It is the center of the Vidarbha region, which includes most of eastern

Maharashtra. Vidarbha is the most backward region of Maharashtra. The Maharashtra State Legislative Assembly holds its Winter Session at Nagpur in the month of December at which time the entire political community of Maharashtra descends on Nagpur for the two week duration of the session.

Nagpur is a very important road and railway junction, a transit for almost all the trains that span the country lengthwise or breadthwise, including all four of India's major metropolitan cities. Many trains connect Nagpur to the state capital Mumbai, of which The Vidarbha Express is most popular. Nagpur has two major railway stations—Nagpur railway station and Ajni railway station. Nagpur is home to the India Zero Mile Stone, from which distances throughout India are measured.

Nagpur is also the next most favoured IT destination in Maharashtra after the saturation in Mumbai and Pune. The Butibori industrial area near the city is one of the biggest in the country in terms of area. An international cargo hub is also coming up in Nagpur. Nagpur also houses the Maintenance Command of the Indian Air Force and has an ordnance factory for Indian Armed Forces.

The city can be roughly divided into two distinct parts; one consisting the developed areas, in which mostly the affluent reside, and the un-developed areas, in which the poorer sections of society reside. The Vidarbha region has witnessed a massive rise in the numbers of poor farmers commiting suicide due to inability to pay of mortgages. Many factions in the city are fighting for a separate state of Vidarbha, the benefits of which no one can assure, with Nagpur as the state capital.

Nagula Chaviti : This is observed on the fourth day of the bright fortnight in the month of either Sravana or Kartika in Andhra. This is a pre-historic celebration of

Naga or Serpent-worship observed throughout Andhra. Every village in Andhra has some or other Naga idol carved in stone or wood. Generally the women fast on this day and propitiate Nagas by offering fresh, un-boiled cow's milk.

Many families have ant—hills which have been worshipped for generations. Miniature silver eyes and hoods of the Serpent God are placed on the ant—hills and coconuts are broken. Some people have gold and silver images along with their family deities for daily worship. Charimidi, Pamakam and Vada Pappu are the special dishes for this day. After praying to the Naga for protection of the family and children, particularly from snake bite, people smear their eyes and ears with the earth from the ant—hills. There are many Telugu folk songs sung in the praise of the Serpent God.

Nagunur Fort: Nagunur Fort's ramparts were once alive with the sounds of a bustling town and people of the Kakatiya Empire. The fort is testimony to the imperial powers of the Kakatiyas. It was one of the most important forts of the emerging Kakatiya Empire and contains ruins of a cluster of Kalyana and Kakathiya temples.

The pillars and galleries around the Shiva temple here are worth seeing. The most important temple in the complex is the Shiva temple which has three shrines. The main entrance to the temple is on the northern side and the three shrines face the other three directions.

The beams of the temple have sculptured images of musicians playing on Mridangam and other instruments. Panels are carved with visuals of dancers in graceful poses. The village of Nagunur is just about 8 km from Karimnagar Town.

Nahan : Nahan is a town in Himachal Pradesh in India and is the capital of the Sirmaur District. A well-laid out picturesque town, Nahan is situated on an isolated ridge in the Shiwalik Hills, overlooking green fields. Traditionally, saints and princes are linked with the origin of Nahan. The city was founded as a capital by Raja Karan Prakash in 1621. Another version recalls a saint who lived with a companion named Nahar on the site where the Nahan palace now stands. "Nahar" means lion and the town probably takes its name from this saint.

At an altitude of 932 m, Nahan is a good base for visits to the surrounding areas such as Renuka, Paonta Sahib, Trilokpur temple and the Suketi Fossil Park. It has a pleasant climate throughout the year and is watered by a man-made lake and decorated with temples and gardens.

Naina Devi's Temple : Since time immemorial, people from all walks of life have been visiting Naina Devi's temple for a darshan of Maa Naina Devi (Mother Goddess). They come with hope—chanting Jai Mata Di, and pray to get their wishes fulfilled.

According to legend, Lord Shiva's consort Sati once burnt herself alive in Yagna to avenge an insult to Lord Shiva. The distraught Shiva picked her corpse and gyrated his horrified dance. Then Lord Vishnu unleashed his Chakra and cut the Sati's body into fifty one pieces to save the earth from Shiva's wrath. All the fifty one places—where parts of Sati's body fell, became known as Shakti Peeths. It is believed that Sati's eyes fell at the place where this temple is situated. Therefore, this temple is called Naina Devi.

The word Naina is synonymous with Sati's eyes. Since then, devotees started visiting this temple. Once the devotee reaches the hill top, prasad can be bought from any of the various shops or it can also one's own offerings from home. After crossing the main gate, there is a big Peepal tree on the left side. On the right side of the temple there are idols of Lord Hanuman Ji and Ganesh Ji. After reaching the main entrance of the temple, there are two statues of lions. Temple of Shri Naina Devi Ji is situated on hill top in Bilaspur Distt. of Himachal Pradesh in India. This famous temple is connected with National Highway No. 21.

Nainital : Nainital is a town in the Nainital District in the state of Uttaranchal, India. It is situated in the foothills of the outer Himalaya and is dotted with lakes and hill stations. The most famous of these has been named after the district itself. Situated at an altitude of 1938 m above sea-level, Nainital town has a pleasurable climate in the summer and sees a flux of tourists coming mainly from the plains of Northern India. Nainital town finds reference in several ancient mythologies of India. One of the earliest references called the Nainital lake Tri-Rishi-Sarovar in reference to the three sages or rishis who dug a hole at the location of the lake and siphoned water from the holy lake of Manasarovar. It is referred to in the Manas Khand of the Skand Puran as such. With the British colonisation of India, Nainital town became a popular hill station and remains so to this day.

Nakashi Art : Nakashi art is an art form that is practised in Cheriyal of Warangal district in the state of Andhra Pradesh, India. They are basically scrolls of narratives from mythology and folklore. They are used in storytelling. The art is believed to be brought to India by Mughal emperors who brought Usta artists.

Nakashi art usually contain bright hues (most primary colors) with a predominance of red in the background. They are easy to relate to—as the themes and stories are familiar—drawn from the storehouse of ancient literary and folk traditions. Nakashi scrolls and dolls were originally used for story telling. These days, they are being used to adorn the walls in homes.

Nal Sarovar Bird Sanctuary : Nal Sarovar Bird Sanctuary, primarily comprising of a huge lake and ambient marshes, is situated about 64 km to the West of Ahmedabad, in Gujarat state of India. Mainly inhabited by migratory birds in winter and spring, it is the largest wetland bird sanctuary in Gujarat, and one of the largest in India.

The lake measures 123 km^2, attracts over 210 species of birds in the winter, and harbours a variety of flora and fauna. Thousands of migratory waterfowl flock to this sanctuary just after the Indian monsoon season. The shallow area and ponds on the outer fringes of the lake attract the wading birds that feed in the shallow waters. Besides a few mammalian species including the endangered wild ass and the blackbuck, its migratory bird population includes Rosy Pelicans, Flamingoes, White Storks, Brahminy Ducks and Herons.

Nalanda : Nalanda is a historical place in central Bihar, India, 90 km south-east of the state capital of Patna. It is the place where one of the best known Universities of India existed. It existed for around 600 years, reaching its zenith under the Gupta rule, which is often calld the Golden period of ancient India. The Chinese pilgrim Xuanzang recorded that Nalanda was home to students from various countries at its zenith. It is not inhabited now, and the nearest habitation is a village called Bargaon. Nalanda is important to the history of India, and that of Buddhism. Nalanda literally means the place that confers the lotus.

The Jain Tirthankara Mahavira attained Moksha at Pavapuri, which is located in Nalanda. However, the site is better known for its importance in Buddhist history. The famous Nalanda University had been established at the site by the 5th century BCE and the Buddha is believed to have visited it and given sermons near "the Mango Grove of Pavarika". Later, Nalanda University became an important Buddhist centre of learning, at its peak accommodating up to 10,000 students. Among the famous teachers there was Nagarjuna. The Tang Dynasty Chinese pilgrim Xuanzang left detailed accounts of the university in the 7th century.

In 1193, the Nalanda University complex was destroyed by Turkish Muslim invaders under Bakhtiyar Khalji; this event is seen as the final milestone in the decline and near extinction of Buddhism in India. Many buddhist monks from Nalanda fled towards and into Tibet to escape the desecrating armies of Bakhtiyar Khalji. Those that remained were put to the sword. It is said that Khalji asked if there was a copy of the Koran at Nalanda before he destroyed it. The destruction of the universities at Nalanda as well as the destruction of many temples and monasteries throughout northern India which housed centers of learning, is considered by many historians to the responsible for the sudden demise of ancient Indian scientific thought in mathematics, astronomy, alchemy, and anatomy.

A vast amount of what is considered to be Tibetan Buddhism (Vajrayana) actually stems from the late (9th-12th century) Nalanda teachers and traditions. Other forms of Buddhism, like the Mahayana followed in Vietnam, China, Korea and Japan, found their genesis in the hallowed portals of the ancient university. Theravada, the other main school of Buddhism, followed in Sri Lanka, Myanmar, Thailand, Cambodia, and elsewhere, and later the mystic Theravada schools also developed here.

A number of ruined structures survive. Nearby is the Surya Mandir, a Hindu temple. The known and excavated ruins extend over an area of about 150,000 square metres, although if Xuanzang's account of Nalanda's extent is correlated with present excavations, almost 90% of it remains unexcavated. In 1951, a modern centre for Pali (Theravadin) Buddhist studies was founded nearby, the Nava Nalanda Mahavihara. Presently, this institute is pursuing an ambitious program of satellite imaging of the entire region. The Nalanda Museum contains a number of manuscripts, and shows many examples of the items that have been excavated.

Nalgonda : Nalgonda is a town in Nalgonda District in Andhra Pradesh, India. The town has a population of 110,651 (agglomeration 111,745) (2001 census). The district has a population of 3,238,449 and covers an area of 14,240 km^2. The literacy rate is 58%. Other towns in the district include Suryapeta, Kodad, Miryalguda, Kattangur, Bhuvanagiri, Alair, Narketpalli, Huzurnagar, Devarakonda, Yadagirigutta and Nakrekal. The rivers Krishna, Musi, Aleru, Peddavagu, Dindi and Paleru flow through the district of Nalgonda.

Nama Pass : Nama pass is a Himalayan pass located in eastern Kumaun region of the Pithoragarh district of Uttaranchal, India.It is located at an altitude of 5,500 M. It links Kuthi and Darma valley as crosses Nama and Kuthi villages. This was once the busy trade route to Tibet.

Namagen : This dance is performed in September to celebrate the autumn. The dancers themselves sing while musicians play the instruments. The most picturesque amongst these are the dances of the Gaddis.

Namakaranam (Naming the Child) : It is like the baptism in Christianity and is done on the12th day after the birth of the child in Kerala. It is done by the father who calls the name of the child in its right ear. The mother also joins in certain rituals. Among the Nayars, Ezhavas it is done on the 28th day.

Namakkal : Namakkal district, headquartered at Namakkal is one of the 30 administrative districts of Tamil

Nadu state in South India. The district has 4 taluks (subdivisions)—Tiruchengode, Namakkal, Rasipuram and Paramathi-Velur (in descending order of population). The district is known as a transportation hub, connecting the west of Tamil Nadu with the capital city Chennai. It is best known for its transport companies, including trucking services, accounting for a bulk of goods traffic from the southern region. The district is also well known for its poultry and dairy industries, accounting for a bulk of supply of poultry products to neighbouring industries. It has also made its mark in recent years, as a major centre for high school education

Namal Dam : Namal Dam is located in Mianwali, Punjab, Pakistan. This dam was constructed in 1913. Namal Dam is situated some 32 km from Mianwali city. The Namal Lake is major area for recreation. The water is used to irrigate farmland and provide drinking water to Mianwali city.

Namal Lake : Namal Lake is located in Mianwali, Punjab, Pakistan. This lake was created Namal Dam was constructed in 1913. Namal Lake spread over 5.5 sq km, in Namal valley. Namal Lake is an ideal abode for the migratory birds in winter season when thousands of water fowls, including Russian ducks and Siberian cranes, land in the lake water.

Namboothiris : The Namboothiris are the Brahmins of Kerala. They adhere to the Advaita philosophy propounded by Sri Adi Shankaracharya and are Smartha's. Indeed, Sri Adi Shankaracharya himself was born into this community (though he disowned them). In Malayalam, the word Namboothiri is derived from Nambu meaning sacred or trustworthy, and thiri meaning Light.

According to the Aryan Invasion Theory, the Namboothiris are thought to have migrated from North

India, or countries further north, into Kerala during the 7th century AD. The Namboothiris' own mythology holds that Sri Parashuraaman created the land (of Kerala) and bestowed it upon them. Parasurama myth also exits amongst Brahmins of coastal regions of Karnataka, Konkan and Gujarat. Hence it has to be seen as a myth not exlusive to Namboothiris and Kerala alone. However, this myth also exist in an old Chera lore about King Velkezu Kuttavan. According to this myth, the king flings his spear into the sea to claim land from it. This lore was modified later in Malayalam language by the Namboothiris as part of their campaign to establish themselves in Kerala. In the Namboothiri version, Parashuraaman uses his Parashu (Axe), to create new land for the Brahmins.

Namchi : Namchi is the capital of the South Sikkim district in the state of Sikkim, India. The appellation Namchi means Sky High in Nepali. Namchi is situated at an altitude of 1675 m (5500 feet) above sea level. It is situated at a distance of 78 km from the state capital Gangtok and 100 km from the town of Siliguri, the nearest railhead and airport. Namchi lies off the road between Melli and Jorethang. Namchi is well connected to other towns in Sikkim and West Bengal. Jeeps and buses regularly ply between Namchi to Gangtok, Pelling, Jorethang, Kalimpong and Siliguri.

Namchi is fast becoming a major tourist spot and pilgrimage centre. The Namchi monastery, Ralong monastery and Tedong Hill are important Buddhist pilgrimage centres. The world's largest statue (at 118 feet) of the Buddhist Guru Rinpoche, the patron saint of Sikkim is just on the hill opposite Namchi.

Namdapha Flying Squirrel : The Namdapha Flying Squirrel (Biswamoyopterus biswasi) is the sole species placed in the genus Biswamoyopterus. It is a flying squirrel endemic to India. It is listed as a critically endangered species due to habitat loss.

Namdapha National Park : Namdapha National Park is located in the Changlang District of Arunachal Pradesh on the India Burmese border a few km from the entry point, Miau. It was designated as a National Park in 1983 under the Wildlife (Protection) Act. The same year, it was also declared as tiger reserve under Project Tiger. With a total area of 1985 sq kms, this is the largest national park in the north-east and one of the larger protected areas in the country. In fact, this was among the earliest national parks established in the seven states of north-east India.

The park watered by the Noa- Dehing and the Namdapha rivers, is largely inaccessible, with diverse habitats of flora and fauna. The vegetation ranges from the wet evergreen tropical and sub-tropical forests to temperate and alpine forests. A variety of wild tree species and crop plants including banana, mango, citrus and medicinal and ornamental plants including wild orchids are found here. The inaccessibility has helped the forests to retain its pristine ness.

The fauna of the park comprises elephant, tiger, leopard, snow leopard, clouded leopard, golden cat, wild dog, endangered Hoolock gibbon, Namdapha Flying Squirrel, wild buffalo, guar, hog deer, sloth bear, bison, Himalayan Tahr, Bharal, python, King cobra,, the wild goats; takin peculiar to the Patkoi range, Serow and Goral etc. The park is rich in bird life. The important birds are Indian Horn bill, the state bird of Arunachal, white winged wood duck, cheer pheasants etc.

The park is unique in its altitude, which varies around 200 metres (nearly sea level) in the valleys to more than 4,500 metres of snow covered mountain peaks. Perhaps no other national park in the world can boast of such phenomenal altitudinal variation. The park is also ideal for trekking and hiking. From Miau the entry point, a forest road stretching over 28-km gives access to the protected area up to a place called Deban where accommodation is available. Beyond this there is no road and one has to go on foot. It is a challenging trek through dense forests and steep hill ranges with rivers flowing in between and the varying climatic conditions from tropical to cold and temperate conditions.

Namdapha Tiger Reserve : Namdapha Tiger Reserve is located in Changlang district of Arunachal Pradesh, India. The reserve forms part of Project Tiger and it is the easternmost habitat of the tiger in India. It covers an area of 1985 sq km, rising from the plains to 4500 m in the Eastern Himalaya. It is the only reserve in India where four big cats can be found—the tiger, leopard, snow leopard and clouded leopard. Other wildlife includes the Great Indian Hornbill, the Red Panda and the Hoolock gibbon.

Nameri National Park : Nameri National Park covering an area of about 200sq. kms is located at the foothills of eastern Himalayas about 35km from Tezpur, the nearest town. The park is the second Tiger reserve of Assam. The park consists of deciduous forests, hills and the river Jia Bhoroli flows through it. Nameri was set up as a sanctuary on 18th September 1985 with an area of 137 sq km which was actually a part of Naduar Forest Reserve. Later another 75sq km was added to it making it an area of 212 sq km and on 15th November, 1998 it was officially established as a National park.

Namik Glacier : Namik Glacier is situated in the Pithoragarh district of Uttaranchal state of India. The glacier situated on Kumaon Himalayas at an altitude of 3,600 m. This glacier feeds the Ram Ganga River which originates from here.The glacier is surrounded by peaks like Nanda Devi (7848 m), Nanda Kot (6861 m), and Trishuli (7120 m).The glacier falls on ancient Indo-Tibet trade route. It is 40 km from Munsiyari] and situated at the villages of Gogina and Namik.There are a number of waterfalls and sulphur springs originating and around this glacier. The glacier can be reached by trekking from Bala village on Thal-Munsiyari road near Birthi Fall.It is 129 km from Pithoragarh.'Namik' means a place where saline water springs are present.

Namli Maira : Namli Maira is a collection of small hamlets, the largest being Namli and Maira respectively, nestled on mountain ridges about 20 kilometers from the city of Abbottabad, Pakistan. A mettled road connects Namli Maira to the main Abbottabad-Nathiagali road near Azizabad (Hernoi) and is an alternate route to reach Nathiagali from Abbottabad.

Namli Maira is surrounded by tall mountains. There was a time when much of the area's mountainous slopes were covered with coniferous forests teeming with wildlife. Excessive logging to accommodate farmland and fruit orchards has denuded the hills of the forest cover. Presently, remenants of forests can be seen near the mountain peaks and places still beyond the reach of humans.

Nana Patekar : Nana Patekar (born 1 January 1951 in Maharashtra) is an Indian actor and filmmaker.

While he acted in movies such as *Mohre* (1987) and *Salaam Bombay!* (1988), he was noticed by the mainstream Bollywood industry and audience alike for his portrayal of the villain in the 1989 film, *Parinda.* He was awarded the Filmfare Best Supporting Actor Award for the role (as there was no separate category for Villain roles then). He also won the National Award for Best Actor in 1995.

Nanasaheb Peshwa : Nanasaheb Peshwa (also called Balaji Bajirao) was one of the Peshwa rulers of Pune, India and the most influential person in the development of the city. During his 20 year reign (1740 to 1761), he completely transformed the village into a city. He established many new neighbourhoods (called peths) like Sadashiv Peth, Nana Peth, Shukrawar Peth, etc. He built the famous Parvati temple atop a hill that overlooks the city and built the first permanent bridge across the river Mutha. (That bridge was made of wood, so the new concrete bridge that stands at the same location today is also called LakDi Pool or 'the wooden bridge'). He also established a reservoir at the nearby town of Katraj to provide clean running water to the city. The 250 year old system is still functioning, but parts of it have been destroyed by careless development.

Maratha power in India reached its peak under his reign. Nanasaheb lost his son and brother at the Battle of Panipat. He could not recover from the shock, and died soon after the debacle. He was suceeded by his second son Madhavrao Peshwa.

Nancowry : Nancowry refers both to a single island, and to the group of adjoining islands, that are a part of the Nicobar Islands chain, located in the northeast Indian Ocean between the Bay of Bengal and the Andaman Sea.

Nancowry, like the Nicobar islands generally, is under the sovereignty of the nation of India. It is also part of the Nicobar and Andaman Tribal Reserve Area, which bars non-native people from visiting or conducting business on the island without permission in hopes of preserving the threatened native communities that live there.

With Kamorta (Camorta) Island, which lies just to the North, Nancowry Island forms the "magnificent land-locked" Nancowry Harbour, used by European sailors since at least the 1600s and described as "one of the safest natural harbours in the world". The harbour was apparently used as a base for piracy; in 1868, the British Navy entered the harbour in some force, destroying suspected pirate ships.

The island, like many others in the Nicobar and Andaman islands, was severely affected by tsunamis generated by the 2004 Indian Ocean Earthquake. According to reports from the Andaman and Nicobar Inspector General of Police, S.B. Deol, the Nancowry group islands were among the worst-hit islands in the chain, with thousands missing and presumed dead. Post-tsunami satellite photos and government situation reports indicate that while portions of Nancowry Island were affected, the adjoining islands of Katchall and Kamorta were more severely overrun.

Nanda Devi : Nanda Devi is the tallest mountain within the territory of India and was also the highest mountain in the British Empire at its fullest extent. Its name means Bliss-Giving Goddess and is regarded as the patron-goddess of the Uttarakhand Himalaya, currently in Uttaranchal state. Of geographical interest, Nanda Devi stands guarded by a barrier ring of the highest mountains in the Indian Himalayas, 12 of which exceed 6,400 m (21,000 ft) in height, further elevating its sacred status as the daughter of the Himalayas in local myth and folklore. Its ascent also necessitated fifty years of arduous exploration in search of a passage into the interior of this almost insurmountable ring. In 1934, the British explorers Eric Shipton and H.W. Tilman with three Sherpa companions, Angtharkay, Pasang, and Kusang, finally discovered a passageway. When the mountain was later climbed in 1936 by a British-American expedition, including Tilman and Noel Odell, it became the highest peak climbed by man until the 1950 ascent of Annapurna (8,091 m).

Nanda Devi East : Nanda Devi East is the Himalayan mountain peak in the central part of Uttaranchal at the border of Chamoli and Pithoragarh districts of India.The altitude of the peak is 7,434 M. Nanda Devi West 7,816 M is situated to the west to it. Nanada Devi East has Longstaff Col 5,910 M to south east, Lawan glacier to East. This peak is the part of great Himalayan north- south massif dividing Rishiganga valley from Goriganga valley, lying in the East. Nanda Devi East was climbed for the first time by A.Karpinski from Poland in 1939.

Nanda Devi National Park : This park is also situated in Chamoli district. It was established in1980 covering an area of 630 sq.km. The town of the Joshimath is 23km from here. The nearest rail head is at Rishikash at a distance of 276km and the nearest airport is at Dehra Dum, 295km away.

The animal found in this park are black and brown Himalayan bear, snow leopard, barrel, musk deer, Himalayan thar, goral, panther, sambar, wild boar, monal, pheasant, snow pigeon, green pigeon, etc.

Nanda Dynasty : Nanda dynasty was established by an illegitimate son of the king Mahanandin of the previous Shishunaga dynasty. Mahapadma Nanda died at the age of 88 and, therefore, he ruled the bulk of the period of this dynasty, which lasted 100 years. The Nandas were followed by the Maurya dynasty. The first Nanda, the Mahapadma Nanda has been described as the destroyer of all the Kshatriyas. He defeated Ikshvakus, Panchalas, Kasis, Harhayas, Kalingas, Asmakas, Kurus, Maithilas, Surasenas, Vitihotras, etc.,. He expanded his territory till south of Deccan. The last of the Nandas was Dhana Nanda. Plutarch tells that Chandragupta Maurya had stated that Nanda was hated and despised by his subject on account of the wickedness of his disposition. The bloody fight between the Nandas and the Mauryas overthrew the dynasty of Nandas.

The Nandas who usurped the throne of the Shishunaga dynasty were of low origin. Some sources state that the founder, Mahapadma, was the son of a Shudra mother, others that he was born of a union of a barber with a courtesan. Nandas were the first of a number of dynasties of northern India who were of non-kshatriya origin. The Nandas are sometimes described as the first empire builders of India. They inherited the large kingdom of Magadha and wished to extend it to yet more distant frontiers. To this purpose they built up a vast army consisting of 20,000 cavalry, 200,000 infantry, 2,000 chariots and 3,000 elephants. But the Nandas never had the opportunity to use this army against the Greeks, who invaded India at the time Dhana Nanda, since Alexander's campaign terminated in the Punjab.

The Nandas made the methodical collection of taxes by regularly appointed officials a part of their administrative system. The treasury was continually replenished, the wealth of the Nandas being well-known. The Nandas also built canals and carried out irrigation projects. The possibility of an imperial structure based on an essentially agrarian economy began to germinate in the Indian mind. But further development of the Nandas was cut short by Chandragupta Maurya and his mentor Chanakya. Chanakya dethroned Dhana Nanda in a battle of wits and replaced him with Chandragupta Maurya, a young adventurer. Dhana Nanda was murdered which finally signaled the advent of the Mauryan era in 321 B.C.

Nanda Gond : Nanda Gond is the Himalayan mountain peak situated in the Pithoragarh district of Uttaranchal state of India. It is located in the Milam valley on the east of Milam Glacier. The altitude of the summit is 6,315 M.Ikualari 6,059 M, Nanda Pal 6,306 M, Nital Thaur

6,236 M, are its neighbouring peaks. Unta Dhura Pass is located north to it.

Nanda Kot : Nanda Kot is the name of one of the Himalayan mountain peak in Pithoragarh district of Uttaranchal state in India. It is one among the Nanda Devi group of peaks in the central Kumaun Himalaya. The altitude of the summit is 6,168 M. This peak is situated on the south east ridge of Nanda Devi east.This peak is the outermost peak of Nanda Devi group of peaks, also named as fortress of Goddess Nanda. Nanda Kot ridge forms a divide between Pinder and Gori ganga valleys and Dana Dhura pass connects the both. This peak was for the first time attempted by Dr. T.G.Longstaff in 1905 through Lawan valley crossing Lawan glacier. The peak was for the first time scaled by a Japanese team led by Y. Hotta in 1936. A new route through south face direct was climbed by British expedition led by Martin Moran in 1995. One can take route through Loharkhet-Dhakuri Pass-Khati Village-Dwali base camp.

Nanda Pal : Nanda Pal is the Himalayan mountain peak situated in the eastern part of Uttaranchal state in Pithoragarh district, India.The altitude of the summit is 6,306 M. Nanda Pal is situated on the easten flank of Milam Glacier on north south massif.Other nearby peaks on the ridge are Ikualari 6,059 M, Nanda Gond 6,315 M, Nital Thaur 6,059 M. Unta Dhura pass lies north to this peak.The peak was climbed in 1974.

Nandidrug : Nandidrug or Nandidurg is a hill fortress of southern India, in the Kolar district of Karnataka state. It is 4851 ft. above sea level. Nandidrug hill, known commonly as Nandi Hills, is the source of the Penner and Ponnaiyar rivers. Nandi Hills gets its name from an ancient Nandi temple situated on this hill. This temple has a thousand year old sculpture of Nandi. An ancient lord Shiva and Parvati temple also adorns this hill.

Nandidurg was traditionally held impregnable, and its storming by Lord Cornwallis in 1791 was one of the most notable incidents of the first war against Tipu Sultan of Mysore. It was formerly a favorite resort for British Raj officials during the hot season. Francis Cunningham built the summer residence here for Sir Mark Cubbon.

The hills are now a popular tourist spot during summer. The state horticulture department maintains a garden for the tourists. The pressure of tourists on the environment here is great with a considerable problem of litter, noise and physical disturbance.

Nanga Parbat : Nanga Parbat (also known as Nangaparbat Peak or Diamir) is the ninth highest mountain on Earth. Nanga Parbat means "Naked·Mountain" in Urdu while the Sherpas, localites of the Himalayan region, call it "the maneater" or the "Mountain of the Devil". No other peak has claimed lives with such regularity and the list of tragedies is overwhelming.

Nanga Parbat boasts what is probably the highest vertical cliff in the world: the southern wall (Rupal Face) rises an incredible 4,600 m (15,000 feet) above its base. Another part of the mountain—the Raikot Face—rises 6,700 m (22,000 feet) from the Indus River valley to the summit in just a few miles, the greatest elevation gain in so short a distance on earth.

Nanga Parbat was first climbed on July 3, 1953 by Austrian climber Hermann Buhl of a German-Austrian team. Before this expedition, 31 people had already died trying to make the first ascent. Buhl is the only mountaineer to have made the first ascent of an eight-thousander solo and without oxygen.

In August 2005 Pakistani military helicopters rescued a renowned Slovenian mountaineer, Toma Humar, who was stuck under a narrow ice ledge at 5900 meters for six days. It is believed to be one of the few successful rescues carried out at such high altitude.

Nannayya : Nannayya, popularly hailed as Adi Kavi or the first poet, belonged to Rajamundry, an ancient city on the banks of river Godavari. He is said to have belonged to 1000—1100. Nannayya initiated the gigantic task of translation of the great epic into Telugu. Before translation, he had to revise Telugu by building new grammar rules and increase its vocabulary. Nannayya used many of the Sanskrit words directly in Telugu too. Thus Nannayya made Telugu more Sanskritized. Thus lot of Nannayya's time was gone in building a scaffold for the great activity. He was able to translate the first 2½ parvas (chapters) into Telugu.

Naogaon : Naogaon is a district in the Rajshahi division of Bangladesh with an area of 3435.67 sq km, is bounded by West Bengal of India on the north, Natore and Rajshahi districts on the south, Joypurhat and Bogra districts on the east, Nawabganj district and West Bengal (India) on the west. Annual temperature: maximum 37.8 C and minimum 11.2 C; annual rainfall 1862 mm. Main rivers are Atrai, Punarbhaba, Little Jamuna, Nagar, Chiri and Tulsi Ganga. Guta, Mansur and Dighali Beels are notable. Naogaon subdivision, under Rajshahi district, was established in 1877 and was turned into a district in 1984. It consists of 2 municipality, 11 upazilas, 18 wards, 74 mahallas, 99 union parishads and 2795 villages. The upazilas are Naogaon Sadar, Atrai, Badalgachhi, Dhamoirhat, Manda, Mahadevpur, Niamatpur, Patnitala, Porsha, Raninagar and Sapahar. Paharpur Buddhist Vihara, Jagaddal Vihara, Halud Vihara, Agrapuri Vihara, etc., are some of the important archaeological sites in the district.

Naradada : NaraDada (also known as 228 GB (Gogera branch) is a village in Pakistan, located at the Gojra—

Samundari road.The exact history of the village is not known but this village existed before the partion of India Pakistan. The most of the villagers are Muslim Rajputs who have migrated from India, there are also number of christians living there. Most of the inhabitants of the village are those who migrated from Indian district Hushiarpur's villages Nara and Dada. That is why this village is named Naradada.

Narain Karthikeyan : Kumar Ram Narain Karthikeyan (born January 14, 1977, Chennai, India) is a Formula One driver. He made his debut in 2005 with the Jordan team. He is currently a Williams F1 test driver. He is often given the title of "The Fastest Indian in the World".

He started racing at the age of 16, an age at which you can't legitimately get a driving license. But you're perfectly eligible for a racing license! Initiated by his father G R Karthikeyan who for years was the Indian National Rally Champion, Narain's interest was stimulated from a very early. Though Narain is only twenty-eight year old, he has already achieved a considerable reputation in the sport.

When he was 16 he attended the Elf-Winfield Racing School in France, showing an immediate talent for the sport; he was among the semi-finalists in the Pilote Elf Competition in Formula Renault cars. He was very successful at the Spa Fracorchamps Formula Three championship in Belgium. He has improved a lot over the years and is all geared up to achieve the F1 racing driver distinction.

In 1994 he returned to the UK and drove in Formula Ford Zetec for Foundation Racing as the number two works Vector Driver. He took part in the British Formula Ford Winter Series and by winning this became the first Indian to win a championship in Europe. In 1995, he participated in the Formula Asia Championship for four races. He feels that Formula Asia is an essential step in pursuit of his racing ambitions.

1997 was one of his best years. He competed in the Formula Vauxhall Opel and won the prestigious Donington Park race with a lead from start to finish. This amazing victory prompted the much-acclaimed Autosport magazine to declare in bold headlines—"The Indian Prince rules in the rain".

He studied Business Administration in London. His hobbies include skeet shooting, tennis, wildlife photography and philanthropy. Narain is not only interested in motor racing, but also in tennis. He is all admiration for Boris Becker. He does yoga and meditation and keeps fit through jogging and weight training. His idol is Michael Schumacher and his only ambition is to be the first Indian Formula One Driver.

Naran Valley : Naran Valley is located in North-West Frontier Province, Pakistan. The Kunhar River, swollen by glacier melt, meanders its way through the Naran Valley and Trout is plentiful.

Narasimhachari : Narasimhachari made his debut in Kuchipudi at the tender age of five under the rigorous training of his father Sri Satyanarayanachari. He performed the Burra Katha (a ballad form in Telugu) along with his younger sister and brother. The trio very soon became the most popular group in Andhra Pradesh, so much so that they had the honour of performing for the then President of India, Dr. Rajendra Prasad. Narasimhachari was trained in Bharatanatyam under the expert tutelage of Rukmini Devi at the Kalakshetra.

Narasimhachari is a rare combination of a music composer, choreographer, singer, *nattuvanar*, mridangam player, concert musician, dancer and a highly respected Guru. His wife Vasanthalakshmi specialised in nattuvangam and also contributes the lyrics for their compositions. The Narasimhacharis have produced as many as 21dance-dramas. Natyaveda, one such endeavour, had for its theme the exploration of the Vedic origins of dance as expounded in the Natya Shastra of Bharata. They were on the faculty of the University of Central Oklahoma (UCO) from the year 1995-1998.

Narasimhachari choreographed a special programme titled "Jugal Bandhi" presenting three major classical dance styles of South India – Bharatanatyam, Kuchipudi and Mohiniattam. Of the several dance-dramas choreographed by them, mention may be made of Kambaramayanam, Sivaleela, Saranam Aiyappa, Megha, Sandesa, Girija Kalyanam, Annamacharya, Nrityankita, Bharati Kannamma, Panchatantra, Voice of Ganga, Jesus Christ, Natya Veda and Challenge of Growth.

Narayana Guru : Sree Narayana Guru (1856—1928) was a great sage and social reformer of India. Born in Ezhava/Thiyya caste (Ezhavas were a middle rung caste and have to face social injustices.), he revolted against the brahminical dominance and thereby transformed the social face of Kerala. Narayana Guru is revered for his Vedic knowledge, poetic proficiency, openness to the views of others, non-violent philosophy and most importantly his unnerving resolve to rebel and change wrongdoing in society.

Narayana Guru was instrumental in setting the spiritual foundations for social reform in the current State of Kerala (erstwhile states of Travancore, Kochi and Malabar) and was arguably one the most successful social reformers that tackled caste in India.He demonstrated a path to social emancipation without invoking the dualism of the opressed and the opressor.

In contrast to certain other reformers who critized Brahmins and upper caste Hindus for the conditions of the lower castes, Narayana Guru stressed on the upliftment of a community through its own efforts by the establishment of schools and temples. In the process he brushed aside the Hindu religious conventions based upon Chaturvarna. His transformation of the social face of Kerala relied on emphasizing the Advaita philosophy.

Narayanganj : Narayanganj is a district in central Bangladesh. It is a part of the Dhaka Division. The main city of the district is also called Narayanganj. A historic place located in Narayanganj is the ancient city of Sonargaon. It is the capital of Isa Khan, a medieval ruler of Bengal. Sonargaon is also famous for producing Muslin, a delicate and fine cloth made from cotton. The Dhaka-Narayanganj-Demra (DND) embankment surrounds Narayanganj district and protects it from flooding. Narayanganj is also home to the Bangladesh Engineering and Ship Building Corporation, established in 1925 at Sonakanda on the east bank of the Shitalakshya River.

Narayanganj : Narayanganj is a district in central Bangladesh. It is a part of the Dhaka Division. The main city of the district is also called Narayanganj. A historic place located in Narayanganj is the ancient city of Sonargaon. It is the capital of Isa Khan, a medieval ruler of Bengal. Sonargaon is also famous for producing Muslin, a delicate and fine cloth made from cotton. The Dhaka-Narayanganj-Demra (DND) embankment surrounds Narayanganj district and protects it from flooding. Narayanganj is also home to the Bangladesh Engineering and Ship Building Corporation, established in 1925 at Sonakanda on the east bank of the Shitalakshya River.

Narcondam : Narcondam or Narcondum (coordinates: 13.43° N 94.25° E) is a small volcanic island located in the Andaman Sea. Its central peak rises some 710 m above mean sea level. It is considered to be part of the Andaman Islands, the main body of which lie approximately 114 km to the west. The island is part of the Indian union territory of Andaman and Nicobar Islands. The island is small, approximately 3 km×4 km.

The island is formed from an volcano, which is not known to have been active in recent times. However on June 8, 2005 there were reports of "mud and smoke" being ejected from the volcano. The 2004 Indian Ocean earthquake is thought to have caused magma to move underground and may be related to the current activity. It is currently classified as a dormant volcano by the Geological Survey of India. Further to the south east (approximately 150 km) lies the active volcanic island of Barren Island, the only active volcano in the region. The name means "pit of hell", although this may be the result of confusion between it and Barren Island.

Narendra Modi : Narendra Damodardas Modi was born on September 17, 1950, Gujarat, India. He became the Chief Minister of Gujarat on October 7, 2001.

He was born in Vadnagar, a town in the northern Mehsana district of Gujarat, to a middle-class Hindu family. As a young man, he joined the Rashtriya Swayamsevak Sangh. He became a fulltime worker and organiser for it, and was later nominated by it to be a representative on the Bharatiya Janata Party. He participated in the rise to political dominance of the Bharatiya Janata Party in Gujarat as its elections organiser in the early 1990s, a period which led to its election in 1995. He became Gujarat's Chief Minister in 2001, promoted to that office when his predecessor Keshubhai Patel resigned, following the defeat of the BJP in by-elections. A hate figure among the Muslims and a popular personality among the Hindus, the state leader of the

Bharatiya Janata Party, came back to power in 2002. He won re-election as chief minister with 126 seats in the 182-member assembly.

Nargis : Nargis (June 1, 1929 - May 3, 1981) was an Indian actress who will always be remembered as Radha in the Oscar-nominee film *Mother India*.

Nargis was born as Fatima Rashid, the daughter of dancer/actor Jaddanbai. Nargis began acting as a child in the 1935 film, Talashe Haq and was credited as "Baby Nargis." In later years, Nargis starred in many popular Hindi movies of the 1950's such as Andaaz and Awaara. She was a recipient of the Padma Shri award in 1958.

Narmada : The Narmada or Nerbudda is a river in central India. It forms the traditional boundary between North India and South India, and is a total of 1,289 km (801 mi) long. It is one of only three major rivers in pensinsular India that run from east to west, along with the Tapti and the Mahi river. It is the only river in India that flows in a rift valley. It rises on the summit of Amarkantak Hill in Madhya Pradesh state, and for the first 320 kilometres (200 miles) of its course winds among the Mandla Hills, which form the head of the Satpura Range; then at Jabalpur, passing through the 'Marble Rocks', it enters the Narmada Valley between the Vindhya and Satpura ranges, and pursues a direct westerly course to the Gulf of Cambay. It flows through the states of Madhya Pradesh, Maharashtra, and Gujarat, and empties into the Arabian Sea in the Bharuch District of Gujarat.

Narmada Bachao Andolan (NBA) : Narmada Bachao Andolan (NBA) (Save Narmada Movement) is a people's movement that mobilised tribal people, adivasis, farmers, environmentalists and human rights activists against the Sardar Sarovar Dam being built across the Narmada river, Gujarat, India. Narmada Bachao Andolan, together with its leading spokespersons Medha Patkar and Baba Amte, was the 1991 recipient of the Right Livelihood Award.

Narmada River : The Narmada or Nerbudda is a river in central India. It forms the traditional boundary between North India and South India, and is a total of 1,289 km (801 mi) long. It is one of only three major rivers in pensinsular India that run from east to west, along with the Tapti and the Mahi. It rises on the summit of Amarkantak Hill in Madhya Pradesh state, and for the first 320 kilometres (200 miles) of its course winds among the Mandla Hills, which form the head of the Satpura Range; then at Jabalpur, passing through the 'Marble Rocks', it enters the Narmada Valley between the Vindhya and Satpura ranges, and pursues a direct westerly course to the Gulf of Cambay. It flows through the states of Madhya Pradesh, Maharashtra, and Gujarat, and empties into the Arabian Sea in the Bharuch District of Gujarat.

Narmada Valley : The Narmada or Nerbudda is a river in central India. It forms the traditional boundary between North India and South India, and is a total of 1,289 km (801 mi) long. It is one of only three major rivers in pensinsular India that run from east to west, along with the Tapti and the Mahi. It rises on the summit of Amarkantak Hill in Madhya Pradesh state, and for the first 320 kilometres (200 miles) of its course winds among the Mandla Hills, which form the head of the Satpura Range; then at Jabalpur, passing through the 'Marble Rocks', it enters the Narmada Valley between the Vindhya and Satpura ranges, and pursues a direct westerly course to the Gulf of Cambay. It flows through the states of Madhya Pradesh, Maharashtra, and Gujarat, and empties into the Arabian Sea in the Bharuch District of Gujarat.

The Narmada Valley is a graben, a linear block of the earth's crust that dropped down relative to the blocks on either side due to ancient spreading of the earth's crust.

Two normal faults, known as the Narmada North fault and Narmada South fault, parallel the river's course, and mark the boundary between the Narmada block and the Vindhya and Satpura blocks or horsts which rose relative to the Narmada Graben. The Narmada's watershed includes the northern slopes of the Satpuras, and the steep southern slope of the Vindhyas, but not the Vindhyan tableland, the streams from which flow into the Ganges and Yamuna.

Its longest tributary is the Tawa, which joins the Narmada at Bandra Bhan in Hoshangabad District, Madhya Pradesh. After leaving Madhya Pradesh and Maharashtra, the river widens out in the fertile district of Bharuch. Below Bharuch city it forms a 20 kilometre wide estuary where it enters the Gulf of Cambay. The Narmada river is not only used for irrigation, but for navigation. In the rainy season boats of considerable size sail about 100 kilometres above Bharuch city. Seagoing vessels of about 70 tons frequent the port of Bharuch, but they are entirely dependent on the tide.

Narmada Valley Dry Deciduous Forests : The Narmada Valley dry deciduous forests are a tropical dry forest ecoregion of central India. The ecoregion lies mostly in Madhya Pradesh state, but extends into portions of Chhattisgarh, Maharashtra, and Uttar Pradesh states.

These forests cover an area of 169,900 km^2 (65,600 square miles) of the lower Narmada River Valley and the surrounding uplands. The Narmada Valley is an east-west flat-bottomed valley, or graben, that separates two plateaus. The Vindhya Range forms the northern edge of the Narmada Valley, and separates the Narmada Valley from the Malwa plateau and Bundelkhand upland, which lie to the north. The Satpura Range encloses the Narmada Valley on the south, and separates the Narmada Valley from the Deccan plateau. The ecoregion includes the western portion of the Satpuras, and also extends to the southeast along the eastern flank of the Western Ghats range. The ecoregion lies between moister forests to the northeast, southeast, and southwest, which receive greater rainfall from the southeast monsoon, and the drier forests and scrublands of the Deccan to the south and Malwa and Gujarat to the west and northwest.

Narsingarh : Narsingarh is a formerly princely state of India, administratively under the Bhopal Agency subdivision of the Central India Agency. The state covered an area of 1901 square kilometers and had a population of 92,093 in 1901. Its rulers were styled "Raja", and were entitled to an 11-gun salute. The principality was founded in 1681 by the Hindu Umat dynasty. After Indian independence in 1947, the rulers of Narsingarh acceded to the Union of India, and the principality was incorporated into the new state of Madhya Bharat, which subsequently became Madhya Pradesh state on November 1, 1956.

Narsingpur District : Narsingpur District is a district of Madhya Pradesh state in central India. The town of Narsinghpur is administrative headquarters of the district. The district has an area 5,133 sq. km., and a population 957,399 (2001 census), a 22% increase from 1991. The district is part of the Jabalpur Division of Madhya Pradesh. It is bounded on the north by Sagar and Damoh districts, on the east by Jabalpur District, on the southeast by Seoni District, on the south by Chhindwara District, on the west by Hoshangabad District, and on the northwest by Raisen District. The administrative seat and chief town is Narsinghpur; other towns include Barman, Chaugan, Jharna, and Soteshwar. The district sits in the basin of the Narmada River, which forms the northern boundary of the district. The Satpura Range forms the district's southern boundary. The main rail line from Mumbai to Calcutta (Kolkata), which follows the Narmada River valley, runs through the district from west to east.

At the beginning of the 19th century, Narsinghpur District in the domain of the Maratha Bhonsle Maharajas of Nagpur, but was ceded to the British Raj in 1818. Narsinghpur District was part of the Nerbudda (Narmada) Division of the Central Provinces and Berar, which became the state of Madhya Pradesh after India's independence in 1947.

Narsinh Mehta : Narsinh Mehta (1414 - 1481) was a poet-saint of Gujarat, India, notable as a bhakta, an exponent of Hindu devotional religious poetry. He is especially revered in Gujarat, where he is acclaimed as its Adi Kavi (Sanskrit for "first among poets").

One of the most important features of Narsinh's works is that they are not available in the language in which Narsinh had composed them. They have been largely preserved orally. The oldest available manuscript of his work is dated around 1612, and was found by the noted scholar K.K.Shastri from Gujarat Vidyasabha. Because of the immense popularity of his works, their language has undergone modifications with changing times.

Naseer Ahmad Nasir : Dr. Naseer Ahmad Nasir, was a notable Islamic scholar and philosopher from Pakistan. His biography of Prophet Muhammad (PBUH), Paighambar e Azam O Aakhir, was one of the most important biographical works in Islam of recent times, and in 1978 it was selected as one of the best biographies of Prophet (PBUH) by Rabita al-Alam al-Islami (World Muslim League), at Saudi Arabia. He also wrote numerous books on philosophy, aesthetics, and Islam. In 1977 he was appointed the Vice Chancellor of Islamia University, Bahawalpur.

Naseeruddin Shah : Nasiruddin Shah (b. 20 July 1950) is an Indian movie actor. He has seen success in both mainstream Bollywood movies as well as in art films. orn in 1950 and educated at the National School of Drama in Delhi, Naseeruddin Shah is now one of the icons of New Indian Cinema along with Smita Patil, Shabana Azmi and Om Puri; indeed, he is arguably one of the finest actors in the world today, though the nature of world culture is such that the most mediocre American actors are more widely known around the world. Though his use of hesitant speech and casual gesture to signify psychological complexity sets him apart from mainstream actors, he has gained a fair amount of success in commercial cinema too.

Like many of the other actors of his genre, Naseeruddin Shah was first noticed by Shyam Benegal. He acted in Benegal's Nishant (1975), Manthan and Bhumika (1976). One of his most intense performances was given in Saeed Mirza's Albert Pinto Ko Gussa Kyon Aata Hai ("What makes Albert Pinto angry?", 1980). In the movie, he plays a garage mechanic from Goa who dreams of the expensive cars that he repairs but that are far beyond his reach. The film is set in a Catholic setting, primarily because Mirza did not have the courage to tackle Muslim issues. Naseeruddin Shah has also acted for other New Indian Cinema directors including Mrinal Sen (Khandan, 1983) and Sai Paranjpye (Sparsh, 1979). Besides these "serious" roles, he has a penchant for comedy.

His roles in Ketan Mehta's films and also in films like Mandi, Jaane Bhi Do Yaaron, and Mohan Joshi Hazir Ho! (1983), have endeared him to the Indian public. He has also not shied away from accepting roles in mainstream Hindi movies where he has played a variety of characters, though his slight frame has ensured that he is most often cast in a comic role. However, directors also utilize his great acting talent when a "character role" has to be played. What is surely most arresting about him is the sheer versatility of his talent. Naseeruddin Shah has also played and directed English and Hindi plays. This is not unimportant, since many of the most brilliant film actors came to the cinema after a long stint as theater actors. With his wife Ratna Pathak, Naseeruddin Shah continues to act regularly in plays, often at Shashi Kapoor's Prithvi Theatre.

Nashik : Nashik or Nasik (in marathi) is a city in India's Maharashtra state. Nashik is in the northwest of Maharashtra, 200 km from Mumbai (Bombay) as well as Pune. Nashik is the administrative headquarters of Nashik District and Nashik Division. The city, located in the Western Ghats, has become a center of attraction because of its beautiful surroundings and cool and pleasant climate. Nashik has a personality of its own due to its mythological, historical, social and cultural importance. The city, vibrant and active on the industrial, political, social and cultural fronts, has influenced the lives of many a great personalities. The Godavari River flows through the city from its source lies to the west-southwest of the city, in the holy village of Trimbakeshwara.

Historically the city has been a religious center - it is one of the four cities in India that hosts the massive Kumbh Mela. Temples and ghats (steps) on the banks of Godavari have made Nashik one of the holiest places for Hindus all over the world. Nashik is also famous for its grapes, and ongoing efforts are underway to promote the growth of an export-oriented wine industry in the district.

It is believed that, Nashik got its name during the Ramayana period. Shurpanakha, the sister of the demon Ravana had proposed to marry Rama.Hearing this Rama ordered Laxmana to cut off shurpanakha's nose (Nasika).Thus 'Nasik' got its name. Nashik is famous for the ghats around Panchavati, the area of 5 banyan trees. Sita was abducted by Ravana from this place.

Recent industrial growth has brought about modernization and development. The city is home to an important thermal power plant (Eklahare) and a National Treasury Printing Press (India Security Press in Nashik Road). There are three 'Industrial Estates' in the metropolitan Nashik area and outskirts (Satpur, Ambad and Sinnar). Among various companies that have operations in these industrial estates are Mahindra and Mahindra, MICO (Bosch), VIP, Crompton Greaves, Glaxo, L&T etc.

Nasim Hasan Shah : Born in Lahore on 15th April 15, 1929 to Syed Mohsin Shah, an eminent advocate and political activist, Dr. Justice Nasim Hasan Shah, a former Chief Justice of Pakistan, gained international respect and recognition when he restored the sovereignty of the Parliament in Pakistan; the first such instance in the country's turbulent constitutional history.

The Supreme Court held that dissolution order was based on an incorrect appreciation of the role assigned to the president and of the powers vested in him by the constitution.The Prime Minister is not answerable to the President. In fact, it is the president who is obliged to act on the advice of the Prime Minister except when he enjoys discretionary powers. An inspiring man physically 56 inches tall and 50 inches in girth, he overcame his handicap to become the Chief Justice of the Supreme Court of Pakistan from April 17, 1993 to April 14, 1994.After a brilliant academic career and a Doctorate of Law (with distinction) from Paris University, he had a successful legal practice when he was appointed a High Court Judge at the age of 39, and retired from Supreme Court at 65, the longest tenure by any judge in the history of the Indo-Pak subcontinent.

Nasirabad : Nasirabad is a district in the center west of Balochistan province of Pakistan. Nasirabad's headquarters are at Dera Murad Jamali. The district was notified in 1974. For three years, from July 1987 to

December 1990, it was known as Tamboo district. Tamboo is a small village 40 km west of Dera Murad Jamali. The district has two sub-divisions, D.M. Jamali and Chattar and 1 tehsil, Tamboo. It is further divided into 163 sub-tehsils and 14 mozas. One moza exists of 1 to 5 villages. Over 99% of the people of the area are Muslims.

Nasiruddin Mahmud Shah : Nasiruddin Mahmud Shah (1435-1459), sultan of Bengal, was a descendant of Sultan Shamsuddin Iliyas Shah and ascended the throne of Bengal under the title of Nasiruddin Abul Muzaffar Mahmud Shah in 1435 (839 AH). His accession to the throne marks the restoration of the House of Iliyas Shah after a gap of about twenty three years. During his reign there was a steady expansion of Muslim colonisation and settlement in different parts of Bengal.

Nataraja Temple : This temple is situated in the middle of the town. The complex of the temple covers an area of 40 acres and It is said to be the oldest complex in southern India. It surrounded by four broad "chariot" streets. The tower designed in canonical texts and built of granite upto the ceiling with the structure of seven storeys in brick and mortar. There is a 1000-pillared hall, the Nritta Sabha court carved out like a gigantic chariot. The main image of Nataraja is within a rectangular shrine, covered with copper tiles and gold and it is called the "The Golden Hall". The 108 poses of Bharathanatyam classical dance are carved on the walls of eastern tower. The annual festival held in December/January. In February/March, leading dancers from all parts of India congregate and dance in the temple as an offering to Nataraja.

Nath Sampradaya : The Sanskrit word Nath is the proper name of a siddha sampradaya (initiatory tradition) and the word itself literally means Lord, Protector, or Refuge. The related Sanskrit term Adi Nath means first or original Lord, and is therefore a synonym for Shiva, Mahadeva, or Maheshvara, and beyond these mental concepts, the Supreme Absolute Reality as the originator of all things.

The Nath tradition is a heterodox siddha tradition containing many sub-sects. It was founded by Matsyendranath and further developed by Gorakshanath. These two individuals are also revered in Tibetan Buddhism as Mahasiddhas (great magicians) and are credited with great powers.

The Nath Sampradaya, a development of the earlier Siddha or Avadhut Sampradaya, is an ancient lineage of spiritual masters. Its founding is traditionally ascribed to Shri Bhagavan Dattatreya, considered by some to have been an incarnation of Lord Shiva. However, the establishment of the Naths as a distinct historical sect began around the 8th or 9th century with a simple fisherman, Matsyendranath.

Nathaniel Brassey Halhed : Nathaniel Brassey Halhed (1751-1830) an orientalist and grammarian, is credited with being the first grammarian to write a Bangla grammar using Bangla texts and letters for illustration. Earlier, some rudimentary forms of Bangla grammars and lexicographies had been attempted in Roman script by Portuguese missionaries. Halhed, however, was the first grammarian who attempted to compile a Bangla grammar systematically.

Nathdwara : Nathdwara is a town in Rajasthan state of western India. It is located on the Banas River in Rajsamand District, 48 km north of Udaipur. This holy town is famous for its temple of Krishna which houses the Shrinathji, a 12th century image (murti) of Krishna. The idol was moved in the 17th century from Govardhan hill, near Mathura, to protect it from the Mughal emperor Aurangzeb's campaign against Hindu worship in his empire. The Haveli of Shrinathji (as the temple is called), was once a royal palace of the Sesodia Rajput rulers of Mewar.

This modest temple attracts Krishna devotees from all over the world including various parts of India, but is significantly important to the Gujarati people of India and thus making it one of the wealthiest temples around. The town is often called Shrinathji rather than its original Nathdwara. During any major Hindu festival it is common to see enormous crowds packing the entire town and the temple complex.

Nathiagali : Nathiagali is one of the mountain resort towns of the Galyat, an area centered on the hill station of Murree, a city in the Rawalpindi District of Pakistan. Nathiagali itself is in the Abbottabad District. The main tribe of Nathiagali is karlal.

Nathula Pass : Nathula Pass is a pass on the Indo-China (Tibet) border in the state of Sikkim. The pass forms part of an offshoot of the ancient Silk Route. Nathula Pass is located at an elevation of 4,310 m (14,200 feet) above mean sea level. The route leading up to the pass is one of the world's highest navigable roads, and is maintained by the Border Roads Organisation, a wing of the Indian Army. On the Pass the Indian army and the Chinese border guards are within touching distance of each other. Since both nations have frosty relations with each other, the border is not open to exchange between Indian and Chinese nationals. To visit the Indian side of Nathula, a visitor's permit must be made one day in advance, which is done by any travel agency.

The pass is 56 kilometres east of the capital Gangtok. Although just 5 km north of the Jelepla pass, the Nathula pass is not navigable in winters as it receives heavy snowfall. Temperatures in Nathula regularly dip to -25 °C in winters. The pass is open only to Indian nationals on Wednesdays, Thursdays, Saturdays and Sundays. On other days is it in use for exclusive military use. A no man's land is absent, and the border consists of a barbed wire fence. Every Thursdays and Sunday post between the two nations are exchanged, a tradition dating back many decades.

The road leading to Nathula from Gangtok is a scenic one and the scenery changes from sub-tropical forests to temperate to wet and dry alpine to cold tundra desert devoid of vegetation. On the way one passes the refulgent Tsongmo Lake. Yaks are found in these parts, and in many hamlets are the beasts of burden. On the Tibetan side the pass leads to the Chumbi Valley of the Tibetan Plateau.

During the 1962 Sino-Indian War, the pass witnessed major skirmishes between the two armies. However with the recent thawing in relations between India and China, the pass was scheduled to be opened on 2005-10-02, but was postponed at the last minute to April 2006 due to last minute infrastructure problems on the chinese side. The opening is expected result in an economic boom for the region.

Nathuram Vinayak Godse : Nathuram Vinayak Godse (May 19, 1910 – November 15, 1949) born at Baramati, Poona District, is best known as the assassin of Mahatma Gandhi, the principal leader of the Indian Independence Movement. He was a Marathi Chitpavan Brahmin.

Nathuram attended the local school at Baramati up through the fourth standard. Then he was sent to live with an aunt in Pune so that he could study at an English-language school. In 1930, Nathuram's father was transferred to the town of Ratnagiri. While staying with his parents at Ratnagiri, the young Nathuram first met Veer Savarkar, a proponent of Hindutva. Godse dropped out of high school and became an activist with the Hindu Mahasabha. They were particularly opposed to the separatist politics of the All India Muslim League. Godse started a Marathi newspaper for Hindu Mahasabha called Agrani, some years later renamed Hindu Rashtra.

The Hindu Mahasabha had initially backed Gandhi's campaigns of civil disobedience against the British government. Godse himself had actively participated in the civil disobedience movement; he had been imprisoned by the government on charges of tree-felling. However, Godse and his mentors later rejected Gandhi. They felt that Gandhi was sacrificing Hindu interests in an effort to appease minority groups. They blamed Gandhi for the bloody Partition of India, in which hundreds of thousands of people died.

The immediate motive for the assassination is usually ascribed to Gandhi's January 13, 1948 decision to fast to the death, a term of which was that the Indian central government reverse a decision to withhold the transfer of 55 crore (550 million) rupees to the government of Pakistan. The transfer had been specified in the partition agreement, but the Indian government had refused to complete it, complaining of the Pakistani military occupation of part of the disputed state of Kashmir. The Indian government immediately reversed its decision to withhold the funds, which infuriated Godse and his friends.

It is far from clear whether or not the decision to assassinate Gandhi was taken by Godse alone, or whether he had consulted with other Mahasabha members, or even received their help in carrying out the assassination. Mahasabha resolutely denied all complicity, and Godse took full responsibility. However, many critics believe that Godse did not act alone. Godse assassinated Gandhi on

January 30, 1948, approaching him during a public appearance, bowing, and shooting him at close range. The gun used by Godse was a Beretta M1934 semi-automatic pistol in.380 ACP caliber, serial number 606824.

Following his assassination of Gandhi, Godse, who did not try to flee, was captured, tried and executed. Godse stood trial on November 8, 1949. During the trial, he spent five hours reading out a ninety-page treatise justifying his decision to kill Gandhi. Godse was sentenced to death for the killing and hanged on November 15, 1949. Nathuram Godse's alleged ties to the Rashtriya Swayamsevak Sangh (RSS) led to its ban (reversed a year later) soon after Gandhi's assassination. The RSS to this day deny any connection with Godse and dispute the claim that he was a member; they say that Godse was definitively a member of the Congress Party, and that if any party should be blamed, it should be the Congress, not the RSS. Savarkar was also charged with conspiracy in the assassination of Gandhi, but was acquitted and subsequently released.

Nati : Several forms of Nati dance are prevalent in the Kulu, Sirmaur, Mandi, Mahasu and Chamba areas in Himachal. In Kulu this is known as Siraji Nati. It is like the Kathak dance and embraces a number of dances like Dheeli, Dekhi, Feh, Bakhali, Kahika, Dohari, Lahauli, Chambiyali, Banthada and Loodi. Rhythm is the main feature of this dance. The instruments that accompany this dance range from Drums, Shehnai, Cymbals and Ranasinga (an instrument similar to a trombone). The Shehnai played by the Hesis is the life of the Nati dance. It not only provides a rhythm but also puts life into the entire performance.

The Nati is not a dance for professional dancers but is open for participation by all age groups. It is a slow-moving dance from Lasya variety and lasts through three or four days and nights. The costume for this comprises of Chola (top coat), Ghaghra (skirt), Gachi, Lachhi, a floral shawl and Boomani with silver chains, tight churidar pyjamas, socks and shoes. The women wear heavy armlets and silver and gold ornaments known as Tunki and Chanki around their necks. The men and women hold an ornate fan in one hand and a colourful handkerchief in another and clap as they dance. Earlier the men and women danced separately but now they dance in unison.

National Flower of Bengladesh : Water Lily (shapla) is the National Flower of Bengladesh. It is an aquatic plant of the genus Nymphaea which has large, disk-like, floating leaves and showy flowers. There are about 50 species growing in different countries. In Bangladesh there are two species: N. nouchali (blue variety) and N. pubescens (white variety). Both species grow abundantly as a mixed population in almost all shallow natural waterbodies, but the latter is more frequent and popular in Bangladesh and has been designated as the national flower.

It is seen in abundance in the monsoon season. The peduncle is a popular vegetable to villagers; the tuberous rhizomes are also eaten. Seeds on frying are eaten as puffed-grains in some places. The giant water lily or Amazon water lily (Victoria amazonica) is occasionally grown in some gardens for its enormous (about 2m in diametre) orbicular floating leaves.

National Fruit of Bengladesh : Jackfruit is the National Fruit of Bengladesh. It a large fruit of a milky-juice tree, Artocarpus heterophyllus, of family Moraceae.

The fruit, botanically named sorosis, is a modification of the entire pistillate catkin and contains 100-500 large, oily seeds. The edible, pulpy part represents the parianth. The close relatives of jackfruit are champedak (A. champenden), monkey jack (A. lakoocha), and breadfruit (A. altilis). Of these, monkey jack is grown in Bangladesh.

Jackfruit originated in the forests of the Western Ghats (India), where it still grows in the wild, as well as in the evergreen forests of Assam and Myanmar. The plant is now grown throughout the lowlands of the tropics and the subtropics. It is seen throughout Bangladesh but is grown in abundance in Naogaon, Dinajpur, Savar, Madhupur and Sylhet.

National Animal—Tiger : The magnificent Tiger, Panthera Tigris (Linnaeus), is a striped animal. It has a thick yellow coat of fur with dark stripes. The combination of grace, strength, agility and enormous power has earned the tiger its pride of the species known, The Indian race, the Royal Bengal Tiger, is found throughout the country except in the north -western region and also in the neighboring countries, Nepal, Bhutan and Bangladesh.

National Anthem : Playing time of the full version of the national anthem is approximately 52 seconds. A short version consisting of first and last lines of the stanza (playing time approximately 20 seconds) is also played on certain occasions. The following is Tagore's English rendering of the anthem.

Thou art the ruler of the minds of all people, dispenser of India's destiny. Thy name rouses the hearts of Punjab, Sind, Gujarat and Maratha, Of the Dravida and Orissa and Bengal; It echoes in the hills of the Vindyas and Himalayas, mingles in the music of Jamuna and Ganges and is chanted by the waves of the Indian sea. They pray for thy blessings and sing thy praise. The saving of all people waits in thy hand, thou dispenser of India's destiny. Victory, victory, victory to thee.

National Archives of Bangladesh (NAB) : After 1947, the National Archives of Pakistan (NAP) was established in Karachi in 1951 under the Directorate of Archives and

Libraries, which had no branch whatsoever in East Pakistan. The government of Bangladesh founded the National Archives of Bangladesh (NAB) in Dhaka in 1973. It was placed under the Directorate of National Archives and Libraries, and initially was housed in a rented building at Elephant Road near the Dhaka University campus. In 1985 the office of NAB and its collections were temporarily shifted to a newly completed building of the National Library complex located in Agargaon at Sher-e-Bangla Nagar in Dhaka. Since then, it has remained there.

National Assembly : The National Assembly is the name of either a legislature, or the lower house of a bicameral legislature in some countries. The best known National Assembly, and the first legislature to be known by this title, was that established following the French Revolution in 1789, known as the Assemblée nationale. Consequently, the name is particularly common in Francophone countries, but is also found in some Commonwealth countries.

It was also the name of the legislature during France's First Republic and the Consulate, and since 1946 has been the lower house of the French parliament, first under the Fourth Republic, and from 1958, the Fifth Republic.

National Assembly of Pakistan : The National Assembly is the lower house of the bicameral Parliament of Pakistan. The Speaker of the House presides over the Assembly, and acts as the president of the country if both the President and the Chairman of the Senate are not present. The leader of the largest party in the Assembly often serves as the Prime Minister of Pakistan.

National Awami Party : National Awami Party From the mid-1950s the Awami League suffered a growing conflict between two of its leaders, HS Suhrawardy and Abdul Hamid Khan Bhasani around the issues of foreign policy and regional autonomy. Bhasani, a populist leader of great influence among the peasants and workers, opposed HS Suhrawardy for his pro-American foreign policy and his lack of support to the autonomy of East Bengal. This eventually led to a split within the Awami League when Bhasani in a convention held in Dhaka on 25-26 July 1957, floated the National Awami Party (NAP) with the support of the left-leaning leaders and workers of the AL. Bhasani was elected the president of the new party. Within a short time after its formation and then after its revival in March 1964, NAP emerged as an important left party of the country.

The party, however, fragmented into the NAP (Bhasani) and the pro-Moscow NAP (Wali) in 1967 following the Sino-Soviet conflict. The pro-Chinese party led by Maulana Bhasani had its major support in former East Pakistan, while the pro-Moscow NAP was strong in former West Pakistan. Maulana Bhasani remained a popular leader and his party played an important role in the mass movement of 1969. It was the first party to oppose the Awami League in 1972. But by 1988, the party split into as many as 13 separate parties and factions. The pro-Moscow NAP also underwent a similar process of fragmentation during the 1970s and 1980s.

National Bank of Pakistan : The National Bank of Pakistan has its headquarters in Karachi, Pakistan. It has branches throughout Pakistan as well in USA, Canada, Germany, France, Bahrain, Egypt, Bangladesh, Hong Kong, Japan, South Korea, The Peoples Republic of China, Afghanistan, Turkmenistan, Kyrgyz Republic, Kazakhstan, Uzbekistan and Azerbaijan. The bank provides both commercial and public sector banking services.

National Bank of Pakistan : The National Bank of Pakistan has its headquarters in Karachi, Pakistan. It has branches throughout Pakistan as well in USA, Canada,

Germany, France, Bahrain, Egypt, Bangladesh, Hong Kong, Japan, South Korea, The Peoples Republic of China, Afghanistan, Turkmenistan, Kyrgyz Republic, Kazakhstan, Uzbekistan and Azerbaijan

National Bird of Bangladesh : Magpie-robin (doel) is a black-and-white bulbul-sized, long-tailed bird, Copsychus saularis, of the family Muscicapidae, order Passeriformes.

The bird has been designated as the national bird of Bangladesh. The upper part of the male is glossy blue-black, its wings are blackish brown with a prominent long white patch; throat and breast are blue-black; the rest of its underparts are white; and the tail is black with white outer rectrices. Black portions are replaced by brown and slaty grey in the female. They are found solitary or in pairs; feed largely on grounds, and are usually not afraid of human habitations.

National Birdof India : The Indian Peacock, Pavo Cristatus, the national bird of India, is a colourful, swan -sized bird, with a fan shaped crest of feathers, a white patch under the eye and a long, slender neck. The male of the species is more colourful than the female, with a glistening blue breast and neck and a spectacular bronze-green train of around 200 elongated feathers. The female is brownish, slightly smaller than the male, and lacks the train.

The peacock is widely found in the Indian sub-continent from the south and east of the Indus river, Jammu and Kashmir, east Assam, South Mizoram and the whole of the Indian peninsula.

National Cadet Corps (NCC) : The National Cadet Corps (India) is the Indian military cadet corps. It is open to school and college students on voluntary basis. The National Cadet Corps in India is a voluntary organization which recruits cadets from high schools and colleges. The Cadets are given basic military training in small arms and parades. The officers and cadets have no liability for active military service. The motto of NCC is "Unity and Discipline". The Param Vir Chakra is an Indian military decoration given for valour in combat operations. It is India's highest military honor. The name is sometimes abbreviated as PVC. It literally means 'Wheel (or Cross) of the Ultimate Brave' (Sanskrit: Param, Ultimate; Vir, Brave; Chakra, Wheel, or its western equivalent, Cross). Equivalent awards in the United States are the Medal of Honor and the Victoria Cross in the United Kingdom.

National Calendar : The National calendar based on the Saka Era with Chaitra as its first month and a normal year of 365 days was adopted from 22 march 1957 along with the Gregorian calendar for the following official purposes Gazette of India News broadcast all India radio Calendars issued by the government of India and Government communications addressed to the members of the public. Dates of the national calendar have a permanent correspondence with dates of the Gregorian calendar; Chaitra falling on 22 march and on 21 march in leap year.

National Capital Territory of Delhi (NCT) : The National Capital Territory of Delhi (NCT) is a special Union Territory of India. The territory encompasses three census towns: New Delhi (the capital of India), Old Delhi and Delhi Cantonment, along with 214 villages. The term is also used informally to refer to the national capital region (NCR) which is a metropolitan region and includes the surrounding satellite cities of Faridabad, Gurgaon, Ghaziabad and NOIDA.

The NCT was set up as a federally administered Union Territory on 1956-11-01. In December 1991, the NCT was given a Legislative Assembly headed by a Chief Minister.

The territory is not classified as a true Union territory, though the Central Government does have limited control over the functioning of the territory much like other Union territories. Delhi is to eventually become a full fledged state. The NCT is unique in India in that the municipal control is handled by a locally elected government, while major areas like police, and administration are handled by the Central Government. The establishment of a NCT was with a desire to fuel development of surrounding areas into urban centers. This would help in the de-congestion of the main city which already suffers from an over burden by a constant in-pouring of people from all over India.

National Chambal (Gharial) Wildlife Sanctuary : The National Chambal (Gharial) Wildlife Sanctuary in India was founded in 1978 and is part of a large area co-administered by the states of Rajasthan, Madhya Pradesh and Uttar Pradesh, within an area of 5,400 square kilometres along the Chambal River. Approximately 400 km of the river is within the reserve, forming the core area. Apart from the Ganges River Dolphin (Platanista gangetica), the other inhabitants of the sanctuary include magar (crocodile) and gharial (Gavialis gangeticus). Stretch of crystal clear water also supports Marsh Crocodile, Smooth Coated Otters, 6 species of Terrapins/Turtles plus 250 species of birds.

Migratory birds from Siberia forms its rich avian fauna.One of the rare bird present here is Indian Skimmers. Black-bellied Terns, Red-crested Pochard and Ferruginous Pochard, Bar-headed Goose, Sarus Crane, Great Thick-knee, Indian Courser, Pallas's Fish Eagle, Pallid Harrier, Greater Flamingos and Lesser Flamingos, Darters, and Brown Hawk Owl and many other birds are part of the sanctuary's rich fauna.The sanctuary is protected under India's Wildlife Protection Act 1972. The sanctuary is administered by the Department of Forest under the Project Officer with headquarter at Morena, Madhya Pradesh.Part of the sanctuary is under heavy illegal sand mining, which is endangering its fragile ecosystem.

National Democratic Alliance (NDA) : The National Democratic Alliance (NDA) is a coalition in India. It is led by the Bharatiya Janata Party and had 13 constituent parties at the time of its formation in 1998. The convenor of NDA is George Fernandes, and its honorary Chairman is former Prime Minister Atal Bihari Vajpayee. The NDA formed the Government in 1998, which collapsed within a year due to the AIADMK pulling out, but it won the 1999 elections and formed a stronger majority.

The NDA governed under Prime Minister Vajpayee for a full five years hence, and was widely expected to win the 2004 elections. But the BJP, the chief party lost too many key seats along with the major allies and the Alliance could not bid for power. Former Deputy Prime Minister and BJP chief Lal Krishna Advani heads the NDA as Leader of the Opposition.

National Emblem of Bangladesh : The National Emblem of Bangladesh was adopted shortly after independence in 1971. Located on the emblem is a Water Lily, that is bordered on two sides by rice sheaves. Above the water lilly are four stars and a flower bud.

The water lilly is the country's national flower, and is representative of the many rivers that run through Bangladesh. Rice represents its presence as the staple food of Bangladesh, and for the agriculture of that nation. The four stars represent the four founding principles that were originally enshrined in the first constitution of Bangladesh in 1972: nationalism, secularism, socialism, and democracy.

National Emblem of India : The national emblem of India is an adaptation of the Buddhist Lion Capital of

Asoka at Sarnath, near Banaras in the north Indian state of Uttar Pradesh. It has been taken from the stupa at Sanchi. It has four lions, resting on a circular abacus. The fourth lion is on the rear and hence hidden from view. The emblem symbolizes power, courage and confidence. The abacus is girded by four smaller animals—guardians of the four directions: the lion of the north, the elephant of the east, the horse of the south and the bull of the west.

The abacus rests on a nelumbo nucifera in full bloom, exemplifying the fountainhead of life. The emblem forms a part of the official letterhead of the Government of India, and appears on all Indian currency as well. It also sometimes functions as the Coat of Arms of India in many places and appears prominently on the diplomatic and national Passport of the Republic of India.

National Fish of Bengladesh : Locally known as Ilish, Hilsa has been designated as the national fish of Bangladesh. It belongs to the genus Tenualosa of the family Clupeidae, order Clupeiformes.

The body is strongly compressed and moderately deep with dorsal and ventral profile equally convex. The upper jaw has a distinct median notch. Regularly arranged medium-sized scales cover the metallic silver-coloured body. Body length may reach up to 60 cm, but commonly found specimens measure 35 to 40 cm. A large-sized hilsa weighs about 2.5 kg. Females grow faster, and are usually larger than males. The hilsa is known to be a fast swimmer, and attains maturity in one to two years.

National Flag of Idia : The national Flag is a horizontal tricolour of deep saffron at the top, White in the middle and dark green at the bottom in equal proportion. The ratio of width of the flag to its length is two to three. In the center of the white band is a navy blue wheel which represents the 'Chakra'.

Its design is that of the wheel which appears on the abacus of Saranath Lion Capital of King Ashoka. Its diameter approximates to the width of the white band and it has 24 spokes. The design of the National flag was adopted by the constituent Assembly of India on 22 July in 1947. Its use and display are regulated by the Indian Flag code.

National Flag of Bangladesh : The national flag of Bangladesh was adopted officially on January 17, 1972. It is based on a similar flag used during the Bangladesh Liberation War of 1971. This flag depicted a map of Bangladesh over a red sun.

The map was later deleted from the flag, most likely to simplify the design. The current flag resembles the flag of Japan, except that it has a green field instead of a white one. A red disc is on top of the green field, offset slightly toward the hoist so that it appears centered when the flag is flying. The red disc represents the sun rising over Bengal, and also the blood of those who died for the independence of Bangladesh. The green field stands for the lushness of the land of Bangladesh.

National Flag of Pakistan : The national flag of Pakistan was designed by Amir-ud-Din Khidwai based on the 1906 flag of the All-India Muslim League. It was adopted on August 11, 1947, three days before independence. The flag comprises a dark green field (representing Muslims) with a vertical white stripe in the hoist (left side) (representing non-Muslim minorities). In the centre is a white crescent (symbolising progress) and a white five-pointed star (symbolising light and knowledge). A common name for the Pakistani flag is 'Sabz Hilali Parcham' which is Urdu for 'Green Flag with the Crescent'.

National Flower of India : Lotus (Nelumbo nucifera) is the National Flower of India. It is a sacred flower and occupies a unique position in the art and mythology of ancient India and has been an auspicious symbol of Indian culture since time immemorial.

National Fruit of India : The fruit Mango,of the tree Mangifera indica, is one of the most widely cultivated fruits of the tropical world. This juicy, delicious fruit is a rich source of Vitamins A, C and D. In India there are hundreds of varieties of mangoes, in different sizes, shapes and colours etc. Mangoes, have been cultivated in India since time immemorial. The famous Indian poet Kalidasa sang its praises.King Alexander relished its taste, as did the Chinese traveller Hieun Tsang. Akbar, the Moghal emperor planted over 100,000 mango trees in Darbhanga, known as Lakhi Bagh(India).

National Library of Pakistan : The National Library of Pakistan was established on August 24, 1982, almost 46 years after the country's independence was granted. Over a short span of seven years the library has acquired numerous collections through purchases, copyright deposits, gifts, exchanges, and donations.

National Remote Sensing Agency of India : National Remote Sensing Agency is an autonomous institution supported by Department of Space of India. It is responsible for acquisition, processing and supply of data from remote sensing satellites. It runs the Indian Institute of Remote Sensing at Dehra Dun. The agency is part of efforts to harness the Remote Sensing capabilities developed by ISRO. It also manages a satellite monitoring station at Shadnagar, near Hyderabad. It is responsible for collecting information from different Indian and International satellites (IRS, LandSat, ERS) and interacting with International agencies (NOAA).

National Revolution and Solidarity Day : In Bangladesh, November 7 is celebrated as the National

Revolution and Solidarity Day. This commemorates the 1975 uprising formed by people and soldiers. The uprising, led by Colonel Abu Taher, ended the three day coup organised by General Khaled Mosharraf. It also helped put General Ziaur Rahman, founder of Bangladesh Nationalist Party, in power. November 7 is a national holiday in Bangladesh.

National Security Guards (NSG) : The National Security Guards (NSG) is India's prime counter-terrorist force. The NSG's roles include protecting VIPs, conducting anti-sabotage checks, rescuing hostages, neutralizing terrorist threats to vital installations, engaging terrorists and responding to hijacking and piracy. The NSG has a strength of 7,500 personnel, and consists of the Special Action Group (SAG) and the Special Rangers Group (SRG). The SAG is the offensive wing and draws its members from the Indian Army, whilst the SRG, which draws its members from central police organizations, supports the SAG in isolating target areas.

The NSG was established under the National Security Guard Act of 1986, in response to the 1984 Operation Bluestar, the storming of the Golden Temple by the Indian military, which caused widespread damage to the temple and heavy casualties, including civilians. The operation highlighted the need for a special force to conduct counter-terrorist operations with greater efficiency. The NSG has been deployed only rarely since its birth. Recently, it achieved considerable success in eliminating the terrorists who infiltrated the Akshardham Temple in Gandhinagar, Gujarat. The NSG is much sought after for VVIP security for high-risk VVIPs in India. This task is done by the SRG of the NSG.

National Song : The song 'Vande Matharam', composed in Sanskrit by Bankimchandra Chaterji, was a source of inspiration to the people in their struggle for freedom. It has an equal status with 'Jana-gana-mana'. The first political occasion when it was sung was the 1896 session of the Indian National Congress.

National Stock Exchange of India (NSE) : The National Stock Exchange of India (NSE), is one of the largest and most advanced stock markets in India. The NSE is the world's third largest stock exchange in terms of transactions. It is located in Mumbai, the financial capital of India. The NSE VSAT terminals, 2799 in total (31st December 2005), cover 320 cities in India.

National Tree of India : The Banyan Tree -Called the Indian fig tree(Ficus bengalensis) grow over a large area. The roots then give rise to more trunks and branches. Because of this characteristic & longevity, the Banyan tree is considered immortal & sacred and is an integral part of the myths and legends in India. Even today, the banyan tree is the focal point of village life and the village council meetings under the shade of this huge shade-giving tree.

National University of Modern Languages (Pakistan) : National University of Modern Languages is located at Islamabad, Pakistan. National University of Modern Languages started as language institute in 1970. During the last 35 years, the university has matured into a national university offering various programmes through non-formal education system throughout the country. It has crossed several barriers and now teaches 23 languages in addition to many emerging arts and sciences.

Nationalist Congress Party (NCP) : The Nationalist Congress Party (NCP) is an Indian political party. It was formed on May 25, 1999, by Sharad Pawar, P.A. Sangma, and Tariq Anwar after they were thrown out of the Congress Party due to their stating their belief that a person of foreign origin should not become the Prime

Minister of India. This is the first ever political site was introduce in India by Mumbai nationalist congress Party members with the ideai of shri Sharad Chandra Pawar.

In January 2004, Sangma quit the NCP because he felt Sharad Pawar was getting closer to the Congress Party in spite of no change of leadership in the Congress. For a brief period Sangma's fraction tried to claim the right to the name and symbol of NCP. The Election Commission acknowledged Pawar's group as the genuine NCP. Following the decision of the Election Commission, Sangma's group merged with AITC to form the Nationalist Trinamool Congress. The NCP advertises itself a progressive, secular party that stands for "democracy, Gandhian secularism, equity, social justice, and federalism." It positions itself as a moderate, left-leaning alternative to the Bharatiya Janata Party (BJP) and the Congress. The party's election symbol is an analog clock that reads 10:10. The party is in power in the state of Maharashtra in alliance with Congress(I). Since 2004 NCP is a member of the United Progressive Alliance, which governs the country.

Natore : Natore is a district located in northern Bangladesh. It borders the metropolitan city of Rajshahi, and used to be part of Rajshahi district. With an area of 1896.05 sq km, the district is bounded by Naogaon and Bogra districts on the north, Pabna and Kushtia districts on the south, Pabna and Sirajganj districts on the east, Rajshahi district on the west. Average annual temperature: maximum 37.8 C, minimum 11.2 C; annual rainfall 1862 mm. Rivers: 10 most noted of which are Atrai, Baral, Narod, Nandakunja; Chalan Beel is notable. Natore subdivision was established in 1845 under Rajshahi district and it was turned into a district in 1984. It consists of 6 upazilas, 4 municipalities, 36 wards, 93 mahallas, 52 unions, 1272 mouzas and 1377 villages. The upazilas are Natore

Sadar, Bagatipara, Baraigram, Gurudaspur, Lalpur and Singra. Indigo resistance movements were held in this district during 1859 to 1860. During the War of Liberation in 1971 a direct battle was fought between the Pak army and the freedom fighters on 29 March in which about 40 members of the Pak army including Major Aslam and Capt Ishaq were killed.

Natya Shastra : The Natya Shastra or Natyasastra is the principal work of dramatic theory in the Sanskrit drama of classical India. It is a set of precepts on the writing and performance of dance, music and theatre. The Natya Shastra was written by the sage Bharata Muni who, it is claimed, was directly inspired by the god Brahma. It is believed to have been written during the period between 400 BC and 200 AD. Some scholars believe it was written by various authors at different times.

The text is written in the Sanskrit language, and consists of 6,000 sutras, or verse stanzas, incorporated in 36 chapters. There are some passages that are composed in a prose form. The name can be loosely translated as The Textbook on Drama. Natya, or nataka means drama, and in contemporary usage does not include dance. However, nataka originally derives from the word meaning "dance" (root: nat). This suggests that in traditional Sanskrit drama, music and dancing, as well as acting, were important.

Naulakha pavilion : The Naulakha pavilion is a marble building located at the Sheesh Mahal courtyard, which is itself located at the Lahore Fort in Lahore, Pakistan. Its western face provides a panoramic view of the ancient city of Lahore. When it was built in 1631 A.D. by the Mughal emperor Shahjahan, it cost Rs.900,000, an exorbitant amount at the time. It is called Naulakha because that word in Urdu means 'worth 9 lakhs' (one lakh equals 100,000).

Navagraha : In Hindu astrology, the Navagraha are the nine chief celestial beings:

—Surya (Sun)

—Chandra (Moon)

—Chevaai (Mars)

—Budhan (Mercury)

—Guru (Jupiter)

—Shukran (Venus)

—Shani (Saturn)

—Rahu (Head of Demon Snake)

—Ketu (Tail of Demon Snake).

"Nava" means "nine". "Graha" is sometimes translated as "planet", but the Sun, Moon, and Ragu and Ketu are not "planets" according to western astronomy. "Graha" is sometimes translated as "celestial body", but Ragu and Ketu are not celestial bodies by western astronomy either. A third translation is celestial god or demi-god, but again, Ragu and Ketu are Asuras not Devas.

Navagraha Temple : Navagraha temple or temple of nine planets is situated on Chitrachal Hill to the east of the town. It was the ancient seat of study of astronomy and astrology. The nine planets are represented by the nine linga's inside the main temple. This temple just 3 km from the railway station is still a center of Astrological and Astronomical research. It was for this temple Guwahati was named Pragjyotishpur (the city of Astrology).

Navanna : Navanna [nava + anna, literally, new food] a harvest festival celebrating the harvesting of aman paddy. All agricultural societies celebrate the harvesting of the main crop. At Wazirabad in North-West India a harvest festival is observed in the month of Baishakh to welcome the new wheat crop. Such festivals are also held in South India. The object is to pray for more crops, timely rain, children and cattle.

Tribal communities in Bangladesh also celebrate the harvest. The santals observe the soharay festival in the months of Paus-Magh after the winter crop is harvested. The celebration lasts for 7 days and 7 nights and includes drinking, singing and dancing. The Usui tribes observe the mailukma festival to welcome Laksmi, the goddess of crops. The Mru tribes observe the chamoinat festival during which they sacrifice hens and entertain guests with new rice. The Garo tribes observe the wangalla festival during which they feast, drink, sing and dance.

Navaratri or Nadahabb : This festival starts on Bhadrapad Amavasya and continues for about 10 days in Karnataka. On the 9th day weapons, implements of labour etc. are offered worship. On the 10th day which is known as Vijayadashami, the deities of Shidlingappa and Hanuman are taken to the Banni tree in front of Shidlingappa temple. The tree and the sword of the village servants are offered worship by the Police Patil and then the Police Patil cuts a branch of the Banni tree with the sword. This is followed by the exchange of Banni leaves by all the persons who have gathered there. The Banni leaves symbolise Gold and with the exchange of such gold, all past differences, animosities etc. are expected to be forgotten. On this day they arrange special dances by Vagayyas at Sri. Billadeva temple where the deities of Hanuman and Shidlingappa are taken. The following day some people are fed at this temple.

Naveen Patnaik : Naveen Patnaik is the Chief Minister of Orissa, India. He is the son of former Chief Minister of Orissa and Gandhi era freedom fighter Biju

Patnaik. Shri Naveen Patnaik was born on October 16, 1946 at Cuttack, Orissa to Shri Biju Patnaik and Smt. Gyan Patnaik. He went to Welham Preparatory School for Boys in Dehradun when he was seven years old. After that he studied at the The Doon School, Dehradun till he passed out with a Senior Cambridge Certificate at 17 years. He excelled in History, Oil painting and athletics in this school. He went on to Delhi University when he got his Bachelor's Degree in Arts at the age of 20 years.

Earlier Shri Patnaik was elected as Member of the 11th Lok Sabha in by-election from Aska Parliamentary Constituency. He was a member of the Consultative Committee of Ministry of Steel & Mines, Member of Standing Committee on Commerce, and Member Library Committee of Parliament. In 1998 he formed the Biju Janata Dal Party in Orissa and was elected to the 12th Lok Sabha from the Aska Parliamentary constituency.

Navi Mumbai : Navi Mumbai (erstwhile: New Bombay) is a satellite twin of the city of Mumbai, India. It is the largest planned new city in the world,with an area of 344 km². It is a city of its own, Navi Mumbai lies on the mainland on the eastern seaboard of the Thane Creek. The city limits stretches from Airoli near Thane in the north, to Uran in the south. The length of the city is almost the same as Mumbai. The Vashi and Airoli Bridges connect Navi Mumbai to Mumbai. There is now a new Railway link from Vashi to Thane via Airoli, Ghansoli, and Kopar Khairane

Navnath : Navnath are the nine saints in the Hindu mythology. They belong to the Nath Sampradaya. The nine saints who are collectively referred as Navnath are, Machindranath, Gorakhnath, Jalandernath, Kanifnath, Charpatnath, Nageshnath, Bharatnath, Revannath and Gahininath.

Navroz : The *Navroz* festival of the Shia Muslims comes a week after the New year day in Kashmir. They celebrate this nine-day festival with good eating and activities showing a spirit of gay abandon, in contrast to recitation of religious dirges that characterise most of their festivals. During the month of April they celebrate *Durga Ashtami*, followed by *Ramnavami*. It is the birthday of Lord Rama. For the Kashmiri pandits the day is also connected with goddess Durga, and they celebrate it with a feast of rice and meat viands, after the prayers. In the middle of April or on the Baisakhi day, starts the New year of the *Vikrami Samvat*. The day presents a grand spectacle of colour and gaiety on the Dal lake and in the gardens that flank it.

Nawab : Nawab was originally the subadar (provincial governor) or viceroy of a subah (province) or region of the Mughal empire. The term is Urdu, derived from the Arabic word Naib, meaning deputy. In some areas, especially Bengal, the term is pronounced Nabob. This later variation has entered the English and other foreign languages. Since most of the Muslim rulers of the subcontinent had—like most otherwise titled Hindu (Maha) radjas and other princely states—accepted the authority of the Mughals at the height of this empire the term Nawab is often used to refer to any Muslim ruler in the subcontinent. This is technically imprecise, as it was also awarded to others and not applied to every Muslim ruler. With the decline of that empire, the title and the powers that went with it became hereditary in the ruling families in the various provinces.

Nawab Mohsin-ul-Mulk : Nawab Mohsin-ul-Mulk (Dec 9, 1837 - 1907), also known as Syed Mehdi Ali was one of the founders of All India Muslim League. He was born to a family of Barah Syeds at Etawah. His early education was at Etawah. In 1867, he sat for the Provincial Civil Service examination and topped the list of successful candidates. He was appointed as Deputy Collector in U.

P. It was here that he met Sir Syed Ahmad Khan. In 1874, Mehdi Ali proceeded to Hyderabad and for his meritorious services, he was conferred the titles of Munir Nawaz Jang and Nawab Mohsin-ud-Daula by the Nizam of Hyderabad.

In 1893, Mehdi Ali came to Aligarh and offered his services to Sir Syed Ahmad Khan to assist him in spreading the message of Aligarh. Upon the death of Sir Syed, he was appointed as the Secretary of the Muslim Educational Conference. Towards the beginning of 20th century, the Hindi-Urdu controversy arose in the United Provinces. Mohsin-ul-Mulk took up the pen in defense of Urdu in collaboration with the Urdu Defense Association.

Nawab Mohsin-ul-Mulk, being a farsighted and politically conscious leader, carried on correspondence with the private secretary of the Viceroy to give his point-of-view on the necessity of separate representation for the Muslims in all legislatures and local bodies. In 1906, he, along with Nawab Viqar-ul-Mulk, was asked to draft the constitution of the Muslim League. He died on October 16, 1907 from chronic diabetes.

Nawab Nauroz/Nowroz Khan : Nawab Nauroz/ Nowroz Khan, commonly known by Balochs as Babu Nowroz, was the head of the Zarakzai tribes of Balochistan. He started an armed struggle against the occupation by Pakistan of Baloch lands (Balochistan). He was later arrested by the Pakistani army while he came for negotiations to the army. He and his followers, including his sons and nephews, were taken to Hyderabad Jail, where his sons and nephews were hanged, while due to his old age he was held in prison, where he later passed away.

Nawabganj : Nawabganj is a district in the Rajshahi division of Bangladesh. With an area of 1744.33 sq km, the district is bounded by West Bengal of India on the north, south and west, Rajshahi and Naogaon districts on the east. The district lies under Barind Tract and consists of diaras and charlands (sandbars develop in riverbed). Main rives are Ganges, Mahananda, Pagla, Moraganga and Punarbhaba. Beel Bhatia, Beel Choral, Beel Hogla, Beel Singra, Sukrabari Damos, Maricha Dara, Beel Putimari, Beel Anal, Kumiradaha are the noted depressions. Annual average temperature: maximum 37.8 C, minimum 11.2 C; annual rainfall 1862 mm. Until 1947, Nawabganj was a thana under the district of Maldah (India). At the time of partition, it was upgraded to a Subdivision under Rajshahi district and again upgraded to a district in 1984. The district consists of 3 municipalities, 33 wards, 134 mahallas, 5 upazilas, 45 union parishads, 830 mouzas and 1136 villages. The upazilas are Bholahat, Gomastapur, Nachole, Nawabganj Sadar, Shibganj; municipalities are Nawabganj Sadar, Shibganj, Rohanpur.

Nawabshah: Nawabshah city (established in 1912) is located in the centre of Sindh, Pakistan, and is therefore often known as the Heart of Sindh. Nawabshah is famous for sugarcane and banana production; its climate is hot and dry. Nawabshah has an airport near the city, where General Pervez Musharraf, President of Pakistan, was once asked to be arrested on a flight from Colombo (Sri Lanka) the day former Prime Minister of Pakistan Nawaz Sharif was ousted. The MPA of Nawabshah is Mr.Tariq Masood Arain, and belongs to PPP Nawabshah possesses various institutes for training in engineering or medical fields

Nawabzada Nasrullah Khan : Nawabzada Nasrullah Khan (1918-2003) was a senior political figure in Pakistan. Just before his death, he was the Chairman of Alliance for Restoration of Democracy (ARD) working tirelessly for the restoration of democracy in Pakistan against General Pervez Musharraf. Mr. Khan's political career spanned over half a century. His willingness to forge alliances with opposing political parties became an almost permanent feature of his leadership.

Mr. Khan often served as a rallying point for Pakistan's opposition parties in their fight against military rulers

Nawajish Khan : Nawajish Khan medieval Bangla poet, writer of Gule Bakawali. The bhanita (prefatory self-introduction) of the poem mentions that he was born in Amirabad under Satkania thana of Chittagong. His father, Muhammad Yar Khondakar, is noted as the founder of Amirabad. Selim Khan, the poet's great grandfather, came from Gauda and settled at Silimpur. Nawajish Khan was inspired to write Gule Bakawali by a local zamindar named Badyanath Roy.

Nawalgarh : Nawalgarh (also known as Hindur or Nalagarh) is a town in Himachal Pradesh, India. In the early twentieth century, Nawalgarh was one of the Simla hill states, under the government of the Punjab. The country was overrun by the Gurkhas for some years before 1815, when they were driven out by the British, and the Raja was confirmed in possession of the territory. Grain and opium have, in the past, been main agricultural products.

Nawegaon National Park : Established in 1975, the Nawegaon National Park is situated in Bhandara district in an area of 134sq.km. The nearest town is Gondia 100km from the park. The nearest airport is Nagpur, 30km from the park and the railhead is Deolgaon, one km away from the park.

The fauna consist of leopard, tiger panther, sloth bear, fishing cat, four horned antelope, sambar, nilgai, python, peafowl and migratory birds. There is a lake in the park which attracts a large number of migratory birds during the period from January to April.

Naxalbari : Naxalbari is a village in northern region of the state of West Bengal, India. It is famous for being the site of a revolutionary peasant uprising in 1967, which began with the "Land to tiller" slogan and it inspired similar revolts in other parts of the India.

Naxalite : Naxalite or Naxalism is an informal name given to revolutionary communist groups that were born out of the Sino-Soviet split in the Indian communist movement. The term comes from Naxalbari, a small village in West Bengal, where a leftist section of Communist Party of India (Marxist) (CPI(M)) led by Charu Majumdar and Kanu Sanyal led a militant peasant uprising in 1967, trying to develop a "revolutionary opposition" in order to establish "revolutionary rule" in India. Mazumdar greatly admired Mao Zedong of China and advocated that Indian peasants and lower classes must follow in his footsteps and overthrow the government and upper classes whom he held responsible for their plight. In 1967 'Naxalites' organized the All India Coordination Committee of Communist Revolutionaries (AICCCR), and broke away from CPI(M). Uprisings were organized in several parts of the country. In 1969 AICCCR gave birth to Communist Party of India (Marxist-Leninist). After the internal revolt led by Satyanarayan Singh in 1971 and the death of Mazumdar in 1972, the movement was fragmented into many competing factions.

Practically all Naxalite groups trace their origin to the CPI(ML). A separate tendency from the beginning was the Maoist Communist Centre, which evolved out of the Dakshin Desh-group. (MCC later fused with People's War Group to form Communist Party of India (Maoist).) A third tendency is that of the Andhra revolutionary communists, which was mainly presented by UCCRI(ML), following the mass line legacy of T. Nagi Reddy. That tendency broke with AICCCR at an early stage.

Today some groups have become legal organisations participating in parliamentary elections, such as Communist Party of India (Marxist-Leninist) Liberation. Others, such as Communist Party of India (Maoist) and Communist Party of India (Marxist-Leninist) Janashakti, are engaged in armed guerrilla struggles. Typically, there is a groundswell of public support for such activities, though it seems to have come down in recent years with counter-movements such as those led by Mahendra Karma becoming popular. Many groups combine both legal and illegal methods of work.

Nazar Mohammed Rashid : Nazar Mohammed Rashid (1910 – October 9, 1975), commonly known as Noon Meem Rashid or N.M. Rashid, was an influential poet of modern Urdu poetry.

He was born in Gujranwala, Punjab, and did his masters in economics from the Government College Lahore. He served for the UN and remained in many countries. He retired to England in 1973 and died in a London hospital in 1975. His first book of free verse, Mavra, was published in 1940 and established him as a pioneering figure in Urdu literature.

Nazia Hassan : Nazia Hassan and Zoheb Hassan were a singing sensation and pioneers of the Pakistani pop music scene during the 1980s. The brother and sister duo released their first album Disco Deewane in 1980 and became an instant hit with the title song reaching the top of the local charts. They released their second album in 1981 titled Boom Boom. It was a sensation both in the United Kingdom as well as in South Asia. But they shot to true stardom and fame as a result of the song Aap Jaisa Koi which Nazia Hassan sang for the Indian movie

Qurbani made by actor/producer Feroz Khan when she was just fifteen.

Nazim Hussain Siddiqui : Nazim Hussain Siddiqui served as Chief Justice of the Supreme Court of Pakistan, from December 31, 2003 to June 29, 2005. Justice Siddiqui was born on June 30, 1940.His father was Late Mukarram Hussain Siddiqui.He did his BA, LLB from the University of Hyderabad and LLM from the University of Karachi. Presently, he was also serving as chairman Central Zakat Council of Pakistan. Member, Board of Governors of Aga Khan University Hospital, Karachi;Member, Selection Board of the Quaid-i-Azam University, Islamabad.

Nazimabad : Nazimabad is a suburb of Karachi, Sindh, Pakistan. Nazimabad was developed in the early 1950s to settle Muslim refugees in Pakistan. This suburb was named after Khawaja Nazimuddin who was the second Governor-General of Pakistan, and later the second Prime Minister of Pakistan as well. In late 1950s, the northern extension of Nazimabad, North Nazimabad, was developed as a residential area for federal government employees. But in the early 1960s the capital of Pakistan was transfered from Karachi to newly developed capital Islamabad

Nazrul Geeti : Nazrul Geeti, literally meaning "music of Nazrul", are the works of Kazi Nazrul Islam, national poet of Bangladesh and active revolutionary during Indian Independence Movement. Nazrul Geeti incorporate revolutionary notions as well as more spiritual and philosophical themes. Kazi Nazrul Islam used his music as a major way of disseminating his revolutionary notions, mainly by the use of strong words and powerful, but catchy, tunes. Among the revolutionary songs, Karar Oi Louho Kopat (Prison-doors of Steel) is best known and has been used several movies—especially those made during the pre-independence period of Bangladesh.

N Chandrababu Naidu : Nara Chandrababu Naidu (born April 20, 1951) was the chief minister of Andhra Pradesh during 1995-2004. He holds the record of being the longest serving chief minister of A. P. He is currently the leader of the Telugu Desam Party, the second largest party in Andhra Pradesh.

Mr. N. Chandrababu Naidu was born in the Naravaripally village of Chittoor district on 20th April, 1950. He did his Masters in Economics from the Sri Venkateswara University, Tirupati. He was working towards a Ph.D. degree at the same university, when he took to politics.

Naidu has won numerous awards including 'IT Indian of the Milleneum' (India Today) Business Person of the Year (Economic Times) member of the World Economic Forum's Dream Cabinet and South Asian of the Year (Time Asia). Naidu was chosen as one of 50 leaders at the forefront of change in the year 2000 by the Business Week magazine for being an unflinching proponent of technology and for his drive to transform the State.

Nehru Administration (1952 - 1964) : Prime Minister Nehru led the Congress to major election victories in 1957 and 1962. The Parliament passed extensive reforms that increasing the legal rights of women in Hindu society, and further disempowered caste discrimination and untouchability. Nehru advocated a strong initiative to enroll India's children to complete primary education, and thousands of schools, colleges and institutions of advanced learning, such as the Indian Institutes of Technology were founded across the nation. Nehru advocated a socialist model for the economy of India—no taxation for Indian farmers, minimum wage and benefits for blue-collar workers, and the nationalization of heavy industries such as steel, aviation, shipping, electricity and mining. An extensive public works and industrialization campaign resulted in the construction of major dams, irrigation canals, roads, thermal and hydroelectric power stations

Nehru Planetarium : It has a seating capacity of 200 and conducts special shows for schools. The lectures and shows on astronomy are a regular features. It is closed on Mondays and 2nd Tuesdays. Just opposite to Nehru Planetarium, is a new attraction "Musical Dancing Fountain" in Karnataka

Nehru Trophy Boat Race : Nehru Trophy Boat Race, the most colourful water sport in Kerala, is conducted at PUNNAMADA LAKE in Alappuzha on the second saturday of every August. This prestigious cultural event of Kerala has been attracting people from all over the world. Nehru Trophy Boat Race is a festival for the people of Alleppey the main attraction of which is the sportive sprits among the participants of the race.

This trophy named as NEHRU TROPHY was donated by the late Prime Minister of INDIA Jawaharlal Nehru to the winners of the first boat race which was an impromptu one conducted in 1952 in honour of Panditji who visited Alappuzha. This aquatic festival fosters a sense of unity and fraternity and sports man spirit event and attaching foreign tourists also.

In the year 1952, Pandit Jawaharlal Nehru visited the erstwhile Travancore-Cochin. On his way to Alleppey from Kottayam he was given a roaring reception by the people of Alleppey, escorted by the huge snake-boats. Having gone through the tremendous excitement of sailing in a snake-boat popularly known as Chundan, Jawaharlal Nehru donated a rolling trophy to be awarded to the winner.

The trophy is a replica of a snake-boat in silver, placed on wooden abacus on which the following words of Panditji are inscribed above his signature.

Nehru Zoological Park : Nehru Zoological Park is the largest Zoo in India. It is located near the Mir Alam Tank in Hyderabad, Andhra Pradesh. It was established in 1963 and named after the first prime minister of the country, Jawaharlal Nehru. It is spread over an area of 300 acres (approx. 1.2 square Km). It has a wide selection of animals—nearly 1,500 species of birds, animals and reptiles are housed here. It is closed on mondays.

Nek Chand Saini : Nek Chand Saini is an Indian outsider artist, famous for building the Rock Garden of Chandigarh, a forty acre (160,000 m^2) sized sculpture garden in the city of Chandigarh, India.

Nek Chand Saini was born in 1924 in the village of Berian Kalan, Tehsil Shakargarh, an area belonging today to Pakistan. His family moved to Chandigarh, India in 1947 during the Partition. At the time, Chandigarh was being redesigned as a modern utopia by the Swiss architect Le Corbusier. It was to be the first planned city in India, and Chand found work as a roads inspector for the Public Works Department in 1951.

In his spare time, Chand began collecting materials from demolition sites around the city. He recycled these materials into his own vision of a divine kingdom, choosing a gorge in a nearby forest for his work. The gorge had been designated as a land conservancy, a forest buffer that nothing could be built on. Chand's work was illegal, but he was able to hide it for eighteen years before it was discovered by the authorities in 1975. By this time it had grown into a twelve acre complex of interlinked courtyards, each filled with hundreds of pottery-covered concrete sculptures of dancers, musicians, and animals.

His work was in serious danger of being demolished, but he was able to get public opinion on his side, and in 1976 the park was inaugurated as a public space. Nek

Chand was given a salary, a title ("Sub-Divisional Engineer, Rock Garden"), and a workforce of 50 laborers so that he could concentrate full-time on his work. It even appeared on an Indian stamp in 1983. The Rock Garden is still made out of recycled materials; indeed, with the government's help Chand was able to set up collection centers around the city for waste, especially rags and broken ceramics.

Nelapattu Bird Sancturay : A must-visit for all bird lovers, this world-renowned sanctuary on the banks of Pulicat lake in Sullurpeta, is spread over 486 sq.km. Here you can sopt the famous Siberian Cranes and nearly 160 species of birds from different countries.

Nelliampathi : Nelliampathi is a popular hill station 60 km away from Palakkad district in Kerala a small state in south India. It is famous for its tea and coffee plantations and the excellent weather condition. It is called as the 'Poor man's Ooty'. The journey to Nelliampathi itself is an experience. The only route is from Nemmara, from where the first town of Nelliampathi, namely Kaikatty junction, is at a distance of 26 km. At the 9th kilometer is the Pothundi Dam, a small irrigation dam which provides water for the rice fields in the surrounding area. The dam is at the foot of the Nelliampathi hills. From here, the road winds up for the next 17 km, with many hairpin turns on the way.

Immediately after Pothundy dam, comes the government forest, where one can see massive teak trees. The road is very narrow and requires a skilled driver behind the wheels. On the way, one can see wild animals like monkey, deer and porcupine. The view of the Pothundy dam from the height is a breathtaking sight. There will be many waterfalls by the roadside during the rainy season.

Nelliampathi : Nelliampathi is a popular hill station 60 Km. away from Palakkad district in Kerala a small state in south India. It is famous for its tea and coffee plantations and the excellent weather condition. It is called as the 'Poor man's Ooty'.

Nellore : Nellore city is the headquarters of Nellore District, the southernmost coastal district in the state of Andhra Pradesh, India. The population of the city is 378,947 (agglomeration 404,922) (2001 census). It is situated in the south east corner of Andhra Pradesh, on the south bank of the River Pennar. The area of the district is 13,076 km^2. The district is bounded by the Bay of Bengal to the east, the district of Cuddapah to the west, the district of Prakasam to the north and the state of Tamil Nadu to the south.

Neora Valley National Park : The Neora Valley National Park, spread over an area of 88sq.km. in the Darjeeling district of West Bengal was established in April 1986. The park, a unique area of rich bio-diversity lies in the Himalayan foothills and is bordered on the east by Western Bhutan and the forests of Sikkim.

Nepali : Nepali (Khaskura) is an Indo-Aryan language spoken in Nepal, Bhutan, and some parts of India and Burma. It is the official language of Nepal and Sikkim. Roughly half the population of Nepal speaks Nepali as a mother tongue, and many other Nepalese speak it as a second language.

New Delhi : New Delhi, an urban area within the metropolis of Delhi, is the seat of the Government of India. It is one of the three municipal corporations of the National Capital Territory of Delhi. Delhi is an independent State (province) of India.New Delhi was laid out to the south of the older city constructed by Shah Jahan, which is now often referred to as Old Delhi. However, New

Delhi overlays many of the previous cities constructed there; hence it includes many monuments of previous cities, and constructions.

Much of New Delhi was planned by Sir Edwin Lutyens, who laid out a grandiose central administrative area as a testament to British imperial pretensions. Rajpath—then Kingsway—stretched from the War Memorial—now India Gate to the Viceregal Palace—Rashtrapati Bhavan atop Raisina Hill. In its scale, extravagance and magnificence, it was not unlike Washington, or Haussmann and his patron Napoleon III's Paris, both cities designed to awe the newcomer with the power of the central State. Tucked away are other clues to the worldview of the designers; Herbert Baker's Parliament House is barely visible from Rajpath, as deliberative democracy was not a central part of the United Kingdom's plans for India; in fact, the main entrance to the Central Secretariat North Block declares "Liberty does not descend to the people; they must raise themselves to it."

New Delhi Television Limited (NDTV) : NDTV (founded in 1988) is one of India's largest television production houses. After producing numerous news and current affairs programs including the highly successful "The World This Week", NDTV inked a production agreement with Rupert Murdoch's STAR to set up India's first 24-hour news channel (STAR News, English/Hindi News) launched in February 1998. The parties parted ways after five years and NDTV launched its own channels, NDTV 24x7 (English News) and NDTV India (Hindi News). STAR retained the STAR News brand, but the channel continued in Hindi. NDTV subsequently launched NDTV Profit which focuses on business news.

NDTV currently has more than 1,000 employees producing news from over twenty plus locations nationally and internationally. The company is owned (54%) by Dr. Prannoy Roy and his wife Mrs. Radhika Roy and has a market capitalisation of about Rs. 1,500 crore. NDTV has decided to enter into an agreement with Astro Broadcast Corporation Ltd. that proposes to establish a joint venture company to set up and broadcast 24-hour channels in South East Asia. NDTV, will open a branch of its networks in Canada, to be known as NDTV Canada, to be owned and operated by Asian Television Network.

New Karachi Town : New Karachi Town is a small densely populated town in the northern part of Karachi, located between the Lyari River, the Manghopir Hills and two major roads—Surjani Road to the north and Shahrah-e-Zahid Hussain to the south. To the north and west lies the town of Gadap, and to the south lie the towns of Gulberg and North Nazimabad. The population of New Karachi Town was estimated to be more than 680,000 at the 1998 census, of which 99% are Muslim. There are several ethnic groups including Urdu speakers, Punjabis, Sindhis, Kashmiris, Seraikis, Pakhtuns, Balochis, Memons, Bohras and Ismailis.

New Okhla Industrial Development Authority : New Okhla Industrial Development Authority, or Noida, is a department of the government of Uttar Pradesh. New Okhla Industrial Development Area is a highly industrialised city with various amenities available, and is considered to be one of the more modernised suburb districts of Uttar Pradesh. It was developed near Delhi in the 1970s as a modern industrial city under the UP Industrial Area Development Act, 1976. Noida came into existence on 19th April, 1976 and celebrates 19th April as "Noida Day". Incidentally, Sanjay Gandhi was responsible for setting up Noida, as part of a major urbanisation thrust during the infamous Emergency period (1975-1977).

New Okhla Industrial Development Authority : New Okhla Industrial Development Authority, or Noida, is a department of the government of Uttar Pradesh. New Okhla Industrial Development Area is a highly industrialised city with various amenities available, and is considered to be one of the more modernised suburb districts of Uttar Pradesh. It was developed near Delhi in the 1970s as a modern industrial city under the UP Industrial Area Development Act, 1976. Noida came into existence on 19th April, 1976 and celebrates 19th April as "Noida Day". Incidentally, Sanjay Gandhi was responsible for setting up Noida, as part of a major urbanisation thrust during the infamous Emergency period (1975-1977).

Neyyar Dam : Neyyar dam is a dam in Thiruvananthapuram district of Kerala, South India. Its only 32 km from Thiruvananthapuram city. It is lying against the southern low hills of the Western Ghats and is a popular picnic spot with a beautiful lake.

Niaz Morshed : Niaz Morshed (b. 1966) is a Bangladeshi chess player. He was the first Grandmaster to emerge from South Asia. After finishing his education, Niaz returned to the world of chess. But things were not easy as they were before. In the new world of information technology he failed to cope with the new information chess. Though he failed to return to his past form, time to time Niaz earned some significant result in internatianal competition. Among them were- 1st in the Goodric, India in 1991, 2nd in the GM Tournament, Cebu, Philliphines, in 1992, 3rd in the Doha Chess Festival, Qatar in 1993, shared 1st place with two other contestants in the zonal tournament 1993, but lost in the tie-break, and finally, shared 2nd place in the Commonwealth Chess Championship in 2004.

Nicobar District : Nicobar district is a district of India, one of two districts in the Indian Union Territory

(UT) of Andaman and Nicobar Islands. The district's administrative territory encompasses all of the Nicobar Islands, which are located in the Indian Ocean (Bay of Bengal, bordering with the Andaman Sea). The district government is headed by a Deputy Commissioner, who in turn reports into the Lt. Governor of the Andaman and Nicobar Islands.

Nicobar Islands : The Nicobar Islands are an island chain in the eastern Indian Ocean, and are part of India, located southeast of the Indian subcontinent, separated by the Bay of Bengal by about 1,300 km.

The Nicobars are separated from the Andaman Islands to the north by the 150 km wide Ten Degree Channel and are 189 km from the Indonesian island of Sumatra to the southeast. The Andaman and Nicobar islands separate the Bay of Bengal from the Andaman Sea. Until the 2004 Indian Ocean earthquake, Indira Point, south of Great Nicobar, was the southernmost point in India.

The Nicobar islands include 22 islands of various sizes, the largest being Great Nicobar. The total land area of the chain is 1841 km^2. The highest point on the Nicobars is Mount Thullier at 642 m.

The population of the islands was 42,026 in 2001, roughly 65% of whom are indigenous peoples (the Nicobarese and Shompen peoples, listed among the Scheduled Tribes of India), and 35% migrants from India and Sri Lanka.

Nicobar Long-tailed Macaque : The Nicobar Long-tailed Macaque (Macaca fascicularis umbrosa, popularly known as the Nicobar Monkey) is a subspecies of the Crab-eating Macaque (M. fascicularis), endemic to the Nicobar Islands in the Bay of Bengal. This primate is found on three of the Nicobar Islands — Great Nicobar,

Little Nicobar and Katchal Island, in biome regions consisting of Tropical and subtropical moist broadleaf forests.

Nicobarese Languages : The Nicobarese languages form an isolated group of six closely-related Mon-Khmer languages from the Austro-Asiatic language family, which are spoken by the indigenous inhabitants of the Nicobar Islands of India. They have a total of about 30,000 speakers (22,100 native). The majority of Nicobarese speakers use the Car language. The morphological similarities between Nicobarese languages and Austronesian languages have been used to help support the Austric hypothesis.

Nihari : Nihari is a Pakistani stew made from beef or lamb and curry. Nihari is known for its spiciness and taste. Nihari is also known in India as the breakfast curry, as it is traditionally eaten before a day of manual labor. It has since become more of a delicacy throughout South Asia with myriad variations on spiciness and texture.

Originally prepared from the upper thigh/hip meat of goats and cows, Nihari was cooked overnight in various vessels, often buried under soil for the duration, to yield extremely tender morsels of meat. Tradional Nihari recipes call for 6-8 hours of cooking time, in addition to the preparation of the ingredients. This is much less common today with the use of more tender cuts of meat (i.e. sirloin) instead of the tougher thigh/hip meat.

Famous Nihari shops in Pakistan are located in Lahore and Karachi; some examples are Waris Nihari Shop, Baoo Nihari House, Muhammadi Nihari House, Javed nihari and Sabri Nihari. The Hyderabadi version of the Nihari contains bones and tongue of the lamb as well.

Nijera Kari : Nijera Kari is a non-government organisation established after the famine of 1974, when many destitute rural women made their way to the cities in search of food and work. Nijera Kari means we do it ourselves. Destitute women constituted the target group of the organisation. Its aim was to rehabilitate these women. The organisation formed a team of people who had work experience at field level and who felt that the increasingly service-based approach of NGOs would simply create dependency among the clients.

Nijhum Dwip : Nijhum Dwip (Char Osman) is a cluster of islands (mainly, Ballar Char, Kamlar char, Char Osman and Char Muri, with a total landmass of about 14050 acres) emerged in the early 1950s as an alluvium in the shallow estuary of the Bay of Bengal on the south of Noakhali. These new sandbanks first drew the notice of a group of fishermen, who named it Baular Char (literally, the alluvium of sand) later transformed into Ballar Char. During the winter, thousands of migratory birds flocked to it. The fishermen used the airy and sunny land as an ideal place for drying their catches from the sea. Sometimes many also constructed straw huts on the islands as seasonal residence.

Nikobarese Dance : This dance is performed by the Nikobarese tribals from the Car Nicobar Islands. It is performed during the Ossuary Feast or the Pig Festival, which is dedicated to the departed head of the family.

Nilgiri Biosphere Reserve : The Nilgiri Biosphere Reserve is an International Biosphere Reserve located in the Western Ghats and Nilgiri Hills ranges of southern India. The reserve encompasses 5,520 km^2 in the states of Karnataka (1527.4 km&sup2), Kerala (1455.4 km^2), and Tamil Nadu (2537.6 km^2). The Mudumalai National Park, Wayanad Wildlife Sanctuary, Bandipur National Park, Nagarhole National Park, Mukurthi National Park and Silent Valley National Park are protected areas within this reserve, which also includes zones open to forestry and tourism.

The reserve extends from the tropical moist forests of the windward western slopes of the Ghats to the tropical dry forests on the leeward east slopes. Rainfall ranges from 500 mm to 7000 mm per year. The reserve encompasses three ecoregions, the South Western Ghats moist deciduous forests, South Western Ghats montane rain forests, and South Deccan Plateau dry deciduous forests. The habitat types include montane rain forest, semi-evergreen moist forest, thorn forest and scrub, montane grassland, and high-elevation Shola forests. Rare animals include the tiger, Asian Elephant, and Nilgiri Tahr.

Nilgiri Langur : The Nilgiri Langur (Trachypithecus johni) is a lutung (a type of Old World monkey) found in the Nilgiri hills of the Western Ghats in South India. Its range also includes Kodagu in Karnataka, Palani Hills in Tamil Nadu and many other hilly areas in Kerala. This primate has glossy black fur on its body and golden brown fur on its head. It is similar in size and long tailed like the gray langurs.

Females have a white patch of fur on the inner thigh. It lives in troops of five to 16 monkeys. The animal is often seen encroaching into agricultural lands. Its diet is comprised of fruits, shoots and leaves. The species is endangered due to deforestation and poaching for its fur and flesh, the latter believed to have aphrodisiac properties.

Nilgiri Mountain Railway (NMR) : The Nilgiri Mountain Railway (NMR) connects the town of Mettupalayam with the hill station of Ooty (correctly Udhagamandalam), in the Nilgiri Hills of southern India. Both towns are in the state of Tamil Nadu. It is the only rack railway in India

The Nilgiri Mountain railway is one of the oldest mountain railways in India. Under consideration since 1845, the line was finally opened by the British in 1899, and was initially operated by the Madras Railway Company. The railway is one of the few in the world to be dependant on steam locomotives. The Palghat division of the Indian Railways, which operates the NMR, incurs an annual shortfall of Rs 4 crores, (~1 million USD). During the Centenary celebrations of Nilgiri Mountain Railway in 1999 the then Railway Minister Nitish Kumar announced that the line would soon be electrified. In July 2005, UNESCO declared the NMR a World Heritage Site after it satisfied the necessary criteria, thus forcing abandonment of modernisation plans.

Nilgiri Tahr : The Nilgiri Tahr (Nilgiritragus hylocrius) ungulate native to the Nilgiri Hills and the southern portion of the Western Ghats range in Tamil Nadu and Kerala states of southernmost India. It is known locally as the Nilgiri Ibex or simply ibex. Its closest relatives are sheep (genus Ovis). Until 2005, it was placed with the Himalayan Tahr (Hemitragus jemlahicus) and the Arabian Tahr (Arabitragus jayakari) in the genus Hemitragus. However, Ropiquet & Hassanin placed it in a new genus Nilgiritragus, because it is genetically more similar to members of the genus Ovis (sheep) than to other tahrs.

The Nilgiri Tahrs are stocky goats with short, coarse fur and a bristly mane. Males are larger than the females, and have a darker color when mature. Both sexes have curved horns, which are larger in the males, reaching up to 40 cm for males and 30 cm for females. Adult males weigh 80–100 kg and stand about 100 cm tall at the shoulder.

The tahrs inhabit the open montane grassland habitat of the South Western Ghats montane rain forests ecoregion. At elevations from 1200 to 2600 m (generally above 2000 m), the forests open into grasslands interspersed with pockets of stunted forests, known as sholas. These grassland habitats and are surrounded by dense forests at the lower elevations. The Nilgiri Tahrs formerly ranged over these grasslands in large herds, but hunting and poaching in the nineteenth century reduced their population to as few as 100 animals by the early 20th century. Since that time their populations have increased somewhat, and presently number about 2000 individuals. Their range extends over 400 km from north to south, and Eravikulam National Park is home to the largest population. The other significant concentration is in the Nilgiri Hills, with smaller populations in the Anamalai Hills (Periyar National Park), Palni Hills and other pockets in the Western Ghats south of Eravikulam, almost to India's southern tip.

Nilgiris : The Nilgiris or Blue Mountains, often called The Queen of Hills are a range of mountains and a district in the south-Indian states of Tamil Nadu and Kerala. The highest point is the mountain of Dodda Betta (the Doddabetta Peak), with a height of 2637m.

The altitude of the Nilgiris results in a much cooler wetter climate than the surrounding plains, and so the area is popular as a retreat from the summer heat. The rolling hills of the Downs look very similar to the Downs in Southern England, and were used for similar activities such as hunting. The principal town of the area is Udhagamandalam, although the old British name of Ootacamund, shortened to Ooty, is often used. In the town there are many buildings which look very "British", in particular the Churches. There is even a road junction known as Charing Cross.

Nilima Ibrahim : Nilima Ibrahim (1921-2002) was a Bangladeshi educationist, literateur and social worker. She is well known for her outstanding scholarship on Bangla literature but even more so for her depiction of raped and tortured women in the 1971 Bangladesh Liberation War in her book Ami Virangona Bolchhi.

Nilphamari : Nilphamari is a district in the Rajshahi division of Bangladesh. With an area of 1640.91 sq km, the district is bounded by Kuchbihar district of West Bengal (India) on the north, Rangpur district on the south, Lalmonirhat district on the east and Panchagarh and Dinajpur districts on the west. Annual temperature: maximum 32.3 C, minimum 11.2 C; annual rainfall 2931mm. Main rivers are Tista, Jamuneshwari, Chikni and Dhaigan. The Nilphamari subdivision was established in 1875 and was turned into a district in 1984. The district consists of 6 upazilas, 3 municipalities, 33 wards, 65 mahallas, 62 union parishads, 390 mouzas and 370 villages. The upazilas are Dimla, Domar, Jaldhaka, Kishoreganj, Nilphamari Sadar and Saidpur. The Tebhaga Movement spread over Domar and Dimla in the 1940s. In this movement the activist Tannarayan was shoot dead by the zamindar. Once indigo was cultivated extensively in this district. The Nilphamari region was under the Votmari Chauki during the British period. Later on the Chauki was transferred first to Shekherhat of Badarganj thana and then to Dokra of Domar thana.

Nilsagar : Nilsagar is a famous historical dighi (big pond), which stands at Dhobadanga mauza of Gorgram union about 14 km southwest of Nilphamari district headquarter. During the reign of Raja Birat there were many cow farms at Gorgram. Raja Birat dug a large dighi named as Birat Dighi or Birna Dighi or Binna Dighi for the cows. After the independence of Bangladesh the dighi was renamed as Nilsagar. A Hindu mandir stands on the east bank and an abode of a Muslim darvesh on the west bank of the dighi. The area of the dighi is 21.449 ha and depth ranges from 7m to 12m. The entire dighi is surrounded by brick walls. The main decorated ghat of the dighi was made by Raja Birat. Every year the banks of the dighi are used as a village fair site especially during the occasion of Baruni Snan festival in full moon of the month of Baisakh. Usually in the fair the Harikirtan singers play music with many kinds of kirtan songs. Every year many tourists and various kinds of migratory birds come here. It is well known as a recreation zone and a picnic spot.

Nimar : Nimar is the southwestern region of Madhya Pradesh state in west-central India. The region lies south of the Vindhya Range, and consists of two portions of the Narmada and Tapti river valleys, separated by a section of the Satpura Range, about 15 miles (24 km) in breadth. On the highest peak, about 800 ft (244 m) above the plain and 1800 ft (549 m) above sea-level, stands the fortress of Asirgarh, commanding a pass which has for centuries been the chief highway between Upper India and the Deccan. The Nimar region is home to the Nimadi language, which is related to the Malvi language of Malwa as well as the other Rajasthani languages.

Nine-Dome Mosque : Nine-Dome Mosque is located on the western bank of the Thakurdighi, less than half a km away to the southwest of the tomb-complex of Khan Jahan.

The mosque is now a protected monument of the Department of Archaeology, Bangladesh. It is a brick-built square structure measuring about 16.76m externally and 12.19m internally. The 2.44m thick walls on the north, south and east sides are pierced with three arched-openings on each side; the central one, set within a rectangular frame, is larger than the flanking ones. The mosque is stylistically dated to the time of Khan Jahan. Local tradition ascribes the building to one of Khan Jahan's officers who had his residence nearby on the same bank of the Thakurdighi.

Ningol Chakouba : Observed on the second day of the new moon in the Manipuri month of Hiyangei (November), this festival acts as a mark of family reunion. Married women of the family who were married to distant places come to the parental house along with her children and enjoy sumptuous feast. The festival is also observed by the Pangals (Manipuri Muslims) to a certain extent now a day.

Niqab : A niqab is a veil which covers the face, worn by some Muslim women as a part of sartorial hijab. It is popular in the Middle East but it can also be found in North Africa, Southeast Asia and the Indian subcontinent.

The niqab originated with the need for protection in the harsh desert conditions of Arabia. Its primary use by modern Muslim women is modesty: to keep non-mahram men (those who are not one's father, brother, husband or other intimate relation) from seeing a Muslim woman's face.

The niqab is regarded differently by the various maðahab (schools of Islamic jurisprudence). Some see it as fard (obligatory) or sunna (recommended); others discourage its use and say it should not be worn if it could cause danger to the wearer.

Niranjanananda Saraswati : Swami Niranjanananda Saraswati (born 14 February 1960) is the successor of Paramahamsa Satyananda, founder of Satyananda Yoga, who passed on the worldwide coordination of Satyananda Yoga to Swami Niranjanananda in 1988. Born in Rajnandgaon, Madhya Pradesh, India, Swami Niranjanananda is considered by his followers to be a yogi from birth. He began his training at Bihar School of Yoga in India at the age of four. In 1971, at the age of ten, he toured extensively in Europe, America and Australia. This experience gave him a deep understanding of the Western mind and society. In 1983 he returned to India and was appointed the Head of Bihar School of Yoga. For the next eleven years, he spear headed the research and development activities at Ganga Darshan, Shivananda Math and Yoga Research Foundation.

In 1990, he was initiated in tradition of Paramhamsa and in 1993 he was chosen as the successor of Paramhamsa Satyananda. In 1993, he organized a World Yoga Convention on the occasion of the golden jubilee of Sannyas of his guru. In 1994, he established Bihar Yoga Bharti as the centre for higher studies in the field of Yoga.

Swami Niranjanananda is a modern master of yoga, whose understanding spans both the scientific Western culture and the mystical wisdom of the East. At present he is the Paramacharya of Bihar Yoga Bharati (Institute for Advanced Studies in the Yogic Sciences) in Munger, Bihar.

Nirankari Mission : The Sant Nirankari Mission was started in 1929 by Baba Boota Singh. Their primary belief is that God is one and formless (Nir-akaar). They also believe that the transcendent Satguru is the bestower of the divine vision (brahm—gian) Since mainstream Sikhs believe that the last and final Guru is the Guru Granth Sahib (the Sikh scripture), the Nirankaris are believed to be heretics by Sikhs. They were the target of Bhindranwale's enmity in the late 1970s. The distrust led to violence between Nirankaris and members of the AKJ and other Sikhs on 13 April 1978. This resulted in the death of 13 Sikhs.

When the then head of the Sant Nirankari Mission was asked how many of "his" had died, his response was that "they were all mine", signifying the vision of such a being, indifference between human beings, and acceptance of all mankind as one family, a practical example of a fundamental belief of the Nirankari Mission, there is one father, god, that can be realised, and that we are all gods children The Akal Takht excommunicated all followers of the Sant Nirankari Mission in 1978.

Nirmal Verma : Nirmal Verma (3rd April 1929-25 October 2005) together with Mohan Rakesh, Bhisham Sahni, Kamleshwar, Amarkant and others, is the founder of the Nai Kahani (new short story) in Hindi literature. He is best known for his short stories. His most famous story, 'Parinde' is supposed to be the pioneer of the Nai Kahani Movement. His other famous stories are Andhere Mein, Dedh Inch Upar, and Kavve Aur Kala Pani. He has also written some excellent novels like Lal Tin Ki Chhat and Antim Aranya. His recent story published in Kathadesh was about two gay boys. Nirmal Verma made new experiments with theme as well technique of Hindi short story in the 60s and 70s. He won the Jnanpith award in 1999.

Nirmalendu Goon : Nirmalendu Goon (b. 1945) is a Bangladeshi poet. He was born in Netrokona, Bangladesh. Goon is one of the most popular poets in Bangladesh, lauded by many for his accessible verse in an age where Bangla poetry has become increasingly complex. Nirmalendu Goon was born in Netrokona. Goon is often thought to be one of the few people who openly protested Sheikh Mujibur Rahman's assaisination in 1975 in the following period where even mentioning Mujib was considered dangerous.

His first book of poems was published in 1970. Since then he has published forty-five collections of poetry and twenty collections of prose. Part of the generation of poets of 1960s, Goon's poetry contains stinging criticism of the noveu-rich and a touching description of the contrasting fate of the masses. A love of freedom and faith in the human spirit also permeats many of his poems. Unabashedly marxist, he has written poems urging an upheaval of the poor against the rich. He also has written a number of poems on important personalities, including Rabindranath, Sheikh Mujib, Lenin, Shakti Chattopadhyay and others.

Nishan Sahib : The Nishan Sahib is a Sikh holy flag made of cotton or silk cloth and is triangular in shape. There was a practice of hoisting of flag during the divine ministry of Guru Amar Das, Guru Ram Das and Guru Arjan Dev. The colour of the Nishan Sahib during this phase of the Sikh history was white. Its colour underwent a change, from white to saffron, in the hands of Guru Hargobind and it was hoisted for the first time at Akal Takhat Sahib in the year 1609 CE.

The Nishan Sahib is placed outside every Sikh Gurdwara and is supported by a pole of timber or metal. You may notice the Sikh symbol, the Khanda on it. It is placed high up as a sign for all Sikhs and indeed any other person that they can come and pray in this building. Great respect is shown to this flag which is shown by its washing using milk and water every year in April at the festival of Vaisakhi. This Nishan Sahib, as a matter of religious injunction, must hoist at each and every building of the Gurdwara. It is this Nishan Sahib that is referred to in the daily prayer of the Sikhs asking for its Immortality.

Nishan-E-Haider : The Nishan-E-Haider, (Sign of the Lion), is the highest military award given by Pakistan. It is awarded to select soldiers who display an incredible amount of valor and courage on the battle field in the face of staunch adversity.

Nishi : The Nishi tribe principally inhabit the Indian state of Arunachal Pradesh. Known as the Nishi (alternative transliteration Nisi) in their own language (also called Nisi), they are sometimes called by the disdainful term Dafla by outsiders. They inhabit in the Papumpare, East Kameng and Lower Subansiri district of Arunachal Pradesh, as well as in the Darrang district of Assam. Their population of around 120,000 thus making up one of the most populous tribe of Arunachal Pradesh, consisting about 11% of the state's population. As they are of the Tibetan stock, their language belong to the Tibeto-Burman family.

Most Nishi do not like the idea of intermarriage between the other neighbouring tribes, and Polygamy is prevalent among the Nishi.They trace their descent patrilineally and are divided into several clans.

Nishtar Medical College : Nishtar Medical College is located in Multan, Punjab, Pakistan. Nishtar Medical College was established in 1951. Nishtar Medical College was named after Sardar Abdur Rab Nishtar one of the leaders of Pakistan Movement.

Nitish Kumar : Nitish Kumar (born March 1, 1951, Bakhtiarpur, Bihar, India) is the Chief Minister of the north Indian state of Bihar. He is one of the leaders of Janata Dal (United) party.

Kumar graduated from Bihar College of Engineering, Patna with a Bachelor's degree in Engineering. He was involved in the JP Movement led by Jaiprakash Narayan between 1974 and 77. He was first elected to the Bihar legislative assembly in 1985. In 1987, he became the president of the Yuva Lok Dal. In 1989, he became the Secretary-General of the Janata Dal in Bihar. He was also elected to the 9th Lok Sabha that year. In 1990, he became the Union Minister of State for Agriculture.

In 1991, he was re-elected to the Lok Sabha and became General Secretary of the Janata Dal at the national level and Deputy Leader of Janata Dal in Parliament. He has been a member of the Lok Sabha representing Nalanda continuously since 1989 being re-elected every time. He briefly served as the Union Cabinet Minister for Railways and Surface Transport and then as the Minister for Agriculture. In 2000, he was made the Chief Minister of Bihar but had to resign in 7 days. Later that year, he rejoined the Union Cabinet as Minister for Agriculture. From 2001 to May 2004, he served as the Union Cabinet Minister for Railways in the NDA government of Atal Behari Vajpayee. In November 2005, he led the National Democratic Alliance to a victory in the Bihar Assembly elections bringing to an end the 15-year rule of the Lalu Prasad Yadav-led Rashtriya Janata Dal in the state.

Nizam : Nizam-ul-Mulk was the title of the ruler of Hyderabad state from 1724 to 1949. The state is therefore sometimes referred to as a nizamate. Like their Mughal predecssors, the nizams were Muslims. The title nizam-al-mulk was first used in Urdu around 1600 to mean "governor of the realm", probably in reference to Nizam al-Mulk. It, in turn, derives from the Arabic word, nizam, meaning "order, arrangement". The Nizam was, and often still is, referred to as Ala Hadrat or Nizam Sarkar.

The first Nizams ruled on behalf of the mughal emperors, but as their power waned with the death of Aurangazeb—the last great moghul, the nizams split away to form their own nizamates. This continued until the British who allowed the Nizams to rule their princely states. This was accepted by the Nizams and retained power over Hyderabad state until Indian independence. Even after Indian Independence, the Nizam wanted to join Pakistan or be independent, however the Indian Army launched Operation Polo that resulted in the annexation of the Nizam's territories.

The Nizam's dynasty was known as Asaf Jahi dynasty. Though it is said that dynasty had only seven rulers however there was a period of 13 years after the rule of the first Nizam when three of his sons Nasir Jung, Muzafar Jung and Salabath Jung ruled the dynasty. They are not officially recognized as the rulers and hence there are just seven known Nizams.

Nizam Sagar : At a distance of about 144 km north-west of Hyderabad, a reservoir known by the name Nizamsagar was constructed across the Manjira River, a tributary of the Godavari River, between Achampet and Banjapalle villages of Nizamabad district. The site is noted for its splendid scenic beauty. The most outstanding feature of the project is the gigantic masonary dam sprawling across the river for 3 km with a motorable road of 14ft width over it. There are excellent boarding and lodging facilities for the tourists at this project.

Nizamuddin Dargah : Nizamuddin Dargah is the mausoleum of Delhi's most famous Sufi saint Nizamuddin Auliya. It is visited daily by many of people of all religions.

The tomb of Amir Khusro is also located within the Nizamuddin Dargah Complex. The neighborhood of Delhi where the mausoleum is located is called "Hazrat Nizamuddin" or simply "Nizamuddin" because of this.

Nobanno : Nobanno is the festival of harvest in Bengal. The word translates as "New Rice". The festival takes place in the month of Agrohayon or Aghran of the Bangla Calendar. Festivities include making traditional cakes named "pitha".

Nocte : The Nocte, (literally, village people) is a tribe of a population of 33,000 found in the Patkai hills of Tirap district of Arunachal Pradesh. Ethnically related to the

Konyak Naga, their origins can be traced back to the Hukong Valley in Myanmar, where they migrated from between the 1670 and 1700. They have chiefs who exert control over the village, and they are also consulted by the village elders and priests on all important socio-religious ceremonies.

The Nocte were follwers of Theravada Buddhism and Animism, although they have adopted Hinduism since the 18th century, under the influence of Shri Shankardeva. They worship Jauban (supreme god) who was believed to have created human beings and started miseries, troubles and happiness. Other malevolent and benevolent deities are also worshipped as well. Offerings of food and water are given to the gods in order to appease them.

The Nocte are agriculturalists and have a good planning in their daily diet. Main crops such as rice and maize are planted, as their staple food is rice, which is often supplemented by leafy vegetables, fish and meat. A locally brewed liquor brewed from rice, tapioca and millet proved to be popular among the Nocte, although in recent times tea is consumed as well. However, as staunch Hindus, they do not take beef and mutton.

Nokrek Peak : The highest point of the Garo Hills region of the Meghalaya, Nokrek Peak stands fourteen hundred and twelve metres above sea level. A virgin canopy of thick, tall and lush green forests cover Nokrek and its environs. The mother germo plasm of Citrus-indica have been discovered by science researchers within Nokrek Range. This discovery led to the establishment of the National Citrus Gene Sanctuary-cum-Biosphere Reserve at Nokrek covering an area of forty seven square kilometres. Nokrek can be reached from the Tura-Asanangre-Daribokgre Road. A comfortable three and a half kilometre trek from Daribokgre village leads a visitor to Nokrek Peak. Abundant wildlife including herds of wild elephants, rare varieties of birds and pheasants, besides rare orchids abound in the sanctuary.

Non-Aligned Movement (NAM) : The Non-Aligned Movement is an international organization of over 100 states which consider themselves not formally aligned with or against any major power bloc. NAM focuses on national struggles for independence, the eradication of poverty, economic development and opposing colonialism, imperialism, and neo-colonialism. They represent 55% of the planet's people and nearly two-thirds of the UN's members. Important members include India, Egypt, South Africa and, for a time, the People's Republic of China. Brazil has never been a formal member of the movement, but the country shares many of the aims of NAM and frequently sends observers to NAM summits. While the organization was intended to be as close an alliance as NATO or the Warsaw Pact, it has little cohesion and many of its members were induced or unable to resist aligning with one or another of the great powers. For example, Cuba was closely aligned with the former Soviet Union during the Cold War era.

The Non-Aligned Movement has struggled to find relevance since the end of the Cold War. The successor states of Yugoslavia, a founding member, have expressed little interest in the NAM since the country's break-up, and in 2004, Slovenia, along with Malta and Cyprus, ceased to be a member of the NAM when it joined the European Union. Malta and Cyprus now have the status of observer.

Non-Cooperation Movement : The Non-Cooperation Movement was the first-ever series of nationwide people's movements of nonviolent resistance, led by Mahatma Gandhi and the Indian National Congress. The Movement opened the Gandhi Era in the Indian Independence Movement.

Nongdai Jagoi : The dance of commencing the split in the sky, the splitting of the rainbow in the sky by the Guru Sidaba. The hands are moved skywards in trying to bring the two parts together. In Leitai Dance, The waist is moved in circular movements depicting the spreading of earth dirt on the web-like framework. When the earth was completed and divided into different divisions, the dance started by moving hands from side to side. Leitai Dance depicts the formation of the trace with the dirt from the Guru's navel. The dance steps are done on tiptoes. Lai-Haraoba is performed in worship of gods like Pakhangba, Thangjing etc. It has got three main forms. The Kanglei Lai-Haraoba is celebrated at the palace. The Moirang Lai-Haraoba is celebrated in the honour of Lord Thangjing and the Chakpa Lai-Haraoba which is basically observed by Loi people. Lai Haraoba takes place in Manipuri month of Kalen. It continues for a week. There are certain days of the month which are considered propitious and the festival is celebrated on these dates like 1, 2, 3, 5 and 8. The deities are represented by a pair of bamboo tubes, wooden or brass mark with cloths placed below and above, pieces of wood or iron or a coin etc.

Nongkrem Dance : Popularly known as *Ka Pamblang Nongkrem,* this is the most important dance of the Khasis and is celebrated during autumn essentially as a thanks-giving ceremony to God for the harvest and to pray for peace and prosperity.

Norman Gilbert Pritchard : Norman Gilbert Pritchard was an outstanding athlete from India who went on to star in Hollywood and Broadway. Pritchard was the first Indian athlete to participate in the Olympic Games. He was also the first Indian and first Asian to win an Olympic medal. He won two silver medals in the 1900 Summer Olympics in Paris, France. He came second in the 200 meters behind Walter Tewksbury of the United States and second in the 200 meters hurdles behind the legendary Alvin Kraenzlein of the United States. Pritchard set a world record in the second heat of the 200 metre hurdles which was bettered by Kraenzlein in the final. He reached the final of the 110m hurdles and failed to finish, and participated in 60m and 100m sprint where he failed to qualify for the final.

Pritchard won the Bengal province 100 yards sprint title for seven consecutive years from 1894 to 1900 and set a meet record in 1898-99. He also won the 440 yards run and the 120 yards hurdles. He studied at Saint Xaviers College, Calcutta, and is credited with the first hat-trick in an open football tournament in India, for Saint Xavier's against Sovabazar in July 1897. He served as Secretary of the Indian Football Association from 1900 to 1902. He moved permanently to England in 1905. He later moved to the United States where he became a silent movie actor under the screen name Norman Trevor. He acted alongside Hollywood legends like Ronald Colman in movies like Beau Geste(1927) and Tonight At Twelve(1929). He also appeared in several Broadway shows. He died in *Los Angeles of a brain malady.*

North Button Island National Park : The park is 60km from the long Island town and 200km from the airport of Port Blair, the capital of the Island. Set up in 1979 the park covers an area of.44sq.km. The fauna found here are dugong, dolphin, water monitor, lizard etc. The best months for visiting the park are December-March.

North Goa : North Goa is one of the two districts that make up the state of Goa, India. The district has an area of 1736 km², and is bounded by Ratnagiri and Kolhapur districts of Maharashtra state to the north and east respectively, by South Goa District to the south, and by the Arabian Sea to the west.

The administrative headquarters of the district is Panaji, which is also the capital of the state of Goa. The district is divided into four subdivisions, Panaji, Mapusa, Bicholim, and Ponda, and six taluks, Bardez, Bicholim, Pernem, Ponda, Sattari and Tiswadi.

Goa was a Portuguese colony from 1510 until December 1961, when it was annexed by India. Goa and two other former Portuguese enclaves became the union territory of Goa, Daman and Diu, and Goa was organized into a single district in 1965. On 30 May 1987, Goa attained statehood (while Daman and Diu remained a union territory), and Goa was reorganized into two districts, North Goa and South Goa.

North India : North India is a geographic and linguistic-cultural region of India. In traditional Indian geography, India is divided into three major cultural zones: North, South and East. The Vindhya mountains, in particular the line marked by the Narmada River and the Mahanadi River marks the southern boundary of north India. The line made by the Son river and the Kosi river marks its eastern border. The dominant feature geographic feature of northern India is the Indo-Gangetic Plain.

However, the socio-cultural boundaries of north India have actually surpassed these traditional boundaries. As a linguistic-cultural and political region, North India consists of twelve Indian states: Jammu and Kashmir, Himachal Pradesh, Uttarakhand, Haryana, Punjab, Uttar Pradesh, Bihar, Jharkhand, Chhatisgarh, Madhya Pradesh and Rajasthan. The National Capital Territory of Delhi is also a part of northern India.

North India remains primarily rural, but its vast population has ensured that it has always supported very large cities: apart from the great metropolis of Delhi, the cities of Lucknow, Patna, Kanpur, Allahabad, Meerut,

Jaipur, Chandigarh, Amritsar, Bhopal and Indore would rank with the most populous cities of Europe.

North Nazimabad Town : North Nazimabad Town is a small densely populated town in the northern part of Karachi, named as such in reference to it being north of the suburb of Nazimabad. The town is bordered by New Karachi Town to the north across the Shahrah-e-Zahid Hussain, Gulberg Town to the east across the Gujar Nala stream, Liaquatabad Town to the south, and SITE Town to the west. The population of North Nazimabad Town was estimated to be about 500,000 at the 1998 census, of which 99% are Muslim. There are several ethnic groups including Urdu speakers, Punjabis, Sindhis, Kashmiris, Seraikis, Pakhtuns, Balochis, Memons, Bohras and Ismailis

North Sikkim : North Sikkim is a district of the Indian state of Sikkim. Its capital is Mangan. It is the largest of the four districts of Sikkim. The people are mainly of Nepali descent. Other ethnic groups include the Lepcha and Bhutia communities. Nepali is the most widely spoken language in the district. It also has one of the lowest populated regions of the state. The region has many power projects and enjoys almost uninterrupted electricity. Roads however, are in a poor condition owing to the frequent landslides.

Most of North Sikkim is restricted to travellers and permits are needed to visit these areas. The area, which shares a sensitive border with the People's Republic of China is heavily patrolled by the Indian army. Most of the people of the state reside near Mangan, the district headquarters which is about 2,000 feet above sea level. Further north the elevation increases with the vegetation turning from temperate to alpine to tundra. Temperatures range from about 25° to below -40° in the extreme high reaches where the altitude is in excess of 6,000 metres.

Kanchenjanga is the highest peak at over 8,000 m, straddling its eastern border with Nepal.

North Simlipal National Park : Set up in 1956, the North Simlipal National Park became one of the Project Tiger reserves of India in 1973. It is spread over 2750sq.km in Mayurbhanj district adjoining Bihar and West Bengal. The park consist of hills and valleys, traversed by brooks, perennial rivers and waterfalls. Influenced by the ecology of both the eastern and western parts of the subcontinent on account of its position, the confluence makes the forest home to exceedingly rare and diverse flora and fauna.

North Western Ghats Moist Deciduous Forests : The North Western Ghats moist deciduous forests is a tropical moist broadleaf forest ecoregion of southwestern India. It lies between 250 and 1000 meters elevation in the northern portion of the Western Ghats range, from their northern end in Maharashtra state, through Karnataka to the transitional forests of Wayanad in Kerala. It surrounds the North Western Ghats montane rain forests ecoregion, which lies above 1000 meters elevation.

The ecoregion has an area of 48,200 square kilometers (18,600 square miles). It is bounded on the west by the Malabar Coast moist forests ecoregion, which lies between the 250 meter elevation and the Malabar Coast. At the northern end of the Western Ghats range in southeastern Gujarat, the ecoregion borders the Kathiawar-Gir dry deciduous forests to the west and the Narmada Valley dry deciduous forests to the northeast. The Wayanad forests at the southern end of the ecoregion mark the transition to the South Western Ghats moist deciduous forests to the south. To the east, in the rain shadow of the Ghats, lies the South Deccan Plateau dry deciduous forests ecoregion, whose tropical dry forests cover the Ghats' eastern foothills.

North Western Ghats Montane Rain Forests : The North Western Ghats montane rain forests is a tropical moist broadleaf forest ecoregion of southwestern India. It covers an area of 30,900 square kilometers (11,900 square miles), extending down the spine of the Western Ghats range, from Maharashtra state in the north through Karnataka to Kerala state in the south. The montane rain forests are found above 1000 meters elevation, and are surrounded at lower elevations by the North Western Ghats moist deciduous forests.

Unlike the lowland forests, which are composed largely of drought-deciduous trees, the montane rain forests are predominantly evergreen laurel forest, dominated by trees of the laurel family (Lauraceae), including Litsea, Phoebe, and Cinnamomum.

Northbrook Hall : Northbrook Hall an elegant building known as Lalkuthi (red house), is situated at Wiseghat in Dhaka on the bank of the Buriganga river. It was originally built as a Town Hall and named after Lord Northbrook, Viceroy of India (1872-1876). Later, it was converted into a public library to which a clubhouse was added and called Johnson Hall. The building combines elements of Mughal architecture blended with architectural styles of the European renaissance.

The building's semi-circular horseshoe arches containing entrances on the north, the four octagonal minars at the northern salient, the ornamental parapet and the towering pinnacles above demonstrate the Muslim features. The deep red colour of the grand monument with its graded roofs, pinnacles and parapets presents a magnificent view from the riverfront. The building, however, has lost its attraction now because of the new structures such as assembly halls and community centres that are built in the same premises and surround it from all sides.

North-East India : North-East India is the easternmost region of India consisting of the following states:

1. Nagaland
2. Arunachal Pradesh
3. Mizoram
4. Manipur
5. Meghalaya
6. Tripura
7. Sikkim
8. Assam

Sikkim became an Indian protectorate in 1947 and a full state in 1975. The other states, except Sikkim, form what are called the Seven Sister States. The states border Myanmar, China (Tibet), Bangladesh, Nepal, and Bhutan. However they share only a 50 km common border with the rest of India via the Chicken's Neck. Due to this the states have been away from the Indian mainstream. This has kept them politically and culturally apart.

Religion is also distinctive, as, along with Kerala, this is the primary stronghold of Christianity in India. Due to these factors there is discontent and demands for independence are being raised by the Nagas, ULFA, and Bodos. The residents are more closely related to Mongoloids than they are to people from most other parts of India. The region is known for its unique culture, handicrafts, martial arts, and scenic beauty. Problems include insurgency, joblessness, drugs, and lack of infrastructure.

Northeast India-Myanmar Pine Forests : The Northeast India-Myanmar pine forests is a subtropical coniferous forest ecoregion of northeastern India and adjacent portions of Myanmar. The ecoregion covers an area of 9700 km^2 of the Naga Hills, part of the belt of folded mountains that make up the India-Myanmar border region, The pine forests are found between 1500 and 2500 meters elevation, and occur in three enclaves; the largest straddles the boundary between India's Nagaland state and Myanmar, with two smaller enclaves in the southern portion of India's Mizoram state, near Myanmar border. The pine forests are surrounded at lower elevations by the predominantly broadleaf Mizoram-Manipur-Kachin rain forests.

Northern Black Polished Ware Culture : The Northern Black Polished Ware culture (NBPW/NBP) of the South Asia (ca. 700 BC–200 BC) is an Iron Age culture, succeeding the Painted Grey Ware culture. It developed beginning around 700 BC, or in the late Vedic period, and peaks from ca. 500 BC 300 BC, coinciding with the rise of the Mauryan Empire.

Malik and other scholars have noted similarities between NPB and Harappan cultures, among them the ivory dice and combs and a similar system of weights. Other similiarities include the utilization of mud, baked bricks and stone in architecture, the construction of large units of public architecture, the systematic development of hydraulic features and a similar craft industry. There are however also important differences between these two cultures, e.g. in the NBP culture rice, millet and sorghum become more important. The NBP culture may reflect the first state-level organization in South Asia.

Northern Dry Deciduous Forests : The Northern dry deciduous forests is a tropical dry broadleaf forest ecoregion of east-central India. It covers an area of 58,300 square kilometers (22,500 square miles), extending across portions of Andhra Pradesh, Chhatisgarh, Orissa, and

Jharkhand states. The region extends north and south in the dry western rain shadow of the Eastern Ghats range, which block the moisture-laden monsoon winds from the Bay of Bengal to the east. It is completely surrounded by the more humid Eastern Highlands moist deciduous forests ecoregion.

North-West Frontier Province : The North-West Frontier Province (NWFP) is the smallest of the four provinces of Pakistan and is home to the Pashtuns (Afghans) and various other groups. Neighbouring regions include Afghanistan to the west and north, and the Northern Areas and Azad Kashmir to the northeast and east. The Federally Administered Tribal Areas stand as a buffer between the NWFP and parts of Afghanistan and Baluchistan. Punjab and Islamabad Capital Territory are to the south and east. The principal language is Pashto and the provincial capital is Peshawar. Some Pashtuns refer to the province as Pakhtunkhwa which means 'Land of the Pashtuns' in Pashto, while other Pakistanis sometimes refer to the province as 'Sarhad' in Urdu.

Northwestern Thorn Scrub Forests : The Northwestern thorn scrub forests are a xeric shrubland ecoregion of Pakistan and northwestern India. The ecoregion encircles the Thar Desert and Indus Valley Desert ecoregions. It includes the western half of Gujarat (excluding the mountain of Girnar), and extending through Rajasthan, where it is bounded on the southeast by the Aravalli Range. It encompasses most of Haryana and Punjab states of India as well as the Jammu region of Jammu and Kashmir, extending to the foothills of the Himalayas. In Pakistan, the ecoregion covers most of Punjab province, extending into easternmost Northwest Frontier and Baluchistan provinces and western Sind.

The Northwestern thorn scrub forests are thought to be tropical dry forests that were degraded through intensive agriculture and grazing into stunted and open thorn scrub, dominated by species such as Acacia senegal and A. leucophloea, as well as Prosopis cineraria, Capparis zeylandica, and species of Salvadora, Gymnosporia, Grewia, and Gardenia. Over 90% of the ecoregion has been converted to human use, and the remaining habitat is highly fragmented. This ecoregion, together with the Thar Desert and Indus Valley Desert ecoregions, form Udvardy's "Thar Desert" Biogeographic province.

Noshaq : Noshaq (or Nowshak) is the highest mountain in Afghanistan and the second highest peak of the Hindu Kush, Tirich Mir (7,690 m) being the highest. Noshaq is located in the northeastern corner of the country along the Durand line which marks the border with Pakistan. The first ascent of the mountain was in 1960 by Toshiaki Sakai and Goro Iwatsuboa of a Japanese expedition. The climb followed the southeast ridge from the Qadzi Deh Glacier. Nowadays, the normal route is by the West ridge.

Notre Dame College : Notre Dame College is a renowned higher secondary school situated in Dhaka, Bangladesh, administrated by the fathers of The Congregation of Holy Cross Priest Society. In this subcontinent higher secondary schools that includes class 11th and 12th are called as college.

Nowshera : Nowshera is a district in the North-West Frontier Province of Pakistan that contains the town of Nowshera. In Nowshera District there are 47 Union Council and 5 provincial seats. The district is part of the Peshawar exo-metropolitan region.

N R Narayana Murthy : NR Narayana Murthy, chairman of Infosys Technologies one of the biggest IT empire in India, was born on August 20, 1946 in Karnataka. Murthy obtained his Bachelor of Electrical

Engineering (B.E.) from University of Mysore in 1967 and his Master of Technology (M.Tech.) from Indian Institute of Technology (IIT), Kanpur in 1969.

In the early seventies, Narayana Murthy took up employment with SESA in Paris. He worked with a team to design a real time operating system for handling air cargo for Charles de Gaulle airport. He came back to India after 3 years and took up a job with Patni Computer Systems in Pune. In 1981, Murthy founded Infosys Technologies along with six software professionals which later became one of the leading software company. In March 1999, Infosys became the first India-registered company to be listed on an American stock exchange.

Personally, Murthy is known for his simplicity and helping mentality. He founded the Infosys Foundation, a social welfare trust for helping the needy. He has a liking for Western Classical music and has liberal ideas. Murthy's ability to put forth his viewpoints and all his other qualities make him a unique personality.

Murthy holds several coveted positions. He was the President of National Association of Software and Service Companies (NASSCOM) from 1992 to 1994. He is a member of the National Information Technology Task Force of India, the Prime Minister's Council on Trade and Industry, Asia Society's International Council and Board of Councilors of the University of Southern California School of Engineering. He is a Director on the board of the Reserve Bank of India (RBI) and is also on the Wharton Business School's Asian Executive Board.

Murthy was honoured by 'JRD Tata Corporation Leadership Award' in 1996-97, 'Alumni Award' in 1998, 'The ET Businessperson of the Year Award' in 2000-2001 and 'The Max Schmidheiny Award' in 2001. He was chosen as the Business India's 'Businessman of the Year 1999', the

Indian corporate world's most coveted award. The credit goes to Mr. Murthy for making India one of the known names in the IT world.

N T Rama Rao : Nandamuri Taraka Rama Rao (28 May 1923 – 18 January 1996), more commonly known as N.T. Rama Rao, NTR, was an Indian film actor, director, producer and a Chief Minister of Andhra Pradesh. His repertoire of films included mythological, social and folk themes. He was awarded the Padma Sree by the government of India in the 1960s, recognizing his contribution to the Telugu cinema. After his film career, N.T. Ramarao became a political activist and party leader.

NTR formed the Telugu Desam Party (TDP) in 1982. TDP came into power within 9 months of its formation. During the first term as Chief Minister of AP, he tried to govern the entire state solely on idealogical terms which later proved to be disastrous as he lost the elections after serving a full term of 5 years. NTR lost the subsequent elections held in 1989. Even though he lost the 1989 elections, he shot to fame at the national level and was capable of uniting many regional parties.

NTR stormed back to power in 1994 when he promised he would offer rice at Rs. 2/kg and to make AP an "Alcohol Free" state. True to his word he kept his promises only to burden the state exchequer. He also faced serious problems within his party. Foreseeing the imminent threat of the de-stabilising wave within the party camaraderie, N Chandrababu Naidu lead a sudden revolt and split TDP into two, where the political careers of more than 180 Members of Legislative Assembly (MLAs) was at stake. The break-up of the party, the loss of power and the subsequent events can be summed up as the start of anti-climax in NTR's life. Officially he died of a severe heart stroke but there are conspiracy theorists who believe he had high traces of steroids in his blood which were unacceptable for a man of that age. The entire state was shocked to hear the news of his death and paid homage in a way only a king receives. His funeral was a state-affair which set the then world-record.

NTR Gardens : NTR Gardens is a park built by the ex-chief minister of Andhra Pradesh, Nara Chandra Babu Naidu. He built it in honour of N.T. Ramarao. The samadi (or burial ground) of NTR lies in this park. There are various attractions in this park, like the fruit restaurant, ant hill, vintage cars, the mini train, boat riding and a water slide as well as considerable greenery.

NTR Manasa Sarovaram : This Beautiful recreation centre named after Shri N.T.Rama Rao, is located 6 Kms from Guntur town at Takellapadu. Spread over an area of 55 acres, NTR Manasa Soravaram is exotically landscaped.

NTV : NTV is a Bengali language satellite television channel based in Bangladesh. It started operation in 2003. It was founded by Mosaddeq Hossain Falu, a lawmaker from the ruling Bangladesh Nationalist Party.

Nuala : Nuala is a folk dance of the Chamba valley in Himachal Pradesh. In this a garland is placed upon a pedestal as Shiva's garland and around it many dance dramas depicting scenes from the life of Lord Shiva are enacted. Women possessed of evil spirits are also brought to these gatherings and their antics also add to the general mystery and awesomeness of the spectacle along with the heady fragrance of the incense and the beating of the drums. The chief devotee, Chela, of Shiva dances in a trance and answers questions that are put to him. He predicts dire changes and natural calamities which sends shivers in the crowds and people vow to offer special Puja if these are warded off by the gods.

Nupa Pala : Nupa Pala, which is otherwise known as Kartal Cholom or Cymbal Dance, is a group performance of male partners, using cymbals and wearing snow white ball-shaped large turbans, who sing and dance to the accompaniment of *Pung* or Manipuri Mridanga.

Nur Jehan : Nur Jehan (1577 – 1645) was a Mughal empress. She was born Mehrunissa Begum in Kandahar, Khorasan (today Afghanistan). She married a Turkish/ Persian soldier, Sher Afghan Quli Khan at the age of 17 in 1594 and had a daughter, Ladli Begum. After her husband was executed in 1607, she became the lady-in-waiting for one of Jahangir's court women and the hand-maiden at the imperial harem in Agra. She met Jahangir in the spring festival of Norouz at the Palace bazaar in March 1611. He was so infatuated by her beauty that they were married in May 1611.

The Mughal state gave absolute power to the emperor, and those who exercised influence over the emperor had immense prestige. Nur Jahan was regarded by many as the real power behind the Mughal throne. Jahangir's addiction to opium and alcohol made it easier for her to assert her role. For many years she effectively wielded imperial power. She even gave audiences at her palace and her name was placed on the coinage. She attempted to consolidate her position through her brother Abdul Hasan Asaf Khan, who was the Imperial wazir. She arranged the marriage of her niece Arjumand Banu Begum, (later known as Mumtaz Mahal and the inspiration for the Taj Mahal) to Prince Khurram (who reigned as Shah Jahan), the most powerful of Jahangir's sons.

Shah Jahan rebelled against the throne, and sought shelter in Rajasthan. A war of succession broke out. Due to Shah Jahan's intransigence, Nur Jahan shifted her support to his younger brother, Prince Shahryar, and arranged his marriage to Ladli Begum, her daughter from her first marriage. Emperor Jahangir was captured by rebels in 1626 while he was on his way to Kashmir. Nur

Jahan intervened to get her husband released. Jahangir was rescued but died on October 28, 1627. When Jahangir died, Asaf Khan took the side of his son-in-law Shah Jahan against his sister. Nur Jahan became a prisoner in a small house for the rest of her life. She died in 1645 and is buried in Shadara in Lahore. She sponsored and is often credited with principally designing the mausoleum of her parents: Itmad-Ud-Daulah's Tomb (sometimes called the Baby Taj) in Agra.

Nur Mohammad Sheikh : Nur Mohammad Sheikh (1936-1971) was a Lance Nayek of East Pakistan Rifles (EPR) and a martyr in the war of liberation. Nur Mohammad Sheikh was born on 26 February 1936 at village Maheskhali in Narail district. An orphan in childhood he had to sell his paternal landed property for his livelihood. Nur Mohammad then joined the local Ansar Force. He joined the then East Pakistan Rifles on 14 March 1959. On completion of training he was posted at Dinajpur sector. He was transferred to Jessore sector headquarters in August 1970.

Nur Mohammad joined the War of Liberation in March 1971 while on leave at his village home. During the War of Liberation he fought in Sector 8 in Jessore. He was then in charge of a regular petrol force. The Pak-army having taken position on three sides of the defence post suddenly managed to surround the petrol force on 5 September, and the heroic resistance that followed resulted in the martyrdom of Nur Mohammad. In recognition of his valour and the highest sacrifice in the War of Liberation, he was honoured with the highest state insignia of 'Bir Srestha'.

Munshi Abdur Rauf : Munshi Abdur Rauf (1943-1971) was born in May 1943 at village Salamatpur in Boalkhali upazila of Faridpur district. He lost his father while an infant. Poverty compelled him to seek for a job for the maintenance of his family. In May 1963 Rauf was enrolled with the East Pakistan Rifles as a Lance Nayek. He had been serving in the East Pakistan Rifles in Chittagong till March 1971.

With the beginning of the war of liberation he made himself associated with the Eighth East Bengal Regiment. He embraced martyrdom in a battle fought against the Pakistan army at Kurighat in Chittagong Hill Tracts on 7 April 1971. He was honoured with the highest state insignia of Bir Srestha in recognition of his valour and sacrifice in the War of Liberation.

Nur Qutb Alam : Nur Qutb Alam a saint and saviour personality of the Muslims of Bengal from the oppression of Raja Ganesha. A son and chief disciple of Shaikh Alaul Huq and a grandson of Shaikh Asad of Lahore, he was a guardian saint of Pandua. Both father and son are lying buried in the famous shash hazari dargah (a dargah endowed with a property worth six thousand rupees) of Pandua. Like his father, Shaikh Nur Qutb Alam was a chishtiya saint and has left behind a line of saints who played significant part in the Muslim social life of Bengal for several centuries. Shaikh Alaul Huq was a contemporary of Sultan Shamsuddin Iliyas Shah and his son Sikandar Shah, while Shaikh Nur Qutb Alam was a fellow-student and contemporary of Sultan Ghiyasuddin Azam Shah.

Nurul Amin : Nurul Amin (1897 - 1974), a prominent Bengali leader of the Muslim League, served as Chief Minister of East Pakistan, Prime Minister and Vice President of Pakistan. Nurul Amin was elected as the Chief Minister of East Pakistan in September 1948 when Khawaja Nazimuddin was appointed Governor General on the death of Quaid i Azam Muhammad Ali Jinnah. In the 1954 elections, the Muslim League was comprehensively defeated by the United Front, an alliance between the Awami

League led by Huseyn Shaheed Suhrawardy, the Krishak Sramrik Party of Moulvi A. K. Fazlul Huq, the Nizam i Islam Party of Maulana Athar Ali and the [Ganatantri Dal] led by Haji Muhammad Danish and Mahmud Ali Sylheti.

Even Nurul Amin lost his assembly seat, and the Muslim League was effectively eliminated from the provincial political landscape. In the 1970 elections, Nurul Amin was elected to the National Assembly as one of only two non Awami League members.

Following the declaration of war between India and Pakistan in December 1971, Nurul Amin was appointed Prime Minister by President General Agha Muhammad Yahya Khan on December 6, 1971. However on December 20, 1971 Yahya Khan resigned. and the Deputy Prime Minister (and Foreign Minister) Zulfikar Ali Bhutto was sworn in as the new President.

Two days later, Nurul Amin was appointed as Vice President of Pakistan, the only person to have held this post. He continued to hold this post until the lifting of Martial Law on April 21, 1972.

Nushki : Nushki, a town and district of Baluchistan. The town lies 70 m. southwest of Quetta, and is situated in a plain at the base of the Quetta plateau, 2900 ft. above the sea. From this point the flat Baluchistan desert stretches away northwards and westwards to the Helmund river. The administration of the Nushki district was taken over from the khan of Kalat by the Indian government in 1896, and was leased from him on a perpetual quit rent in 1899. In 1902 a railway of 91 m. was sanctioned from Quetta to Nushki, which was completed in 1905. This railway makes Nushki the starting-point of the caravan route to Seistan. From the strategic point of view a force operating from Nushki would flank any advance from the north on Kandahar, and would also guard the southwest approach to the fortress of Quetta.

Nusrat Fateh Ali Khan : Ustad Nusrat Fateh Ali Khan (October 13, 1948 - August 16, 1997) was primarily a singer of Qawwali, the devotional music of the Sufis, a mystical offshoot of Islam. Traditionally, Qawwali has been a family business. Nusrat's family has an unbroken tradition of performing qawwali for the last 600 years.

NWFP University of Engineering and Technology : NWFP University of Engineering and Technology is a university in Peshawar, Pakistan. It was established in 1952 as a "constituent" college of University of Peshawar, but it was upgraded to a university in 1980. Since then, three satellite campuses in Abbottabad, Bannu and Mardan have been established. The Peshawar campus, however, remains the nucleus of the University. The university's degrees are highly regarded and its electrical engineering department is well known in Pakistan.

Nyaya : The Nyaya school of philosophical speculation is based on a text called the Nyaya Sutra. It was written by Aksapada Gautama at an indeterminate date, but probably in the second century BCE. The most important contribution made by this school is its methodology. This is based on a system of logic that has subsequently been adopted by most of the other Indian schools (orthodox or not), much in the same way that Western science and philosophy can be said to be largely based on Aristotelian logic.

But Nyaya is not merely logic for its own sake. Its followers believed that obtaining valid knowledge was the only way to obtain release from suffering. They therefore took great pains to identify valid sources of knowledge and to distinguish these from mere false opinions. According to the Nyaya school, there are exactly four sources of knowledge (pramanas): perception, inference, comparison and testimony. Knowledge obtained through each of these can of course still be either valid or invalid, and the Nyaya scholars (Naiyanikas) again went to great pains to identify, in each case, what it took to make knowledge valid, in the process coming up with a number of explanatory schemes. In this sense, Nyaya is probably the closest Indian equivalent to contemporary Western analytical philosophy. The later Naiyanikas gave logical proofs for the existence of God and also for his uniqueness, especially during their arguments against the Buddhists who at that time were fundamentally atheistic. An important later development in Nyaya is the system of Navya Nyaya (New Logic).

Nyokum—Nishi Festival : In Arunachal Pradesh, the month of August every year is the time for celebrating Nyokum or the worship of goddess of crops (Lakshmi) and other Gods and Goddess. On the first day, before an altar of images and symbols of the gods and goddess, the priest starts the Puja by chanting prayer and girls dance and sing to propitiate the unseen god and goddess. They sing about abundant crops and good will, health and unity among all the people, joy and mutual co-operation and peace and plenty every year. On the second and concluding day, the villagers of the neighbouring villages perform their Puja in their villages and come in long procession. The sacrificial animals like dogs, pigs and chicken are either carried or hung in long bamboo poles. On the arrival at the place of worship the people go round the altar chanting and the atmosphere seems to be sur-charged with a feeling of devotion and godliness. The animals are sacrificed and after invocation of the blessings, the Puja comes to a conclusion.

O

Oberoi Hotels : Oberoi Hotels is a luxury hotel company extablished in 1934. It has branches in seven countries, including India and Egypt.

Objectives Resolution : The Objectives Resolution states that the future constitution of Pakistan would be modeled on the ideology and democratic faith of Islam. On March 12, 1949, the Constituent Assembly adopted a resolution moved by Liaquat Ali Khan, the then Prime Minister of Pakistan. It was called the Objectives Resolution. It proclaimed that the future constitution of Pakistan would not be modeled on European pattern, but on the ideology and democratic faith of Islam.

Ocean Park : Ocean Park in Hyderabad is an excellent Water Theme Amusement Park modelled on International Standards. It provides a number of amusement rides, water rides and is equipped with facilities like multi-cuisine etc.

Ochchira Kali : This is an annual festival celebrated at Ochchira, a village near Kayamkulam in Kerala. This festival is celebrated in memory of a hard fight between the Rajas of Quilon and Kayamkulam. Only Nairs could take part in it. It is not open to women. It is now conducted on the first and second days of Mithunam or

Avany (June-July). For seven days beginning with the first, it is popularly believed that there will be incessant rain.

Ochre Coloured Pottery Culture : The Ochre Coloured Pottery culture (OCP), is a 2nd millennium BC Bronze Age culture of the Ganga-Yamuna plain. It is a contemporary to, and a successor of the Indus Valley Civilization. The OCP marks the last stage of the North Indian Bronze Age and is succeeded by the Iron Age black-and-red ware and painted-gray ware cultures. Early specimens of the characteristic ceramics found near Jodhpura, Rajasthan date to the 3rd millennium,this site of Jodhpura is in district Jaipur and must not be confused with the city of Jodhpur, and the culture reaches the Gangetic plain in the early 2nd millennium.

Odissi : Odissi, the essence of the state of Orissa. Orissa is the highly inspired, impassioned, ecstatic and sensuous form of dance. Odissi was performed in the temples of Orissa as a religious rite and offering by the Devadasis known as 'Maharis'.

Odissi is a rich and generous cultural gift of the land, well known for its dedication to religion and arts and known in the past as 'Kalinga Desha'. The people of this land raised magnificent temples, each erected as an act of religious faith and embellished by the skills of master craftsmen, sculptures and architects. These temples became the centre of art and culture and it was here that Odissi, one of India's scintillating dance-forms was born, nurtured and nourished.

In Odissi, the technique, the style, its stages, the repertoire and the finale were almost amorphous. Today Odissi is a well established and codified classical dance form of India, a dance of love, delight and intense passion, lyrical, pure, divine and human all rolled into one.

Oil Bath : In most Indian communities, a bath or *snan* is *de rigueur*, a vital part of most cultural traditions. There re ways and ways of bathing but the oil bath prevalent in South India is a sure winner. For the Kannadiga, an oil bath is both a link with the past and a way to ensure longevity, good skin and hair. In most traditional Kannada households, huge copper cauldrons for heating water are a permanent fixture and bespeak of a deep commitment to the fine art of an oil bath.

The ritual of an oil bath is definitely an art form. Contrary to its name, an oil bath is not about bathing in oil – you need a few ounces of gingelly or castor oil and gallons of hot water. It is not an idiosyncrasy on the part of the Kannadiga to have an oil bath but is a practise based on scientific principles. It is believed that regular oil baths help to banish *ushna*, the inner heat of the body, thereby preventing many ailments. The oil bath keeps the mind calm and ensures a healthy, glowing body.

Old Goa : Half a dozen imposing churches and cathedrals and a fragment of a gateway are all that remain of the second capital of the Adil Shahi dynasty of Bijapur and the Portuguese capital that was once said to rival Lisbon in magnificence. Wracked by cholera and malaria epidemics, eroded by monsoon rains and choked by creepers, Old Goa has declined from a vibrant city of over a hundred thousand souls to little more than a handful of potent architectural relics.

Old Goa is still the spiritual heart of Christian Goa, and its most famous building is the Basilica of Bom Jesus, which contains the tomb and mortal remains of the peripatetic St Francis Xavier, credited with introducing Christianity to much of South-East Asia. Also of interest is the Convent & Church of St Francis of Assisi, which has gilded and carved woodwork, murals depicting scenes from the saint's life, and a floor substantially made of carved gravestones. The largest of the churches is the Portuguese-Gothic Se Cathedral, dating from 1562, which houses the so-called 'Golden Bell', whose resonant peal can be heard thrice daily. Other gems include the Church of St Cajetan which was modelled on St Peter's in Rome and the Royal Chapel of St Anthony. Not a single secular building remains standing, so don't say God doesn't work in mysterious ways.

Om Parvat : Om Parvat or Adi Kailash or Chhota Kailash or Baba Kailash or Jonglingkong, is an ancient holy Hindu Himalayan mountain peak at an altitude of 6191 m, in the Himalayan Range lying on the Pithoragarh district of Uttaranchal, India near Sin la pass, similar to Mount Kailash in Tibet. The snow deposition pattern gives the impression of 'AUM' (?) written over it, which is sacred Hindu Mantra or chant. Near Om Parvat, beautiful 'Parvati lake' and 'Jonglingkong lake' is situated.

Om Puri : Om Puri (born October 18, 1950) is a highly regarded and renowned Indian actor of Hindi movies. He was born at Ambala, Haryana, India, and graduated from the Film and Television Institute of India. He was also an alumnus of the 1973 batch of National School of Drama where Naseeruddin Shah was a co-student. Puri has won a few of the prestigious National Awards, and the popular Filmfare Awards for his performances.

In July, 2004, he was awarded an honorary OBE for his performances in English movies as well.

Omkareshwar : Omkareshwar is a Hindu temple in Madhya Pradesh state in India. It is on an island called Mandhata or Shivapuri in the Narmada river. It is one of the 12 revered Jyotirlinga shrines of Shiva. It is about 12 miles from Mortakka in Madhya Pradesh. The shape of the island is said to be like the Hindu Om symbol. There are two temples here, one to Omkareshwar (whose name means "OM-maker-lord") and one to Amareshwar (whose name means "immortal lord" or "lord of the immortals"). Omkareshwar is formed by the sacred river Narmada. This is one of the most sacred of rivers in India and is now home to one of the worlds biggest Dam projects.

Onam : Onam is the national festival of the people of Kerala. It is the festival of flowers, which falls in 'Chingam' or Bhadrapada usually in August or September. It is a harvest festival and goes for 4 colourful days with song and Kathakali dances, feasting and boat races. There is a legend behind Onam. In ancient times Kerala was ruled by an asura King Mahabali who was very wise and greatly loved by the people. Because of jealousy, the king of gods, Indra, hatched a plot to oust Mahabali. To execute the scheme Vishnu disguised himself as a Brahmin boy, Vamana, and went to the asura King. He asked as much land as he could cover in three steps and King Mahabali agreed to the request. Vamana immediately began to grow as big as the universe and with two steps, he covered the earth, the heavens and the nether world. He looked at Mahabali to place his third step and the King offered his head for Vamana to place his foot. Vamana pushed Mahabali down to the ground and before he disappeared Mahabali asked Vishnu for a boon to come to the earth once a year to see his people and the request was granted.

The celebration of Onam is a tribute to Mahabali's sacrifice. Onam celebrations which last ten days begin with a colourful reception to King Mahabali. Mahabali is supposed to visit his kingdom on the 2nd day, which is the most important day of the festival. Earthen mounds, which look somewhat like square pyramids, representing Mahabali and Vishnu are placed in the dung-plastered courtyards and beautifully decorated with flowers. The legend is believed to have happened at Trikkakara, a place

10km from Cochin on the Edapally- Pookattupadi road which according to mythology was the legendary capital of King Mahabali. The temple here, is the only temple in Kerala with the deity of 'Trikkakara Appan' or 'Vamanamurthy' who is Lord Vishnu himself in disguise.

Ongar : Ongar is a Paleolithic site located in in Sindh, Pakistan. Ongar is located a few kilometers south of Hyderabad on the hills, which lie on the right side of the Indus River. At the present state of the research, Ongar is the most important Paleolithic site discovered in southern Sindh. According to the aspect and surface patina of the tools, the flint assemblages can be attributed to the Early, Middle and Late (Upper) Paleolithic periods.

Ongole : Ongole, a town in the state of Andhra Pradesh, India, is the administrative headquarters of Prakasam District. The town has a population of 149,589 (agglomeration 152,945 (2001 census).

The town's history goes back to the era of the Mauryas, and Satavahanas who ruled most of present day Andhra Pradesh. A few inscriptions dating to the Satavahana period were found in a village called China Ganjam, near Ongole. After the Satavahanas, this place came into the limelight again during the Kakatiya dynasty. At that time the nearby towns of Motupalli and Voda Revu served as major seaports.

Ongole is famous for its Ongole breed of oxen which are considered virile and of superior stock. They are one of the major Zebu cattle breeds of the world.

Ooty : Ooty, short for Ootacamund (the official name is Udhagamandalam), is a popular hill station in the state of Tamil Nadu in South India. The word Ootacamund itself is a derivation from the toda tribal word Utaka-mund. It is sometimes referred to as "Queen of Hill stations"

The Nilgiri Hills were supposedly first claimed in recorded history by the Hoysala King Vishnu Varadhan sometime in the 12th century. However, the hills remained isolated from the glare of civilization until they were surrendered to the conquering British by the Muslim king Tipu Sultan of Mysore in the 18th century. The British citizens in neighboring Coimbatore liked the climate of this forested land, and occupied it by taking land from the native tribes (Toda, Irumba and Badaga); often buying up many square kilometres in a day for the price of a few meals. The hills were developed rapidly under the British Raj because they were almost entirely owned by private British citizens, unlike the rest of India. Ooty served as the summer capital of the Madras Presidency, and had winding hill roads and a complicated rack-and-pinion railway system built by influential and enterprising British citizens with venture capital from the Madras government. Following independence, India has come to love it for the same reasons as the British.

Located in the mountainous range called the Blue Mountains or Nilgiris (in the native tongue), it draws swarms of tourists every year. The weather is quite pleasant at a mean of 15 to 20 °C year round, dropping to lows of 0 °C during winter. The hill town suffers from rampant commercialization and erosion of natural resources. The tourism industry has placed an enormous strain on the natural resources resulting in pollution, water shortage and bad roads. The landscape is quite unlike the rest of India, marked by rolling hills covèred with dense vegetation, smaller hills and plateaus covered with tea gardens, and eucalyptus trees. Many portions of the hills are preserved as natural reserve forests, and special permits are needed to camp in noncamp sites. Ooty is not the destination in itself, as much as it is the focal point of attraction. Auto touring the surrounding country side is certainly a must do.

The hilly region also houses smaller towns like Coonoor and Kotagiri. These towns are less than 1 hour away from Ooty, and enjoy the same natural climes, but have fewer tourists and cheaper prices.

Operation Blue Star : The Operation Blue Star (June 4 to June 6, 1984) was the Indian military operation at the Golden Temple in Amritsar, Punjab, the holiest temple of the Sikh religion. The Punjab state in India had seen the rate of murder and overall crime rise in the early 1980's. This was in large part due to the conflict between the Militant Sikhs and the secular government of India. Many Sikhs felt that they were being discriminated against. The distrust between the MilitantSikhs and the government grew. Jarnail Singh Bhindranwale had become the voice of the minority of Sikh's who were militancy against the government.

Following a crackdown on Sikh militants in early 1984, a group of militant Sikhs led by Jarnail Singh Bhindranwale fortified the Golden Temple complex. A majority of the Sikh public in India and abroad did not support this action by the militants. On the 3rd of June, a 36 hour curfew was imposed on the state of Punjab which increased the apprehensiveness of the militants inside the temple that a raid on the temple was imminent, many innocent Sikh pilgims and those residing in the temple areas would be in danger. The period coincided with the weekend of 2nd and 3rd, the anniversary of the martyrdom of Guru Arjan Dev, who built the Golden Temple and compiled the Sikh's Holy book. As a result of this, when the curfew was imposed the temple was filled with worshippers. The Indian government did not warn pilgrims of the coming action, and many many innocent Sikhs were needlessly killed.

The Indian Army had thought the operation would last a few hours at most. However, after the Operation

Bluestar commander Major General Brar visited the Golden Temple complex the day before the operation he realized that the Sikh militants had prepared well and built defensive positions against an attack. The Sikh separatist forces within the Golden Temple were led by former Major General Shabeg Singh (dismissed from the Indian Army in 1976).Maj. Gen. Brar, a Sikh himself, and Lt. Gen. Sundarji, another senior commander, believed there was no way to avoid a violent resolution. Brar went in and briefed all troops.

The Indian army asked the militants to surrender and made a plea to release the trapped civilians inside. The militants however refused to surrender. The army used as much force as it deemed necessary to dislodge the militants and in course desectrated the Sikh's holiest shrine equivalent to the vatican for Catholics.

Eyewitnesses say that the army deployed tanks, armed personnel carriers, rocket launchers, heavy machine guns and helicopters. Many of the buildings surrounding the Temple were reduced to rubble. The damage inside of the temple complex was severe. The Harmindar Sahib [the sanctum sanctorum where the Sikh holy book, the Guru Granth Sahib, is kept during the day] received many bullet holes. The Sikh holy book itself was even hit by a bullet.

The militants in the temple appeared to be armed with machine guns, anti-tank missiles and rocket launchers and resisted the army's attempts to dislodge them from the shrine. The militants also appeared to have planned for a long occupation of the shrine having arranged for water from wells within the temple compound, and had stocked food provisions that would have lasted months. It is intersting to note the Indian Forces could have waited out the militants, cut off electricity, water etc in order to ensure a peaceful non violent end without the loss of life and desecration of the temple.

The fighting between the militants and the Indian military continued throughout the night. Major General Brar a Sikh himself made the decision to bring in tanks to support the military in hopes of finishing the operation before dawn. After two days of heavy fighting with the assistance of superior military equipment the Indian military was able to bring most of the Golden Temple complex under its control.

Operation Blue Star led to India's bitter relations with Sikhs all over the world and continue to this day. It was considered by most Sikhs as a great insult because of the completely unnecessary use of force at their holy place, on one of the most holiest of days. The later assassination of Indira Gandhi by her Sikh bodyguards was said to be in response to desecrating the temple. The events that followed were more horrific. Anti-Sikh riots broke out in North India killing as many as 4000 Sikhs, militancy in Punjab lasted for more than a decade in which many people were killed.

Operation Dwarka : Operation Dwarka also known as Operation Somnath was the popular name given to Pakistan Navy's attack on the Indian coastal town of Dwarka on 7 September 1965. This was the first use of a Navy in the Indo-Pakistan Wars.

As the Indo-Pakistani War of 1965 broke out between India and Pakistan over Kashmir, armies and air forces of both nations were involved in bitter fighting. Pakistan was under attack in Punjab region and were locked in battles in Kashmir. To relieve pressure on the northern front, Pakistan decided to use her navy in the war by launching a quick strike on Indian coast. The primary objective of the attack was to draw out ships out of Bombay for attack purposes and to detroy the radar station and other naval installations at Dwarka. The attack also hoped to divert the Indian Air Force from the north.

On the night of September 7 Pakistan Navy launched its assault on Western Indian shores. Dwarka was chosen for its proximity, relatively less guarded port and historical relevance. The plan called for a fleet of 7 naval vessels of Pakistan to bomb the tiny town of Dwarka. It was aimed at luring the major ships anchored in Bombay to attack the Pakistan ships. The intention was that the submarine PNS Ghazi lurking in the Arabian Sea would then take out the Indian ships. Accordingly a fleet of ships comprising PNS Babur, PNS Khaibar, PNS Badr, PNS Jahangir, PNS Alamgir, PNS Shahjahan and PNS Tipu Sultan set sail for Dwarka and bombed the tiny town. But despite the shellings, none of the primary objectives were achieved. The radar installations remained intact, there were no loss of lives in the town and more importantly the Indian Navy's ships did not take the bait. Soon the Pakistan ships sped away, later claiming a psychological victory.

Operation Gibraltar : Operation Gibraltar was the name given to the failed plan by Pakistan to infiltrate Jammu and Kashmir, India and start a rebellion. Launched in August 1965, Pakistan Army soldiers and guerrillas disguised as locals entered Indian held Kashmir from Pakistan with the intention of fomenting an insurgency among Kashmiri Muslims. However, the strategy went awry from the very outset, as the locals did not respond as expected and the infiltrators were soon found. The debacle was followed by an Indian counterattack that resulted in minor victories.

Operation Polo : Operation Polo was the military operation of annexation of the princely Hyderabad state into India, by the Indian Army in September 1948. It was the first and the largest police action undertaken in Independent India.

Operation Searchlight : It was a planned genocide carried out by the Pakistan Army to curb the Bengali nationalist movement in erstwhile East Pakistan in 1971. This was seen as the sequel to Operation Blitz that was launched in November 1970. The killings which began on March 25, 1971 and ended on 16th of December, 1971 led to death of 3 Million Bangladeshis as well as other atrocities like rape (there is no reliable estimate of how many women and children were raped but some parties put it to around 200,000) and looting. It was part of the genocide of 1971 to snuff out any Bengali opposition to the military dictatorship in Pakistan. After the defeat of the Pakistan Army, there was a call to try nearly 200 POWs for war crimes, but none of the soldiers or officers involved were tried for war crimes

Operation Trident : Operation Trident was a naval attack launched on Pakistan's port city of Karachi by the Indian Navy during the Indo-Pakistani War of 1971, which resulted in a massive victory for India. Casualities of the Pakistan Navy included PNS Khyber, a destroyer, and PNS Muhafiz, a minesweeper, which were sunk. Another Pakistani destroyer, PNS Shajehan, was badly damaged. The Indian attack fleet returned undamaged. The operation was the first successful naval attack since independence in South Asia which saw naval ships being sunk.

Following months of civil unrest in neighboring East Pakistan (now Bangladesh) India decided to intervene on behalf of the Bengalis and entered the war on December 3. The very next day Indian Navy decided to launch a lightning fast naval strike on Karachi port in West Pakistan with the aim of crippling the Pakistan Navy and bottling up the western shores. Accordingly on December 4 a task group of 3 OSA class Missile boats were assembled.

Escorted by two Anti-submarine patrol vessels, the boats set sail for Karachi. Nearing the Karachi port, Indian Navy then detected Pakistani presence and launched its missiles which hit PNS Muhafiz and PNS Khyber which both sank. PNS Shajahan was also severely hit. The missile boats then went on to hit the fuel storage tanks at Karachi harbour that were set ablaze, causing heavy loss. After notching up considerable material and economic damage to the enemy the Indian vessels returned to a hero's welcome.

The success of this operation prompted another attack on Pakistan coast named Operation Python which was also quite successful. Together the Indian operations on the West Pakistan coast had obliterated its main ships and bottled up the region leading to victory in the war. Operation Trident had introduced to the war a number of firsts. It was the first time ever ship launched missiles were used in the region. And it was the first time since independence that saw naval ships being sunk in South Asia. Operation Trident proved to be a huge success, prompting Navy Day to be shifted to this day. Since then, December 4 is officially celebrated as Indian Navy Day.

Operation Vijay : In the 1999 Kargil Conflict between India and Pakistan, Operation Vijay (Victory in Hindi) was the name of the successful Indian operation to push back the infiltrators from the Kargil Sector.

Oppana : It is a Muslim bridal group dance.

Orang National Park (Mini Kaziranga) : Orang national park popularly known as mini Kaziranga, is located on the north bank of the river Brahmaputra. The park covering an area of 72-sq-kms was established as a sanctuary in 1985 and declared a National Park on 13th April 1999. Famous for its natural scenic beauty, the park is about 150-km from Guwahati and 31-km from Tezpur, the nearest town.

Orang Wildlife Sanctury : Covering an area of 72 Sq. Kms. Orang Wildlife Sanctuary in Assam is a miniature Kaziranga. It is situated on the north bank of river Brahmaputra. The animals and birds to be seen in this sanctuary are the great Indian one-horned rhinoceros, Elephant, Leopard, Samber, Barking Deer, Tiger and varieties of water birds, Green Pigeon, Florican, Teal, Gees, etc. Orang is 150 Kms. from Guwahati and 32 Kms. from Tezpur by road. The nearest Airport is Saloni, (Tezpur) and the nearest railhead is Rongapara. Both Govt. and private buses ply regularly from Guwahati. As there is only a small Forest Rest House, having limited capacity, inside the forest, tourists are, therefore, requested to visit Orang form Tezpur. For comfortable stay there is a Govt. tourist lodge, Govt. circuit House and other private hotels of moderate rates at Tezpur.

Oraon : The Oraon are a tribal (Adivasi) people of Bihar, Jharkhand, Orissa, Chhattisgarh and West Bengal, India. Their language, Kurukh, belongs to the Dravidian family, and is most closely related to Brahui and Paharia. About 25 percent of the population are Christians. There are close to two million Oraon (twenty lakhs). The Roman Catholic Archbishop of Ranchi, Cardinal Telesphore Toppo, is Oraon.

Orchha : Orchha (or Urchha) is a town in Tikamgarh district of Madhya Pradesh state, India. The town was the seat of an eponymous former princely state of central India, in the Bundelkhand region. Orchha lies on the Betwa River, not far from Jhansi. Orchha possesses an imposing fort, dating from the early 17th century, which contains a number of palaces and other historic buildings. The most noteworthy of these are the Rajmandir, a massive square building of which the exterior is almost absolutely plain; and the Jahangirmahal, of the same form but far more ornate, a singularly beautiful specimen of Hindu domestic architecture. Elsewhere about the town exist fine temples and tombs, among which may be noticed the Chaturbhuj temple built on a vast platform of stone.

Orchha was founded in the 16th century by the Bundela chief Rudra Pratap, who became the first Raja of Orchha. In the early 17th century, Raja Jujhar Singh rebelled against the Mughal emperor Shah Jahan, whose armies devastated the state. Orchha was the only Bundela state not subjugated by the Marathas in the 18th century. The town of Tehri, presently Tikamgarh, about 40 miles south of Orchha, became the capital of Orchha state in 1783, and is presently the district town. Tehri was the site of the fort of Tikamgarh, and the town eventually took the name of the fort.

Orchids : Because of the profusion of orchids in the state, and Sonitpur has some of the rarest specimen, orchids are part of the life style of the people. They figure in folk songs and folk dances of the Assamese. Any native damsel in a festive mood is not completely adorned till she puts an orchid round her chignon. With over 400 varieties, the orchid centre at Tipi Arunachal Pradesh is just 68 km From Tezpur.

Orissa : Orissa (2001 provisional pop. 36,706,920), 60,162 sq mi (155,820 sq km) is a state situated in the east coast of India. Orissa is bounded on the north by Jharkhand, on the north-east by West Bengal, on the east by the Bay of Bengal, on the south by Andhra Pradesh and on the west by Chhattisgarh. The relatively unindented coastline (c.200 mi/320 km long) lacks good ports save for the deepwater facility at Paradip. The narrow, level coastal strip, including the Mahanadi River delta, is exceedingly fertile. Rainfall is heavy and regular, and two crops of rice (by far the most important food) are grown annually. The state is known for its temples, especially in the cities of Konark, Puri, and Bhubaneswar.

Orissa and Puri are popular tourist destinations. Puri, with Sri Lord Jagannatha's temple on the sea, and Konark, with the Mukhasala of the Sun Temple, are visited by thousands of westerners every year. Along with the Lingaraja Temple of Bhubaneswar, the Sri Lord Jagannatha Temple and the Sun Temple of Konark are the must sees for anyone doing research on the arecheological marvels of India.

Orissa Semi-evergreen Forests : The Orissa semi-evergreen forests are a tropical moist broadleaf forest ecoregion of eastern India. The ecoregion covers an area of 22,300 square kilometers (8,600 square miles) on the coastal plain of Orissa state, bounded on the north and west by the Eastern Highlands moist deciduous forests and on the south and west by the Bay of Bengal.

Oriya : Oriya is one of the Indian languages mainly spoken in the Indian state of Orissa, though there are also significant Oriya-speaking populations in other linguistic regions, such as the Medinpur district of West Bengal and the Saraikela Kharsawan district of Jharkhand. Due to the increasing migration of labour, the west Indian state of Gujarat also has a significant Oriya speaking population with Surat being the second largest Oriya speaking city in India. The language is also an official language of India. Oriya is an Indo-Aryan language and is thought to be directly descended from the Prakrit known as Purva Magadhi that was spoken in eastern India over 1,500 years ago. It bears a very strong resemblance to the modern languages Bangla (Bengali) and Ôxômiya (Assamese). Of all the languages spoken in northern India, Oriya appears to be the least influenced by Persian and Arabic.

Oriya has a rich literary heritage dating back to the thirteenth century. Sarala Dasa who lived in the fourteenth century is known as the Vyasa of Orissa. He translated the Mahabharata into Oriya. In fact the language was initially standardised through a procss of translation of classical Sanskrit texts like the Mahabharata, the Ramayana and the Srimad Bhagabatam. Jagannatha Das translated the Srimad Bhagabatam into Oriya and his translation standardized the written form of the langauage. Oriya has had a strong tradition of poetry, especially that of devotional poetry.

Ormara : Ormara is a port city located in Balochistan province of Pakistan. It is located 450 Km west of Karachi on the Arabian Sea. Jinnah naval base of Pakistan Navy is also located at Ormara. Ormara airport is located at 25° 16' 29N 64° 35' 10E. The population of Ormara is estimated to be over 40,000 in 2005. Over 99% is Muslim. The vast majority of the population of Ormara is Baloch.

Osho Rajneesh : Rajneesh Chandra Mohan Jain (December 11, 1931 - January 19, 1990), better known during the 1970s as Bhagwan Shree Rajneesh and later as Osho was an Indian spiritual teacher or guru. He lived in India and the United States and was the spiritual head of the Osho-Rajneesh movement, a controversial new religious movement.

Osho was known as Acharya Rajneesh (teacher Rajneesh) during his early years as a spiritual teacher. In 1971 he asked his disciples to start calling him "Bhagwan Shree Rajneesh." The Sanskrit word Bhagwan means "Blessed one" (historically, it is used to refer to a Hindu god, such as Bhagwan Ram or Bhagwan Krishna or to a spiritually awakened being in Mahayana Buddhism). It is also used to denote individuals who possess a great wealth of spiritual knowledge. Shree (more commonly transliterated as Shri or Sri) in Sanskrit means "spiritual wealth" and is thus roughly equivalent to the English word "Lord". It derives this meaning from its use as another name Lakshmi, the Hindu goddess of prosperity.

In February 1989, following a request from Swami Harideva, the well known American disciple who had introduced Rajneeshs'work and mediatations to the West in 1971, Rajneesh changed his name to "Osho". 'Osho' is an ancient Japanese term that is used to address a spiritual master in certain Zen traditions. The name "Osho" in this context means "The Friend". It fit how Rajneesh wanted to be known by his followers and lovers.

Osho (Rajneesh) claimed that the greatest values in life are (in no specific order) love, meditation and laughter, and that the sole goal of human life was to reach spiritual enlightenment. He extracted and expounded truth and techniques from various spiritual sources. He was a prolific speaker both in Hindi and English on various spiritual traditions including those of Buddha, Krishna, Jesus, Socrates, Zen masters, Hassid, Sufism and many others. His lectures were mixed with wit and jokes. His discourses have been printed in several hundred books and are available in audio and video recordings. An experienced orator, he used it to convey his message, but insisted that the only reason he kept on talking was to eventually convince his listeners to start on a path of meditation.

Osho was 58 years old when he died. His ashes were placed in a reconstructed meditation hall, at his last home place, his Ashram in Pune, India. The epitaph reads, "Never born, Never died: visited the planet earth between December 11, 1931 and, January 19, 1990."

Other Backward Class : The Other Backward Classes (or OBCs) in India are a group of castes officially recognized as being traditionally subject to exclusion, while still having a higher status than scheduled castes or scheduled tribes. OBCs comprise about half of India's population, and are entitled to 27% of the job reservations in government employment. In India's constitution, OBCs are described as "socially and educationally backward classes", and governments are enjoined to ensure their social and educational development.

Ottantullal : It is a solo dance form of Kathakali, referred as 'poor man's Kathakali'.

Outlook : Outlook is an Indian weekly English newsmagazine in publication since October 1995. It is estimated to be read by 1.5 million people in India, and sells more than 11.2 million copies over the year. Vinod Mehta has been its editor-in-chief from its inception. Outlook has also spawned the specialised magazines Outlook Traveller, Outlook Money and the Hindi Outlook Saptahik. Originally owned by Hathway Investments Private Limited, it is now part of the Rajan Raheja Group.

O V Vijayan : Ootupulackal Velukkuty Vijayan (July 2, 1930-March 30, 2005) was an Indian author and cartoonist, an important figure in modern Malayalam language literature. V. Vijayan was almost certainly India's foremost fabulist in the recent past. An extraordinary writer with enormous range, he wrote everything from a semi-fictional history of his feudal-landlord family, 'Generations' to the scatological 'The Saga of Dharmapuri'.

Ovi Songs : The Ovi songs relating to ceremonies of a profane nature like weddings etc are very much current in Goa among the Hindus, while they have almost disappeared among the Christians with few exceptions. They are sung by women while applying the coconut-pulp milk to the bride and groom, while preparing condiments for dinners etc. The most popular are those that concern with the spirit of fertility in the biblical terms of increase and multiply.

P

Paan : Paan, pan (in Hindi), or bidda (in Tamil) is a type of Indian snack, which consists of fillings wrapped in a triangular package using leaves of the Betel pepper (Piper betle) and held together with a toothpick or a clove. Paan is chewed in India as a palate cleanser, and a breath freshener. It is also commonly offered to guests and visitors as a sign of hospitality. Paan fillings is generally a mixture of various spices, fruits, and sugar. Many paan makers use Mukhwas as an ingredient to their paan fillings. Although many types of paan contain Betel nuts as a filling, many other types do not.

Paba or Milroy Sanctuary : Covering an area of 49 Sq. Kms., Pabha Wildlife Sanctuary is situated in Lakhimpur District in Assam. It is a sanctuary created exclusively for the protection of the magnificent Wild water Buffalo.

Pabitora Wildlife Sancuary : A small wildlife sanctuary, 60 km from Guwahati. Rhino and various species of deer abound here.

Pabna : Pabna is a district in the Rajshahi division of Bangladesh. With an area of 2371.50 sq km, the district is bounded by natore and sirajganj districts on the north, Rajbari and Kushtia districts on the south, Manikganj and Sirajganj districts on the east, Ganges river and Kushtia district on the west. Average maximum temperature 33.9 C, minimum 9.6 C; annual rainfall 1872 mm. Characteristically the soil of the district is divided into four, viz flood plains of the Ganges, Karatoya, Jamuna and Barind Tract. Main rivers are Ganges, Ichamati, Gumani and Hurasagar.

Pabna district was established in 1832. It consists of 9 upazilas, 8 municipalities, 81 wards, 191 mahallas, 72 union parishads, 1321 mouzas and 1540 villages. The upazilas are Atgharia, Bera, Bhangura, Chatmohar, Faridpur, Ishwardi, Santhia, Sujanagar and Pabna Sadar. The municipalities are Bera, Bhangura, Chatmohar, Faridpur, Ishwardi, Santhia, Sujanagar and Pabna Sadar. Once the present area of the Pabna district was a part of the ancient Pundravardhana. Although established in 1832 the contours of the district has been changed many times. The major changes of the boundaries of the district took place in 1877 and 1881 with the major changes of the courses of the rivers Padma and Jamuna. In the 1980s greater Pabna district was divided into two districts: Pabna and Sirajganj.

Pabna Peasant Uprising : Pabna Peasant Uprising was a resistance movement against the oppression of the Zamindars. It originated in the Yusufshahi pargana, which is now the Sirajganj district within greater Pabna. The zamindars routinely collected money from the peasants by the illegal means of forced levy, abwabs (cesses), enhanced rent and so on. Peasants were often evicted from land on the pretext of non-payment of rent.

Pachmarhi : Pachmarhi is a hill station in Madhya Pradesh state of central India. It's widely known as " Satpura ki Rani", situated at a height of 3500 ft. in a valley of the Satpura Range in Hoshangabad district, 32 miles by road from Piparia station on the Indian Railways. Piparia is 2 hrs Train run from Jabalpur. All the trains departing towards Itarsi from Jabalpur pass through Piparia, but only a few halt here. The area was discovered in the modern times by Captain James Forsyth of the British army in 1857 Pachmarhi became a hill-station and sanatorium for British troops in the Central Provinces of India. The population in 1901 was 3020, rising to double that number in the hot summer months. Pachmarhi also served as the summer capital.

Pachmarhi is still a popular tourist retreat; its elevation offers some relief from the summer heat, and the lush forests of the Satpuras, with their streams and waterfalls, are picturesque and home to much wildlife. Pachmarhi lies within the Pachmarhi Biosphere Preserve, created in 1999 to link two forest reserves and Satpura National Park into a larger wildlife conservation area. It also has Dhupgarh- the highest point in Central India.

Padamanabhapuram Palace : Padamanabhapuram Palace complex is located in a small village Padmanabhapuram, around 65 km from Trivandrum, Kerala, India, en route to Kanyakumari, Tamilnadu. The palace complex is inside an old granite fortress around four km long. The place is located at the foot of the Veli Hills, which form a part of the Western Ghats. The river Valli flows nearby.

The palace was constructed around 1601 A.D by Iravi Iravi Varma Kulasekhara Perumal who ruled Travancore between 1592 A.D. and 1609 A.D. In the late 18th century, the capital of Travancore was shifted from here to Trivandrum, and the place lost its former glory. However, the palace complex continue to be the best examples of traditional Kerala architecture, and some portions of the sprawling complex are also the hall mark of traditional kerala / Dravidian building art.

Padayani or Padeni : It is one of the most colourful and spectacular folk dances associated with the festivals of certain temples in Alleppey, Quilon and Kottayam districts of southern Kerala. It involves a series of divine and semi-divine impersonations wearing huge masks or kolams of different shapes, colours and designs. The most important of the kolams usually presented in a Padayani performance are Bhairavi (Kali), Kalan (god of death), Yakshi (fairy) and Pakshi (bird).

Padhar Dance : A rural community living around Nal Lake performs this dance in which the dancers simulate the rhythmic movements of undulating sea.

Padma Bhushan : The Padma Bhushan is an Indian civilian decoration established on January 2, 1954 by the President of India. It stands third in the hierarchy of civilian awards, after the Bharat Ratna and the Padma Vibhushan, but comes before the Padma Sri. It is awarded to recognize distinguished service of a high order to the nation, in any field.

Padma River : Padma river is the downstream of the Ganges, more precisely, the combined flow of the Ganges and the Jamuna after their confluence at Goalandaghat. In Bangladesh the Ganges is popularly known as the Padma from its point of entrance at Manakosa and Durlabhpur unions of Shibganj upazila, Nawabganj district. This name (Padma or Podda) is sometimes applied to the Ganges as far up as the point at which the Bhagirathi leaves its rightbank, and according to the Hindus, it takes the sanctity of the Ganges with it. It is hydrographically more correct to use the name Ganges to refer to the river up to its confluence with the Jamuna (Brahmaputra), and the downstream after the confluence as the Padma. The Padma is also sometimes wrongly referred to as the Ganges. The river between Aricha and Sureshwar (Chandpur) is therefore best called Padma.

Padma Shri : Padma Shri (also spelled Padma Shree, Padma Sree and Padma Sri) is an award given by the Government of India generally to Indian citizens to recognize their distinguished contribution in any sphere of activity including Arts, Education, Industry, Literature, Science, Games, Sports etc. (The word "Padma" (Hindi) means "Lotus".) It stands fourth in the hierarchy of civilian awards after the Bharat Ratna, the Padma Vibhushan and the Padma Bhushan. On its obverse, the words "Padma" and "Shri", in Devanagari, appear above and below the lotus flower. The geometrical pattern on either side is in burnished bronze. All embossing is in white gold.

Padma Vibhushan : The Padma Vibhushan is India's second highest civilian honour. It consists of a medal and a citation and is awarded by the President of India. It was established on January 2, 1954. It follows the Bharat Ratna and precedes the Padma Bhushan. It is awarded to recognize exceptional and distinguished service to the nation in any field, including government service. The award was briefly suspended from July 13, 1977 to January 26, 1980.

Padmanabhapuram : Padmanabhapuram was the old capital of the princely state Travancore in India. The Travancore King, Rama Varma who was popularly known as Dharma Raja, shifted the capital in 1795 from Padmanabhapuram to Thiruvananthapuram. The Padmanabhapuram is near Thuckalai in Kanya Kumari district of Tamil Nadu. The popular Padmanabhapuram Palace, the old palace of Travancore kings is also located here.

Padum : Padum is the largest town and administrative centre of Zanskar in Jammu and Kashmir, India. The town is located at 3,500m (11,640ft) in the Himalayas. There are several small villages around Padum. The traditional heart of the village is below the gompa where two large chortens stand above old buildings. A road was constructed in 1980 across Pensi-La. Padum has several hotels and restaurants meant for tourists. Padum is inhabited by people of Tibetan descent who follow Tibetan Buddhism. There is a sizeable Muslim population, mainly Balti who have settled in Padum since the 17th century. A mosque was built in Padum in recent years to cater the local Muslim population.

Pagal Panthi Movement : Pagal Panthi Movement (1825-1833) is a peasant movement guided by religious merdicants called pagal panthis. At the initial stage it was directed against the zamindars and later assumed the fervour of an anti-British movement. Northern Mymensingh including Sherpur was different from Bengal proper in many ways. Its language, culture and ethnic traits were basically dominated by the hill tribes: the Garos, Hajangs, Dalus, Hudis and the Rajvangshies. Nature worship was their main faith. In course of time Hindu and Muslim elements were also added to their culture and the area began to be inhabited by some Hindus and Muslims as well. For decades the region provided a safe-haven for religious and political rebels. The Pagal Panthis belonged to this category.

Pagla Bridge : Pagla Bridge constructed perhaps during the period of Mirza Moula (Mir Jumla) in the 1660s on the river Pagla, a former course of the Dulai river, about five miles to the east of Dhaka on the road to Narayanganj. Tavernier noticed it in 1666 as 'a fine brick bridge, which Mir Jumla ordered to be built' on the river that ran from the northeast. While visiting Dhaka in 1824, Bishop Heber found the Pagla Bridge in a fairly good condition and identified it as a very fine specimen of the richest Gothic architecture. He gathered from local boatmen that the bridge was built by a Frenchman, a theory not shared by many historians, as Mir Jumla had it built much earlier. Some also do not agree with the view that the pointed arches of the bridge could be called Tudor Gothic.

In Dani's description, even in its damaged condition in the 1960s, the bridge had a romantic appeal, and the construction spoke of the great Mughal taste. The bridge consisted of three open arches, each being four-centred and stilted, and two blind arches at its two ends. The spandrels of the arches were decorated with prominent rosettes and their bases were provided with semi-circular cut-waters. But of great importance were the bridge's four octagonal hollow towers, one at each corner. These towers had arched openings with multiple cusps and were relieved with deep panels while a fluted dome crowned their heads.

Pagla Kanai : Pagla Kanai (1809-1889) mystic folk poet and musician was born in a peasant family in Lebutala village in Jhenaidaha district. His real name was Kanai Sheikh but he is better known as Pagla Kanai. Pagla Kanai lost his parents in early childhood and was brought up by his sister, He did not go to school. He worked for some time at the local indigo factory. He was married but gradually became attracted to an ascetic life. He was a natural poet and could compose songs spontaneously. His itinerant group of singers included Kala Chand Bayati, Hakim Shah, Karim Biswas, Indu Biswas and Karamaddi. They would tour the areas of Jessore, Kushtia, Pabna, Rajshahi and Bogra singing in chorus, occasionally competitively.

Paharganj : Paharganj (literally 'hilly neighbourhood') is a section of Delhi, located just west of the New Delhi Railway Station. It is known for its concentration of affordable hotels, restaurants, and a wide variety of shops catering to both domestic travellers and foreign tourists, especially those travelling on a relatively low budget.

Pahari : Pahari (also known as Pahaari), is a general term for various dialects spoken in the Indian part of the central Himalayan range. The word is derived from 'pahar' or 'pahad' meaning 'mountain'. The term 'Pahaari/Pahari' in Hindi, Urdu, or Punjabi means "language of the mountain people". Pahari dialects are found in the Indian states of Himachal Pradesh and Uttaranchal (traditionally called Uttarakhand). Western Pahari (Himachali) dialects include: Pothohari/Potwari, Kangri, Kullu, etc. The dialects spoken in Uttaranchal/Uttarakhand include Garhwali, Kumaoni and others. Garhwali itself has many dialects spoken in different parts of the state, like Jaunsari, Jadhi, etc.

The words Garhwali and Kumaoni are also used to refer to people speaking those dialects. There are also speakers of various Pahari dialects living in the mountainous north of Pakistan, between Kashmir and Afghanistan—although these dialects are increasingly coming under the influence of the national language Urdu and also Punjabi.

Pahari Painting : Pahari painting (literal meaning a painting from the mountainous regions, pahar means a mountain in Hindi) is a form of Indian painting, which developed and flourished during 17th-19th centuries in certain sub-Himalayan areas of India, particularly Himachal Pradesh. Pahari paintings were done mostly in miniature forms.

Paharia : Paharia is a small ethnic community, very thinly dispersed in northwestern Bangladesh. Paharia is an Indo-Aryan word referring to people living in hills or mountains. Paharias of Bangladesh claim Rajmahal Hills of southern Bihar (India) as their place of origin. In the past, Paharias were notorious bandits engaged in robbing people in the neighbouring areas in the plain or cargo boats in the ganges. Paharias are a historically neglected ethnic minority engaged in cultivation and primitive gathering from forests. At the time of food shortage, they depended on theft, plundering and looting. The British government used a corps of light infantry to keep such mountaineers in order.

Pahariyas : The Sauria Pahariyas live in the inaccessible hilly region and are confined to Godda, Rajmahal and Pakur sub divisions of Bihar. They do not posses any totemic clans. The Mal Pahariyas, a Hinduized section of Pahariya tribe, employ advanced methods of cultivation, invariably using plough and bullocks to till the small tablelands of the plateau on which they raise quite substantial dry crops.

Paharpur : Paharpur is an important archaeological site in Bangladesh, situated in a village named Paharpur (Pahadpur) under the Badalgachhi Upazila of Naogaon district. The village is connected with the nearby Railway station Jamalganj, the district town Naogaon and Jaipurhat town by metalled roads. It is in the midst of alluvial flat plain of northern Bangladesh. In contrast to the monotonous level of the plain, stands the ruins of the lofty (about 24m high from the surrounding level) ancient temple which was covered with jungle, locally called Pahar or hill from which the name Paharpur is derived.

Paika Dance : The Paika Dance is performed by the Munda and Oraon communities of Bihar. It is a stylized presentation of war dance. However, it is danced as a festive dance during weddings and the Dussehra days. The gestures suggest removal of obstacles in the way and of giving protection to honored guests. The martial nature of the dance has been retained through the use of swords, 'steeds' and shields while performing acrobatic feats. The accompanied musical instruments include Dhol, Nagara, Shehnai, Ranbheri and Mandal.

Painted Grey Ware Culture : The Painted Grey Ware culture (PGW) is an Iron Age culture of Gangetic plain, lasting from roughly 1100 BC to 350 BC. It is contemporary to, and a successor of the Black and red ware culture. It probably corresponds to the late Vedic civilization. It is succeeded by Northern Black Polished Ware from ca. 500 BC.

B.B. Lal associated Hastinapura, Mathura, Ahicchatra, Kampilya, Barnawa, Kurukshetra and other sites with the PGW culture, the (post-) Mahabharata period and the Aryans in the 1950s. Furthermore, he pointed out that the Mahabharata mentions a flood and a layer of flooding debris was found in Hastinapura. However, B.B. Lal considered his theories to be provisional and based upon a limited body of evidence, and he later reconsidered his statements on the nature of this culture. The pottery style of this culture is different from the pottery of the Iranian Plateau and Afghanistan. In some sites, PGW pottery and Late Harappan pottery are contemporaneous.

Paisa : A Paisa is a monetary unit currently equivalent to 1 / 100th of a Rupee or Bangladeshi Taka and is used in several countries, including Bangladesh, India, Nepal, and Pakistan. Variant spellings include Poisha (especially in Bangladesh), and Pice, (during British rule). Until the 1950s in India and Pakistan (and before that in British India), the Paisa was equivalent to 3 Pies, 1 / 4th of an Anna, or 1 / 64 of a Rupee. After the transition from a non-decimal currency to a decimal currency, the Paisa was known as a Naya Paisa ("New Paisa") for a few years.

Paites : The Paites are one of the constituent tribes of the Zomi or the Chins who inhabit Myanmar, India and Bangladesh. The Paites are concentrated in Manipur, a northeastern state of India. They are dominant in Lamka Town of Churachandpur of Manipur state.

Pak Sarzamin Shad Bad : "Pak sarzamin shad bad" ("Blessed be the Sacred Land") is the national anthem of Pakistan, adopted in 1954. It is a rendering of a three-stanza composition with a tune based on eastern music arranged so it can be easily played by any band. The lyrics were written by the poet Abu-Al-Asar Hafeez Jullandhuri, and the music was composed by Ahmed G. Chagla. An interesting fact is that the music of the anthem was composed before the lyrics were written and that the anthem is written in ornate literary Urdu, with the overwhelming majority of the vocabulary borrowed from Persian. In fact, only one word in the entire song is of Hindi origins (as opposed to Persian or Arabic).

Pakhal Wild life Sanctuary : Pakhal Wildlife Sanctuary is located 50 Km from Warangal, along the shoreline of Pakhal Lake and is named after it. It is a manmade lake, excavated in 1213 AD by the Kakatiyas.

Pakhavaj : The Pakhavaj is a North Indian wooden, barrel-shaped, two faced percussion instrument. Set horizontally on a cushion in front of a crossed-leg pakhavaji the larger bass-skin is played with the left hand, the treble skin by the right hand. The goatskin membranes are looped with leather thongs around the hollowed barrel, which is widest in the middle. Eight pieces of two inch wooden roundstock are pried between thongs and barrel and are hammered tight. The treble skin is fitted with three concentric rings of dense black hardened paste which helps create a sound resonant with harmonics. The treble skin is tuned with a tuning-hammer, holding the instrument in a vertical position, striking down along the rim over the barrel to raise the pitch, turning the pakhavaj on its vertical axis as it is tuned all along the circumference of the skin. The sound emitted by a particular stroke should merge completely with that of the accompanying tanpura. The bass skin is tuned not by adjusting the tension but by applying a ball of dough from aarta, whole-fiber wheat. Its fundamental tone will be the lower tonic. Traditionally, the pakhavaj has been the favoured percussion instrument for performances of the Dhrupad-style, be it vocal, on Rudra-Veena or on Surbahar. These are all capable of employing low registers so the colours match well.

Pakhtunkhwa : Pakhtunkhwa or Pashtunkhwa a name used historically by Pashtun leaders for the Pashtun areas of Afghanistan and Pakistan. More recently used by Pashtun nationalists in Pakistan as the name they would like to rename the North-West Frontier Province (NWFP).

Pakistan Air Force (PAF) : The Pakistan Air Force (PAF) Pakistan Fiza'ya) is the Aviation branch of the Pakistan armed forces. The Royal Pakistan Air Force (RPAF) was formed in 1947 right after the Partition of the Indian Subcontinent. The RPAF began with 2,332 personnel, a fleet of 24 Tempest II fighter-bombers, 16 Hawker Typhoon fighters (also called Tempest I), two H.P.57 Halifax bombers, 2 Auster aircraft, twelve T-6G Harvard trainers and ten Tiger Moth biplanes. It also had eight C-47 Dakota cargo planes which it used to transport supplies to soldiers fighting in the 1947 War in Kashmir against India. It also started with 7 operational airbases scattered all over the provinces. The prefix Royal was removed when Pakistan became an Islamic Republic on 23rd March, 1956. It has since been called Pakistan Air Force (PAF).

The 1950s saw the PAF join the jet age with the purchase of British-made Attacker jets. While these jets were built for Naval Aviation, the PAF made full use of them in many land based operations. Initially, much of the PAF's equipment came from the United Kingdom. As the Cold War heated up, the government of Pakistan allied itself with the United States against the Soviet Union as part of the CENTO alliance. As a result, they began receiving American defense equipment: notably the F-86 Sabre which would form the backbone of the PAF until the mid-'70s.

Pakistan Army : Pakistan Army is the largest branch of the Military of Pakistan, and is responsible for land based military operations. It is modelled on the United Kingdom armed forces and came into existence after the partition in 1947. It has an active force of 620,000 personnel, although the Army has implemented a plan to reduce the size of the Army by 50,000. Pakistan also has 513,000 men in reserve and they continue to serve until the age of 45. Currently the Military of Pakistan with the total size of 1,000,000 is ranked as the 7th largest in the world.

The Pakistani Army is a complete volunteer force and has fought in many wars with its neighbours and actively contributes in United Nations peacekeeping operations as well as sending a contingent of forces to help the Arab countries during the Arab-Israeli Wars, and the first Gulf War to help the Coalition. Currently, the Pakistan Army as well as the Military of Pakistan is lead by General Pervez Musharraf, who is also the President of Pakistan.

Pakistan Broadcasting Corporation : The Pakistan Broadcasting Corporation (PBC) is the state-run radio service of Pakistan. It was formed on 14th August 1947 when Pakistan became independent. It was a direct descendant of the Indian Broadcasting Company which later became All India Radio. At independence Pakistan possessed three radio stations at Dhaka, Lahore and Peshawar. A major programme of expansion saw new stations opened at Karachi and Rawalpindi in 1948, and a new broadcasting house at Karachi in 1950.

Pakistan Coast Guard (PCG) : The Pakistan Coast Guard (PCG) was recently hived off from the navy. It has recently upgraded its facilities and fleet to counter the threat of smugglers and terrorists. The PCG has a fleet of 23 small craft. The PCG Headquarters are at Bandar Road, Saddar, Karachi. It is commanded by a director-general with the rank of brigadier, seconded from the Pakistan Army.

Pakistan Football Federation (PFF) : The Pakistan Football Federation (PFF) is the governing body of football in Pakistan. It was founded in 1948, and became a member of FIFA in the same year. It is a member of the Asian Football Confederation. Pakistan's core national league has two divisions. The National Football Championship (Division 1) is named as the Pakistan Premier League (PPL) while National Championship (Division 2) is known as the Pakistan Football Federation League (PFF league). Below this are regional leagues. There is also a national knock-out competition called the National Football Challenge Cup.

Pakistan Hindu Panchayat (PHP) : The Pakistan Hindu Panchayat is the leading socio-political representative organization of the Hindu community in heavily Muslim Pakistan. The PHP represents the Hindu community on social and political issues, bringing them together to protect their interests, advance education and opportunity and protect the basic rights and freedoms, especially of worship and assembly, of Hindus all over Pakistan. The task of the PHP has become more difficult in face of increasing Islamization since the 1980s in Pakistan, especially the rise of global Islamic fundamentalism, terrorism and increased tensions with archrival neighbor, India.

The PHP organizes support for the Hindu candidates in Hindu electorates, and lobbies the Government of Pakistan on issues important to Hindus, such as the security of temples, and contentious issues like protests against the abduction of Hindus for ransoms and forcible conversions. The PHP holds an annual national conference, and has branches in all Pakistani provinces. Another important and linked organization is the Pakistani Hindu Welfare Association.

Pakistan Institute of Engineering and Applied Sciences (PIEAS) : Pakistan Institute of Engineering and Applied Sciences (PIEAS) is located at Islamabad, Pakistan. Pakistan Institute of Engineering and Applied Sciences started as a post graduate institute in Nuclear Sciences in 1967. In 1997 PIEAS was given the status of university. PIEAS now has nearly 30 laboratories in different areas for conducting students' experiments as well as for R&D work. Besides the regular academic programmes, PIEAS has conducted a large number of courses on various specialised topics. The length of these courses has varied from 2 to 18 months and the areas covered have included reactor supervision and operation, health physics, medical physics, laser technology, vacuum technology, computer applications and advanced reactor safety. PIEAS is engaged in manpower development programmes at many levels and in many directions, but the major thrust of our efforts is directed towards postgraduate academic work. At this level, research and development activities become an integral part of the educational process.

Pakistan International Airlines : Pakistan International Airlines (PIA), is the national flag carrier of Pakistan with a network of both passenger and cargo operation around the world. Its main hubs are Quaid-e-Azam International Airport, Karachi, the Allama Iqbal International Airport, Lahore and the Islamabad International Airport, Islamabad/Rawalpindi.

Pakistan Movement : Pakistan Movement is a name given to the independence struggle carried out by the Muslims of British South Asia to create a separate homeland. This struggle was led by the Muslim League. Quaid-e-Azam Mohammad Ali Jinnah was head of the movement. The other Muslim League leaders were: Allama Iqbal, Liaqat Ali Khan, Fatima Jinnah, Suhrawardy and Sardar Abdur Rab Nishtar. The Pakistan Resolution was passed in 1940 at Lahore. Muslim League made this resolution its main objective election campaigns.

Soon after World War II, the British were convinced that keeping British colony in South Asia was no longer possible, as the United Kingdom itself was economically shattered by the war. British South Asia was divided into Pakistan and India. The idea of Pakistan was presented by Allama Iqbal in 1930. Iqbal asked Jinnah to focus his energies towards getting an independent homeland for Muslims of the South Asia.

Pakistan Muslim League (N) : The Pakistan Muslim League (N) is a political party in Pakistan. It is led by Nawaz Sharif. It was Pakistan Muslim League, founded in 1962, as a successor to the previously disbanded Muslim League, and gained the (Nawaz) or (N) in 1993 for its leader, Nawaz Sharif. A Pakistan Muslim League (J) was formed in 1986. A Pakistan Muslim League (Q) split from it in 2001, and there are various other parties with similar names. Despite Musharraf best efforts to put aside the party leaders in exile and others in jail,legislative elections on 20 October 2002, the party won 9.4% of the popular vote and 14 out of 272 elected members.

Pakistan National Highway : Pakistan National Highway is the major highway in Pakistan connecting all major cities. The National Highway Authority (NHA) was established in 1991, through an Act of the Pakistani Parliament, for planning, development, operation, repair and maintenance of National Highways and Strategic Roads specially entrusted to NHA by the Federal Government or by a Provincial Government or other authority concerned.

Total length of the federalized roads under NHA now stands at 8780 km, account for 3% of the entire road network and 75% of the commercial road traffic in the country.

Pakistan Navy : The Pakistan Navy is the naval wing of the Pakistan military. Though not as significant as their other military divisions, it does play a vital role given the regional rivalry with India.

The birth of the Royal Pakistan Navy came with the creation of Pakistan on 14 August 1947. Later it was renamed the Pakistan Navy (PN) to reflect the transformation to a republic in 1956. As the Indo-Pakistani War of 1947 involved fighting on land, it was in the Indo-Pakistani War of 1965 that the navy was involved in a conflict for the first time. However, apart from carrying out a bombardment of the coastal town of Dwaraka—codenamed Operation Dwarka—there was no significant action.

The Pakistan Navy has some 24,000 personnel. The force includes a small Naval Air Arm and the approximately 2,000 member paramilitary Maritime Security Agency, charged primarily with protecting Pakistan's exclusive economic zone(EEZ). The naval reserve consists of about 5,000 personnel. Included in this is the Naval arm of the Special Services Group, a marine commando unit stationed at Karachi. The NSSG or SSG(N) as its known is believed to number around 1,000 in troop strength.

The supreme commander of the Navy is the Chief of the Naval Staff. Admiral Shahid Karimullah is the current Chief of the Navy. Pakistan Navy recently began inducting women for combat positions apart from the existing administrative posts, becoming one of the few Islamic Republics to do so.

Pakistan occupied Kashmir (PoK) : Pakistan occupied Kashmir (PoK or POK) is the name given by the Republic of India to a portion of Kashmir controlled by the Islamic Republic of Pakistan and People's Republic of China. PoK borders the Indian state of Jammu and Kashmir to the east, Himachal Pradesh to south-east and Pakistan to the west.

Pakistan Oppressed Nations Movement (PONM) : The Pakistan Oppressed Nations Movement (PONM) is an alliance of Nationalist Parties of Pakistan comprising of Sindh Taraqi Pasand Party, Sindhi Awami Tehreek, Baluchistan National Movement, Pakhtoonkhwa Milli Awami Party, Seraiki Movement. Prominent Leaders of PONAM are Sardar Ataullah Mengal, Mehmood Khan Achakzai, Rassol Bux Palijo, Dr. Qadir Magsi, Syed Jalal Mehmmood Shah and other Sindhi, Baluch, Pathan and Seraiki leaders. Although it is not a political party, but a grouping of nationalist parties, they supported each other candidates in election. They constitute a large group in Balochistan provisional assembly. It is present in Sindh as well, but it is more vibrant in Balochistan.

Pakistan Peoples Party (PPP) : The Pakistan Peoples Party (PPP) is a mainstream political party in Pakistan. It is led by Benazir Bhutto. The Pakistan Peoples Party Parliamentarians (PPPP) is a party formed in 2002 by the PPP for the purpose of complying with electoral rules governing Pakistani parties. At the last legislative elections, 20 October 2002, the party won 25.8 % of the popular vote and 71 out of 272 elected members, thus gaining the second-largest number of seats in the Parliament of Pakistan. The party was founded in 1967, and Zulfikar Ali Bhutto became its first chairman. Now it is known as People's Party Parliamentarians.

Pakistan Railways : Pakistan Railways is the state-owned railway company of Pakistan. It is a large organization under the administration of the Pakistani Government's Ministry of Railways. Pakistan Railways provides an important mode of transportation in the farthest corners of the country and brings them closer for Business, sight seeing, pilgrimage and education. It has been a great integrating force and forms the life line of the country by catering to its needs for large scale movement of people and freight.

Pakistan Resolution : The Lahore Resolution, later called Pakistan Resolution, is a political statement adopted by the All India Muslim League on 23 March 1940. Although the idea of founding the state of Pakistan had been introduced as early as 1930, very few had responded to it. However, the volatile political climate and hostilities between the Hindus and Muslims in British India gave the idea stronger backing. The division of India into two separate sovereign states is sometimes referred as Two Nation Theory.

Pakistan Television Corporation (PTV) : The Pakistan Television Corporation (PTV) is the state-run television service in Pakistan, and has been on the air since 1964. other state-run corporations, the television company was allowed by the Government of Pakistan to raise a sizable amount of private capital to finance the stations. In October 1963, the government signed an agreement with the NEC company in Japan to have NEC operate affiliates for PTV. On 26 November 1964, the first television station commenced broadcasts in the cities of Lahore, and Dhaka (then the capital of East Pakistan). Centres were established in Karachi and Rawalpindi/Islamabad in 1967, and in Peshawar and Quetta in 1974.

Pakistan's Paramilitary Forces : Pakistan's Paramilitary Forces is the second largest branch of the Military of Pakistan and is charged to safe guard Pakistan from external and internal threats and their current strength is approximately 288,000 personnel.

Pakistani Black Metal : Black metal is a musical genre which emerged in the early 1980s predating the great expansion of heavy metal 'extreme' genres. Black metal evolved from thrash metal, as did its sister genre death metal. There are two views on the genre. One views black metal as a very specific form of music that must adhere to a particular 'style' in order for it to be a part of the genre; while the second considers the lyrical and philosophical/political ideology of the music to take more precedence in defining the genre itself, rather than 'style'.

Pakistani Cuisine : Pakistani Cuisine is, for the most part, identical to North Indian cuisine, especially in the regions of Punjab and Sindh. However, due to its location in the northwest of the Indian subcontinent, there is significant regional variation; for example, the western frontier regions of Pakistan have cuisine that is more similar with that of Afghanistan and Iran. Much of the food is referred to as Mughlai cuisine, especially in the east, and varies from its neighbors in that it is spicier than the cuisine of the Middle East and less spicy than that of most of India. One could term it a unique blend of Indo-Iranian, but, more realistically, it is perhaps best described as a nation with many different types of foods, the east and, to some extent, the North West Frontier Province being almost identical to North Indian cuisine and the west being more similar to the cuisine of Iran. Often, both interlap, especially in Mughlai cuisine. The most prominent Pakistani cuisine, though, is the Mughalai cuisine which is also prominent throughout northern India.

Pakistani Rupee : The Pakistani rupee (PKR) is the currency of Pakistan. The Pakistani rupee was put into circulation after the country became independent from India in 1947. For the first few months of independence, Pakistan used Indian coins and notes with "Pakistan" stamped on them. New coins and banknotes were issued in 1948.

Like the Indian rupee, it was originally divided into 16 annas, each of 4 pice or 12 pies. The currency was decimalized in 1961, with the rupee subdivided into 100 paise (singular paisa).

Pakola : Pakola is a line of fruit flavored soft drinks, originally introduced in Pakistan in 1950 by Haji Ali Muhammad. It is produced by Mehran Bottlers (Pvt) Ltd. It is the first nationally branded soft drink of Pakistan. The original green color Pakola Ice cream soda is still popular in Pakistan, however other Pakola soft drinks, like Pakola Lychee have gained increasing popularity.

Pakora : Pakora is a type of Indian cuisine created by deep-frying ingredients such as chicken, onion, eggplant, potato, spinach, cauliflower, tomato, and chilli. These are then dipped in a batter of gram flour and then fried. They are usually served as snacks or appetitizers. They can be eaten as starters in restaurants. When onions are so fried they are also known as onion bhaji. Pakora is sold in fast food takeaways as an alternative to chips or a kebab during the evening and early morning. With the widespread availability of Indian food, pakoras can be purchased from many if not the majority of takeaways and restaurants throughout the world. Pakoras are eaten as snacks with tea in India and Pakistan.

Pala : Pala is a popular cultural institution responsible for the popularisation of ancient Oriya literature. It consists of five or six persons. The drummer plays on the 'mridanga'. Others play on the cymbals, dance and help the chief singer—'Gayaka',—to sing and explain the meaning to the audience. Depth of knowledge, sharpness of intelligence, oratory and keen memory power are put to a severe test when two well-matched groups challenge each other in a 'pala' competition. The drummer displays the skill of his fingers and relates humorous stories to please the audience. The dialogue between the singer and one of the attendants breaks the monotony of long speeches and jugglery of words in the song. Pala owes its origin to attempts at Hindu-Muslim unity.

Pala Empire : The Pala Empire was a dynasty in control of the Bihar and Bengal regions of South Asia from the 8th to the 12th century. The name Pala means "protector" and was used as an ending to the names of all Pala monarchs. The founder of the empire was Gopala. He reigned from 750-770 consolidated his position by extending his control over all Bengal. His successor was Dharmapala (770-781). He made the Palas a dominant power of northern India. The Empire disintegrated in the 12th century under the attacks of the Sena dynasty. The Palas were followers of Mahayana Buddhism. They created many temples and works of art and supported the Universities of Nalanda and Vikramashila. Their proselytism was at the origin of the establishment of Buddhism in Tibet.

Palak Paneer : Palak paneer is an Indian dish, made with spinach, paneer (an acid-set, unaged cheese), and a mixture of spices. It is one of the most popular dishes in Indian restaurants in the U.S., and it is a commonly served in buffets. The spinach often has the consistency of canned spinach. Some cooks would call the same thing saag paneer, though saag could be made with different greens such as mustard and not just spinach.

Palakkad : Palakkad or Palghat is one of the 14 districts of Kerala state in South India. The city of Palakkad is the district headquarters. Palakkad is bordered on the northwest by the Malappuram district and on the southwest by the Thrissur district. To the east lies the Coimbatore district of Tamil Nadu. It is a predominantly rural district. Palakkad is the gateway to Kerala due to the presence of Palakkad Gap, in the Western Ghats. The total area of the district is 4480 km^2 which is 11.5% of the State's area.

In the earlier times Palakkad was also known as Palakkattussery. Some etymologists trace the word "Palakkad" to be from the word Palanilam which means "dry lands". The commonly held belief however is that, it is the fusion of the two Malayalam words, Pala a tree (Alstonia scholaris) which is found abundantly in Palakkad and Kadu which means forest.

Palakkad Gap : The Palakkad Gap (30-40 km) is a low pass through the Western Ghats (960 km long) ranges of southern India, linking Palakkad District of Kerala state with Coimbatore District of Tamil Nadu. The gap is the lowest pass through the Western Ghats ranges, and was an important trade route connecting the east and west coasts of peninsular India since ancient times. The gap is also important in the climate of southern India; it allows the moisture-laden Southwest monsoon winds into the Coimbatore region, which moderates Coimbatore's summer temperature and generates greater rainfall in the region relative to the rest of lowland Tamil Nadu.

Palamau : Palamau is a district of Jharkhand state, India. The district lies between 23°50' and 24°8' north latitude and between 83°55' and 84°30' east longitude. It is bordered on the north by river Son and Bihar, on the east by districts of Chatra and Hazaribagh , on the south by Latehar District and on the west by Garhwa District.

The district is home to the famous Palamau National Park known for its wild life. The park is spread over a core area of 250 square kilometers. The area is rich in flora and fauna but also prone to severe droughts. The Palamau National Park was brought under Project Tiger in the year

1973 and is among the original Tiger Reserves of India. Sal and bamboo are the main vegetation.

World's first tiger-census was done in the Palamau forests in the year 1932. Counting was based on pugmarks. There were around 44 tigers when the last census was done. There are several other wildlife found in the sanctuary — chital, chinkara, common langur, dhole (wild dogs), elephants, gaur, hares, Indian porcupine, nilgai, monkey, mouse deer, leopard, pangolin, panther, sambar, sloth bear, wild boar and wolves. Peafowl, red junglefowl and partridges are the common birds found here. The tourists can drive through dense patches of sal and bamboo in the park. A guide and jeep can be hired from the forest department. Watch towers are there to observe the wildlife in relative safety.

Pali District : Pali District is a district of the state of Rajasthan in western India. The town of Pali is the district headquarters. The Aravalli Range forms the eastern boundary of the district. A zone of foothills lies to the west, through which run the many tributaries of the Luni River. The western portion of the district includes the alluvial plain of the Luni.Pali has an area of 12,387 km^2 and a population of 1,819,201 (2001 census), which increased 22.39% in the decade 1991-2001. It is bounded by Nagaur District to the north, Ajmer District to the northeast, Rajsamand District to the east, Udaipur District to the southeast, Sirohi District to the southwest, Jalore District to the west, and Jodhpur District to the northwest.

Palika Bazaar : Palika Bazaar is an underground, air-conditioned market in the middle of the inner circle of Connaught Place, Delhi, India. It has hundreds of shops selling everything from books to electronics to clothing. It used to be very popular in the 1980s, but has lost its charm for locals now that a lot of new and swanky malls have sprung up all over Delhi. It has its own charm for the foreigners who come to India. If they visit Connaught Place, the first place they visit is Palika Bazaar. One can find great bargains out here. There are many stores selling Indian crafts, clothes and arts.

Palitana : Palitana, a city and former princely state, located 50 km South-West of Bhavnagar city in India's state Gujarat, is a major pilgrimage centre for Jains. The Palitana temples, are considered the most sacred pilgrimage place (tirtha) by the Jain community. There are a total of 1250 temples located on the Shetrunjaya hills, exquisitely carved in marble. The main temple on top of the hill, is dedicated to 1st tirthankar lord Adinath (Rishabdeva).

No one is allowed to sleep overnight including the priest, because the temple city has been built as an abode for the Gods. The town is considered by many Jains to be more important than the temple covered hills of Bihar, Gwalior, Mt Abu and Girnar. Palitana was the capital of a princely state of the Gohil Rajput clan. It is also one of the greatest tourist attractions in Gujarat for foreign tourists. There are hundreds of other temples (besides those on the Shetrunjaya hills) and guest houses (dharmashalas) in Palitana city. It is believed that every Jain should visit Palitana at least once in his lifetime to get "Bhavya" status (fit to attain nirvan or salvation).

Palk Strait : The Palk Strait is a 40-85 mi (64-137 km) wide strait that lies between India's Tamil Nadu state and the island nation of Sri Lanka. It connects the Bay of Bengal to the northeast with the Gulf of Mannar to the south. The strait receives several rivers, most notably the Vaigai River of Tamil Nadu. It is named after Robert Palk, governor of Madras Presidency (1755-1763).

It is studded at its southern end with a chain of low islands and reef shoals that are collectively called Rama's Bridge or Adam's Bridge. Rama's Bridge extends between

Dhanushkodi on Rameswaram Island (also known as Pamban Island) in Tamil Nadu and Talaimannar on the Mannar island in Sri Lanka. The Island of Rameswaram is linked to the Indian mainland by the Pamban Bridge.

The shallow waters and reefs of the strait make it difficult for large ships to pass through, although fishing boats and small craft carrying coastal trade have navigated the strait for centuries. Large ships must travel around Sri Lanka. Construction of a shipping canal through the strait was first proposed to the British Raj government of India in 1860, and a number of commissions have studied the proposal up to the present day. The most recent study of the Sethusamudram Shipping Canal Project, as it is now called, was an Environmental Impact Assessment and a Technical Feasibility Report commissioned by the Tamil Nadu government in 2004. Like the English Channel, the Palk Strait has been taken up as a challenge by many long distance swimmers.

Pallava Kingdom : The Pallava dynasty's greatest kings were Simhavisnu (ruled 575-600) and Narasimhavarman I (ruled 630-668). Their main capital was Kanchipuram, a town southwest of Madras. It is believed that they had two other working capitals in Bhavathri, in Andhra, and in Palakkad, in eastern Kerala. At its peak the Pallava Empire stretched over most of south India, bounded by the Cholas on the south and Cheras on the west and the Chalukyas on the north. At its height it covered an area larger than France, England and Germany combined. It encompassed all the present-day Dravidian nations, including the Tamil, Telugu, Malayali and Kannada tracts within its far-flung borders. The foundations of classical Dravidian architecture were established by these powerful rulers, who left behind fantastic sculptures and magnificent temples which survive to this very day.

Mahabalipuram Shore temple is one of the greatest examples of Pallava architecture. The Pallava dynasty was a time of significant change in South India — in particular, the growth of Jainism, decline of Buddhism and emergence of Bhakti movement. Both the Alvars and the Nayanmars were active during this time. Under the Pallavas, maritime trade with Sri Lanka and Southeast Asia flourished, as did music, painting, literature, and architecture. Structural stone temples replaced rock buildings, the most impressive example being the sculptured Shore Temple at the seaport of Mahabalipuram, dedicated to the god Shiva.

The Pallavas engaged in constant warfare with the Chalukyas of Badami and were finally eclipsed by the Chola kings in the 8th century.As Pallava rule declined, the Kuruba people scattered over a wide area of southern India and became culturally distinct. During this time, the Kurubas survived by hunting, gathering forest produce, or small-scale farming. In time, the majority of Kurubas settled on the plains as small landowners or herdsmen. Classification of Pallava dynasty as "Early", "Middle" and "Later" is based on the language used in their copper and stone engravings. Early Pallavas used Prakrit, middle Pallavas used Sanskrit, and later Pallavas used Tamil in their engravings.

Palni Hills : The Palni Hills (also Palani Hills) are a mountain range in Tamil Nadu state of southern India. The Palni Hills are an eastward extension of the Western Ghats ranges, which run parallel to the west coast of India. The Palni Hills adjoin the high Anamalai range on the west, and extend east into the plains of Tamil Nadu, covering an area of 2068 km^2. The highest part of the range is in the southwest, and reaches 1,800-2,500 meters elevation; the eastern extension of the range is made up of hills 1500-1000 meters high.

The range lies between the Kambam Valley on the south, which is drained by the Vaigai River and its upper tributaries, and the Kongu Nadu region to the north. The northern slopes are drained by the rivers Shanmukha, Nanganji, and Kodavanar, which are tributaries of the Kaveri. The range lies mostly within Dindigul District, except in the western portion, where it forms the boundary between Dindigul and Theni District to the south. The hill station of Kodaikanal lies in the northwestern portion of the range.

The lower elevations of the Palni Hills, between 250 and 1000 meters elevation, are part of the South Western Ghats moist deciduous forests ecoregion. Above 1000 meters elevation, the deciduous forests transition to the evergreen South Western Ghats montane rain forests. In the highest portions of the range, above 2000 meters elevation, the montane rain forests give way to shola-grassland mosaic, made up of frost-tolerant montane grasslands interspersed with pockets of stunted shola forests.

The Palni Hills are currently subject to increasing development pressure. The Palni Hills Conservation Council, a non-governmental organization headquartered in Kodaikanal, was founded in 1985. In the early 1990's the Tamil Nadu Forest Department proposed to the Tamil Nadu state government that much of the range be granted protected status as a wildlife sanctuary or a national park.

Pamba : Pamba is the third longest river in the South Indian state of Kerala and the longest river in the erstwhile princely state of Travancore. Sabarimala temple dedicated to lord Ayyappa is located on the banks of the river Pamba.Pamba originates at Pulachimalai hill in the Peerumedu plateau in the Western Ghats at an altitude of 1650 metres and flows through Ranni, Thiruvalla, Changanassery and Ambalapuzha Taluks and finally empties into the Vembanad Lake. Kuttanad, an important rice cultivating area in Kerala gets the irrigation water from the Pamba river. The Pamba basin is bounded on the east by the Western Ghats. The river shares its northern boundary with the Manimala river basin, while the southern boundary it shares with the Achankovil river basin.

Pamban Bridge : The Pamban Bridge also called Indira Gandhi Bridge lies on the Indian end of the Palk Strait that connects Rameswaram island to mainland India. It actually refers to both the road bridge and the cantilever railway bridge, though primarily it means the latter. It is the longest sea bridge in India at a length of nearly 2.2 km and stands as a fine example of Indian architecture. The bridge was constructed with sufficient elevation and a beautiful scenery of the sea, adjoining Islands and parallel rail bridge below can be viewed from the bridge.

Pamir Mountains : Located in Central Asia, the Pamir Mountains are formed by the junction of the Tian Shan, Karakoram, Kunlun, and Hindu Kush ranges. They are among the world's highest mountains. They are also known by the Chinese name of Congling. The Pamir region is centered in the Tajikistani region of Gorno-Badakhshan. Parts of the Pamir also lie in the countries of Kyrgyzstan, Afghanistan, and Pakistan. South of Gorno-Badakhshan, the Wakhan Corridor runs through the Pamir region, which also includes the northern extremes of the North-West Frontier Province and the northern extremes of the Northern Areas of Pakistan

Panaji : Panaji or Panjim is the capital of the state of Goa in India. It lies in the North Goa district on the banks of the Mandovi estuary and has a population of 65,000, with a metropolitan population of 100,000 if suburbs are included. It is Goa's third largest city after Vasco and

Madgaon. The current official name is Panaji, though in the local language Konkani this gets pronounced as Ponnji, Ponnje, or Ponjhe. The Portuguese name was Pangim. Many mostly English-speaking people use the name Panjim.

Panch National Park : Set up in the year 1975, the Panch National Park is situated in the district of Nagpur 64km away from the park. Sonegaon, Nagpur is the nearest airport to visit the park. The fauna of the park consist of tiger, panther, gaur, sloth bear, barking deer, chital, sambar, four-horned antelope, nilgai, chinkara, jungle fowl and peafowl. The ideal time for visiting the park is April-May.

Panch Pir : Panch Pir is an important development in the concept of Pirism in Bengal. With the spread of Islam to distant lands Muslims came in contact with people of other religions. As a result Islam influenced other religions and likewise others also influenced Islam and the Muslims. The influence was mainly through the Pirs or saintly persons.

The adoration of Panch-Pir (five Pirs) was prevalent in some parts of Bengal, particularly in West Bengal in the districts of Burdwan and Midnapore. Panch-Pir, as family deities, represented by a small mound on a clay plinth erected in the northwest corner of one of the rooms of the house, was worshipped both by Muslims and Hindus, particularly of the lower strata of the society. On the mound was fixed a piece of iron, resembling a human head and five fingers resembling the five pirs. In Sonargaon, there is a dargah known as Panch-Pir dargah, and the sailors of the coastal districts of East Bengal, remember Panch-Pir along with Pir Badar, with a view of averting dangers.

It is difficult to trace the origin of the reverence to the Panch-Pir. The date of the Panch-Pir dargah of

Sonargaon is not known. By the side of the dargah, there is a mosque, with no inscription attached to the mosque and it has been completely renovated so that the date of the construction of the mosque cannot be ascertained. Though the name of Parch-Pir is associated with Pir Badar in the ballads, Pir Badar also cannot be identified. There are several places where Pir Badar is remembered. But if Pir Badar of the ballads is identified with Pir Badar or Badar Shah associated with the Muslim conquest of Chittagong, it may be assumed that the Panch-Pir concept originated in the 14th century. Of course, the Panch-Pir could have been associated with the name of Pir Badar at a later date as well.

It is difficult to ascertain who the five pirs were. Lists of Panch-Pir found at different places differ, they include some local pirs, though one Ghazi Miyan is common, but who is this Ghazi Miyan is not known. Those who are killed in jihad (religious war) are called Shahid (martyr) and those who come out successful are called Ghazi. Ghazi stands for valour and heroism. The poor and lower class village folk, therefore, adored Panch-Pir as symbol of power and they sought asylum under their protection.

Panchagarh : Panchagarh is a district in the Rajshahi division of Bangladesh. This extreme northern district of with an area of 1404.63 sq km is bounded on three sides by 288 km long Indian border, having Darjeeling district on the north, Jalpaiguri and Kuchbihar districts on the northeast, West Dinajpur and Purnea district on the west, Dinajpur and Thakurgaon districts on the south, Nilphamari district on the east. Its soil is sandy, alluvial and bears close affinity with the soil of the old Himalayan basin. On the northern part of the district there exists underground layer of pebbles. Maximum temperature 30.2 C and minimum 10.1 C; annual total rainfall 2931 mm. Main rivers are Karatoya, Atrai, Tista, Mahananda, Tangon,

Dahuk, Pathraj, Bhulli, Talma, Nagar, Chawai, Kurum, Versa, Tirnoi, Chilka.

Panchagarh was a thana under Jalpaiguri district of West Bengal during the British rule. It was under Dinajpur district at the time of the partition of 1947. It was turned into a subdivision in 1980 consisting of Panchagarh, Boda, Debiganj, Atwari and Tentulia thanas. Panchagarh was elevated to a district in 1984. It consists of five upazilas one municipality, 9 wards, 32 mahallas, 43 union parishads and 850 villages. The upazilas are Panchagarh Sadar, Boda, Debiganj, Atwari and Tentulia. The existence of fifteen garhs (fortifications) has hitherto been traced of which the most noted are Bhitar Garh, Hosain Garh, Mir Garh, Rajan Garh and Deven Garh. Panchagarh is named after these five garhs. Archaeological relics include Nayani Burz (bastion), remains of Atwari zamindar-bari and that of katchari-bari of Raniganj Devottvar Estate and the temple therein, Mirzapur Shahi Mosque, Tomb of Bara Awliya, tomb of Arif Shah, Maharaja Dighi (pond) at Bhitargarh, Maidan Dighi, Mughali killah (fort) at Chandan-bari, Vadeswari temple and Boda temple.

Panchakki : It is an impressive pre-Mughal watermill harnessed to operate large grain-grinding stones in Maharshtra. It was built in 1624 to commemorate the memory of the Sufi saint Baba Shah Musafir, whose tomb lies nearby. Panchakki takes its name from the mill which was considered a marvel of engineering at that time.

Panchamighat : Panchamighat a holy place for Hindus, is situated on the western bank of the old Brahmaputra under Bandar thana of Narayanganj district. Thousands of Hindus annually resort to ceremonial baths in Panchamighat and in nearby Langalband in the Bengali month of Chaitra on the 8th day of the bright half of the moon.

Pancharama Kshetras : Pancharama Kshetras are five ancient Hindu temples of Lord Shiva situated in Andhra Pradesh. The Sivalingas at these temples are made from a single Sivalinga. As per the legend, this Sivalinga was owned by the Rakshasa King Tarakasura. Nobody could win over him due to the power of this Sivalinga. Finally Lord Kumaraswamy breaks this Sivalinga into five pieces and kills Tarakasura. The five pieces fall at different places on earth. These five pieces are installed as five different Sivalingas by Indra, Surya, Chandra, Vishnu and Kumaraswamy at the respective places. These places (or araamas) are Amararama, Draksharama, Somarama, Ksheerarama and Kumararama.

Panchari Melam : Panchari melam is a classic performance (melam) of different musical instruments that are unique to temples of Kerala state in south India. The most traditional of all melam's is 'Pandi Melam' which is generally performed outside the temples. But 'Panchari Melam', which is similar to Pandi melam is played inside the temple.

The instruments involved in Pancharimelam are the Chenda (kettle drum), the kuzhal (a kind of trumpet), the ilathalam (cymbals) and the kombu (another kind of trumpet). The most famous Pancharimelam performance in Kerala is that which is performed during the Temple festival at Sri Edakkunni Bhagavathy temple in Ollur , Thrissur District during March—April and in November-December (Vrischikam) at the Sree Poornathrayeesha Temple, Thrippuntithura, in Ernakulam district. Other Places include Peruvanam, Irinjalakuda temples.

Panchatantra : The Panchatantra is a collection of Sanskrit fables in prose and verse. The original version, now lost, was written around 200 BC and is attributed to Vishnu Sarma. The Panchatantra reached its current form in the 4th-6th centuries AD. One of the most influential

Sanskrit contributions to world literature, it was exported to China and South East Asia by Buddhist Monks on Pilgrimage. During Khosrau I of Persia era, his famous minister Burzoe translated Indian Panchatantra from Sanskrit into middle Persian language of Pahlavi and called it Kelileh va Demneh. From the Persian version, it was translated to various languages including Arabic which after Muslim invasion of Persia (Iran) was the first language to be translated to from Persian. From Persian it then transmitted in the 11th century to Greece and thence to the rest of Europe. But it was a 12th century Hebrew translation that became the source of most European versions.

Panchavadyam : Panchavadyam is a classic performance of different musical instruments that are unique to Kerala state of south India, where five instruments are involved in a breathtaking-fastmoving act of percussion (Pancha in Sanskrit means five). "Pancha" means five. The five instruments are Shudha Madhalam, Kombu, Edakka, Elathalam & Timila. The Timila, the Shudha Madhalam and the Edakka are different types of drums. The Elathalam is a cymbal and the Kombu is a type of trumpet. Earlier, different instruments were used in Panchavadyam, but Thiruvilwamala Venkichan Swamy, Annamanada Peethambara Marar, Annamanada Achutha Marar, Annamanada Parameswara Marar and Pattarath SanKara Marar evolved the modern-day Panchavadyam with these five instruments and a new structure.

Panchavadyam is performed during the festivals of the Temples in Kerala, mainly in Central Kerala. The most famous performance is that during the Thrissur Pooram, known as the "Madathil Varavu" Panchavadyam. It is performed by the Thiruvambadi Temple camp.

Panchayat : The Panchayat is an Indian political system that groups five villages in a quincunx (four peripheral villages around a central one were laid out as the '5' side of a die). Each had appointed tasks and responsibilities, such as cart-making or basket-weaving. The central village, usually the largest of the Panchayat, traditionally handled food storage and meetings places for the officials, as well as their residences.

Mahatma Gandhi advocated Panchayati Raj, a decentralized form of Government where each village is responsible for its own actions, as the foundation of India's political system. His term for such a vision was "Gram Swaraj" (Village Self-governance). It was incorporated into the state governments during the 1950s and 60s as various legislations were passed to establish Panchayats in different states. It found a backing in the Indian Constitution which was amended in 1992 to accommodate the Panchayat Raj Institutions. However political and caste undercurrents among the voters have prevented strong adoption of this concept.

Panchchuli Glacier : Panchchuli Glacier is a Himalayan glacier, situated in the Pithoragarh district of Uttaranchal, India.This glacier is located in the easternmost part of Kumaun.This glacier is in the west and east of five peaks of Panchchuli on the Goriganga valley and Darma valley. Uttari Balati glacier is situated north to it.Panchachuli group of glaciers include—1-Meola 2-Sona 3-Uttari Balati 4-Dakshini balati The popular trek is through Darma valley to East Facing glacier. Pithoragarh-Dharchula-Tawaghat-Sobla-Dar-Sela-Bailing-Son-Duktu. Yuli river immerse out of this glacier.

Panchkula : Panchkula is the newly formed 17th district of Haryana state in India. As formed 15 August 1995, it comprises of two sub divisions and two Tehsils named Panchkula and Kalka. It has 264 villages out of which 12 villages are un-inhabited and 10 villages wholly merged in towns or treated as census towns according to census 1991. There are four towns in the district named Kalka, Panchkula, Pinjore and H.M.T. Pinjore. Total population of the district is 319398 out of which 173557 are males and 145841 are females.

Panchmahal : Panchmahal, also Panch Mahal, is a district in the western India, in the eastern portion of Gujarat state. Panch mahal means "five districts", and refers to the five districts that were transferred by the Sindhia Maharaja of Gwalior to the British.

Panchmahal were conquered from the Mughal Empire by the Maratha leader Sindhia in the eighteenth century. The Sindhias became Maharajas of Gwalior, and after 1818 were forced to recognize British sovereignty. The Panch Mahals were transferred in 1861 by the Sindhias to British India, where they became a district in the northern division of Bombay Presidency. The British district consisted of two separate parts, divided by the territory of a princely state. The southwestern portion was for the most part a level plain of rich soil; while the northern, although it comprised some fertile valleys, was generally rugged, undulating and barren, with but little cultivation. The area of the British district was 1606 sq. mi., and the population was 261,020 in 1901. The administrative headquarters were at Godhra, pop. (1901), 20,915.

Pandi Melam : Pandi melam is a classic performance (melam) of different musical instruments that are unique to Kerala state of south India. The most traditional of all melam's is 'Pandi Melam' which is generally performed outside the temples. Another melam called Panchari melam, which is similar to Pandi melam is played when you are inside the temple.

Pandit Bhimsen Joshi : Pandit Bhimsen Joshi, who holds a legendary status in Indian Classical music was born in Gadag (Karnataka) on 14 February 1922. His unique style and mastery over ragas has made him un parallel to any other vocalist in the country.

A conservative schoolmaster's son, Bhimsen Joshi had a passion for music even from his early childhood. The little boy deeply moved by a recording of Abdul Karim Khan, the founder father of the ' Kirana gharana', was later destined to become an accomplished jewel of the gharana. He left home in 1932 and was on the move for the next two years in search of a guru. He travelled to Bijapur, Pune, Gwalior where he tutored under Ustad Hafiz Ali Khan, the well-known sarodiya and father of Ustad Amjad Ali Khan, then to Calcutta, Punjab and back home, only to goad his father into sending him to Sawai Gandharva for training.

In 1936, Joshi started his rigorous training under Sawai Gandharva (Pandit Rambhan Kundgolkar), the eminent Khyal singer student of Abdul Karim Khan at Kundgol, near Gadag. He taught him the basics of Khayal singing. The tutoring spanning several years honed his inborn talent and helped him attain his mastery over ragas.

Bhimsen Joshi sings in the khayal style and has also rendered heavenly thumris and bhajans. Some of his popular numbers are 'Piya milan ki aas', 'Jo bhaje hari ko sada', 'Mile sur mera tumhara' etc. He has improvised and combined ragas to form new ragas like the Kalashri (Kalavati and Rageshri) and LalitBhatiyar (Lalit and Bhatiyar ragas) and has also developed and excelled in an unique style of singing adapting characteristics from other gharanas. Be it a new raga or a bhajan, khyal or kirti he performs with absolute ease moving from one pitch to another in the same breath effortlessly. His first public concert, to mark the shashtyabdipoorti (60th birthday) of his guru Sawai Gandharva, was held in Pune in January 1946. By the early 50's his voice became known throughout the country and then he began to travel extensively in India and abroad giving concerts.

This musical marvel is the recipient of prestigious awards like the Padma Shri from the Indian government, Sangeet Natak Academy Award, the Mysore Sangeet Natak Academy Award etc. Every year he has been conducting a music festival at Pune with performances of famous classical musicians, to observe his Gurus death anniversary. He married twice, the second time to Valsalabai his own disciple who played a big role in his success.

Apart from singing his other passion was automobiles, where he had a definite flair for fixing engines. In his eighties now, the Pundit who had been riding the crest of popularity for the last several decades has announced his retirement plan in a recent concert. Connoisseurs of classical music the world over are going to miss the divine musical experience of hearing this master sing.

Pandit Hariprasad Chaurasia : Pandit Hariprasad Chaurasia is an internationally renowned world class flautist from India. He is credited with popularising Indian Classical music in India and abroad through various experiments and innovations he made with the traditional music.

Born on July 1, 1938 in Allahabad, to a family of wrestlers he was drawn to the sound of the flute even as a small child. He began learning classical vocal music from Pandit Rajaram at the age of 15. Within a year, he switched to flute-playing after hearing Pandit Bholanath, a noted flautist from Varanasi on Radio. He tutored under Pandit Bholanath for eight years and in 1957, moved to Orissa where he became a staff artiste working as a performer and composer for All India Radio in Cuttack, Orissa. He met his wife of 39 years, Anuradha an established singer, there.

Later he was transferred to All India Radio, Mumbai. There he met renowned Surbahar player Annapurna Devi his 'Guruma' and trained under her. She is the daughter of late Ustad Allauddin Khan and sister of famous Sarod player Ali Akbar Khan. He left All India Radio to pursue a career as a flautist and from then on there has been no looking back for him.

He travels around the world giving concerts residing in Holland for almost half a year and making it a point to be at home in Mumbai, India for his 24-hour recital on the 'Janmashtami' day (Lord Krishna's birthday). He has performed with greats like Yehudi Menuhin, John McLaughlin and Jean Pierre Rampal and as a part of his experimentation, he has tried pop, jazz, rock, western classical fusions with the traditional Indian music. He has also released many albums of his compositions and done film music with his friend and Santoor exponent Pandit Shivkumar Sharma for films like 'Silsila', 'Darr' and others earning mass appeal.

In 1984, in recognition of his outstanding contribution to music, he received the National Award of the Sangeet Natak Academy. In 1990, he was awarded the 'Maharashtra Gaurav Puraskar', in 1992, the coveted 'Padma Bhushan' and the 'Konarak Samman' by the Orissa state government. In 1994, he was bestowed the 'Yash Bharati Sanman' by Uttar Paradesh government. This immensely popular humble artiste also gives training to several dedicated students.

Pandit Shivkumar Sharma : Pandit Shivkumar Sharma (born January 13, 1938) is an Indian classical musician, working in the Hindustani classical music tradition. He is a master of the santoor, a folk instrument from the valley of Kashmir. It is a type of hammered dulcimer whose strings are struck with a pair of light carved wooden mallets.

In the early decades of the twentieth century, the santoor or shata-tantri veena as it was called in earlier times, was used as an accompaniment to a specific type of singing called sufiana mausiqi. When Pandit Uma Dutt Sharma, a renowned vocalist from Jammu and a disciple of Pandit Bade Ramdasji of Benaras gharana discovered the instrument, he became interested by its possibilities. After extensive research on the instrument he passed on to his only son Shivkumar the responsibility of establishing it on the concert platform.

Shivkumar Sharma is the master instrumentalist of the santoor, after some years as a student of the tabla and as a vocalist. He is credited with single-handedly making the santoor a popular classical instrument, to the extent that the santoor and Pandit Shivkumar Sharma are synonymous. Sharma modified the Kashmiri folk instrument to make it more suitable for his classical technique, increasing the range of the instrument to three full octaves and making it capable of a smoother meend (the glissando or gliding between notes required in Hindustani classical music to emulate the human voice). Besides, he also created a new technique of playing with which he could sustain notes and maintain sound continuity. Today the santoor is the equal of any classical instrument, well established not just all over India, but across the globe.

Pandu Lena : About 8km south of Nasik, close to the Mumbai road, is a group of 24 rock cut Hinayana Buddhist caves dating from around the 1st century BC. Some of them have excellent carvings on the doorways. Of them, caves 3, 10 and 18 are noteworthy. Cave 3 and cave 10 are viharas with some interesting sculptures. There is a carved Buddha in Cave 10. Cave 18 is a Chaitya, well sculptured with an elaborate facade which is particularly noteworthy.

Pandurang Shastri Vaijnath Athavale : Pandurang Shastri Vaijnath Athavale (1920-2003, affectionately known as dadaji, meaning grandfather or elder brother) was an Indian guru and social reformer who created the Swadhyay movement in India. Swadhyay is the incorporation of the message of the Bhagavad Gita in one's life.

Pandurang Vaman Kane : Dr. Pandurang Vaman Kane (1880-1972) was a famous Indologist and Sanskrit scholar. He was born in a conservative Chitpavan Brahmin family. He hails from the Ratnagiri district in Maharashtra, India. Dr. Kane was revered as Mahamahopadhyay, usually shortened to MM as a prefix in the writings that refer to him. He served as the Vice-Chancellor of Bombay University. His services were requisitioned and enlisted for establishing Kurukshetra University in Indic studies. He was awarded the Sahitya Akademi award in 1956 for History of Dharmaśastra Volume IV for his research under the Sanskrit translation category. He was also an honorary member of the Bharatiya Vidya Bhavan. He was nominated to the Rajya Sabha as a member of Parliament for his distinguished record in the field of academics. The highest accolade bestowed upon him was the Bharat Ratna in 1963.

Pandyan Kingdom : The Pandyan kingdom was an ancient state at the tip of South India, founded around the 10th millenia BCE, traditionally. It was part of the Dravidian cultural area, which also comprised other kingdoms such as that of the Pallava, the Chera, the Chola, the Chalukya and the Vijayanagara. The Pandyans controlled the present districts of Madurai and Tirunelveli and part of southern present day Kerala. The present Madurai was founded by the third Sangam Pandyan king Muda-Thiru-MaaRan. The Pandyas excelled in both trade and learning.

They controlled the important pearl fisheries along the south Indian coast, between Sri Lanka and the mainland, which produced the finest pearls known in the ancient world. They had trading contacts with Ptolemaic Egypt and, through Egypt, with Rome by the first century CE, and with China by the 3rd century at the latest. The 1st century Greek historian Nicolaus of Damascus met at Damascus the embassy sent by an Indian king "named Pandion or, according to others, Porus" to Caesar Augustus around 13 CE.

Paneer : Paneer, is the Persian word for "cheese". It is an unaged, acid-set, non-melting Farmer cheese that is similar to acid-set fresh mozzarella and queso blanco, except that it does not have salt added. Like mozzarella, Bengali paneer is beaten or kneaded. However, other types of paneer are simply pressed. Paneer is the only type of cheese indigenous to the Indian subcontinent, and is most commonly used in Middle Eastern and South Asian cuisine. Paneer is a primary source of protein for Buddhists (typically those of South Asian origin) who adhere to vegetarian but not to vegan diets.

Paneer is known in North India and Pakistan by the same name; however, in Bengal it is known by the name "Chhena" and in south India, by names derived from "Panneer" and "Channa" (not to be confused with Chana, the Bengali name for the chick pea).

Pangal : The Pangal, also known as the "Meitei Pangal", are a subset of the Meiteis, the major ethnic group in the border state of Manipur, India. Their present population is estimated as 150,000, most of whom are under 20. The Pangal are mainly concentrated in and around Imphal, the capital of Manipur. Inhabited localities include Kshetrigaon, Lilong, Khergao, Yairipok, Kairang, Mayang Imphal, Jiri, Cachar, Keirao, and Hapta.

The Pangal have slightly Aryan features. They are thought to be descendants of a group of Muslim warriors from the district of Sileet in Cachar (now in Assam) who intermarried with the local Meitei. Pangals identify themselves as Muslims but their beliefs, practices, and culture reflect the pre-Hindu religion of the Meiteis. Traditional dress for men is lungis and pajamas, and for women is fanek and salwar. Both also wear western attire.

The Pangal suffer from low literacy and poor economic development. A riot involving this community occurred in May 1993. About 150 were killed and an unknown number were injured and displaced.

Panguni Uttiram : The marriage of the god and goddess is the annual event in all temples in Tamil Nadu in the month of Panguni. This month is also noted for the Uttiram festival for Lord Subrahmanya or Muruga for ten days. For villagers, this is a very important festival and as it comes off in the off-season, they participate in it fully and give offerings of paddy to the temples. On the morning of the final day the Vel or the lance, which is the chief weapon of Lord Subrahmanya, is taken out in a procession to the river bank, where devotees make offerings. Along with the deity, a pair of wooden sandals, Kavadi—a palanquin-like structure with bells and other decoration on it and a baton known as the Idumban Thadi are also anointed.

The day following the Panguni Uttiram is set apart for the Idumban festival. On this day, Pujas and offerings are made to Idumban vassal of Lord Subrahmanya. During the course of puja, the deity's spirit is believed to enter many a devotee who will there upon act as though he is in a state of delirium. He will beat himself with the Idumban Thadi and also give out forecasts which can be deciphered only with difficulty. These are said to forecast coming events and the people believe that Idumban himself is doing so through the medium.

Panhwar : Panhwar is a Sindhi tribe in Sindh, Pakistan. Panhwars constitute about 40% of Dadu District, Sindh. Panhwars live in all parts of Sindh and are engaged in agriculture, civil serice and business. The Panhwars have been mentioned in the history several times and in 18th century when the capital of Sindh was Khudaabad Panhwars were rulers of Sindh for a short period of time.

Panini : Panini was an ancient Gandharan grammarian (approximately 5th century BC, but estimates range from the 7th to the 3rd centuries). Panini's grammar of Sanskrit is highly systematised and technical. Inherent in its analytic approach are the concepts of the phoneme, the morpheme and the root, only recognized by Western linguists some two millennia later. His rules have a reputation of perfection — that is, they are claimed to fully describe Sanskrit morphology, without any redundance. A consequence of his grammar's focus on brevity is its highly unintuitive structure, reminiscent of contemporary "machine language" (as opposed to "human readable" programming languages).

Panini uses metarules, transformations, and recursions with such sophistication that his grammar has the computing power equivalent to a Turing machine. In this sense Panini may be considered the father of computing machines. His work was the forerunner to modern formal language theory, and a precursor to computing. Paninian grammars have also been devised for non-Sanskrit languages. The Backus-Naur form (Panini-Backus form) or BNF grammars used to describe modern programming languages have significant similarities to Panini's grammar rules.

Nothing definite is known about Panini's life, not even the century he lived in (he lived almost certainly after the

7th and before the 3rd century BC). According to tradition, he was born in Shalatula, near the Indus river in the current Pakistan, and lived ca. 520–460 BC, a time probably falling within the late Vedic period: he notes a few special rules, marked chandasi ("in the hymns") to account for forms in the Vedic scriptures that had fallen out of use in the spoken language of his time, indicating that Vedic Sanskrit was already archaic, but still a comprehensible dialec

Panipat : Panipat is a historic as well as an ancient city in the Panipat District in Haryana state, India, The city has a population of 216,000. It was one of the five cities (prasthas) founded by the Pandava brothers during the times of Mahabharata; its historic name being Paneprastha.

Panipat was the scene of three pivotal battles in Indian history. The First battle of Panipat was fought in 1526 between Sultan Ibrahim Lodi and Zaheeruddin Babur. The fight was won by twelve thousand soldiers of Babur over one lakh soldiers of Lodhi because of cannons and better organization of force. Babur laid the foundation of Mughal Empire in India. The Second battle of Panipat was fought in 1556 between Hemu and Akbar. Hemu fell unconscious when an arrow hit his eye and his army ran away. He was beheaded by Akbar. The Third battle of Panipat was between Ahmad Shah Abdali and Marathas under Sadashivraobhau, the cousin of Peshwa Nanasaheb, who were protecting the Mughal emperor Shah Alam II. This battle marked the beginning of fall of Mughals and rise of British in India.

Panipat is the city of textiles and carpets. It is also known for its world famous pickle 'Pachranga International'. This city is also famous for its handloom industry. It is also home to many industries such as Indian Oil Co. Ltd. (IOCL) Refinery, NTPC Thermal Power Plant and National Fertilizers Limited. It is the biggest centre for cheap blankets and carpets in India.

Panipuri : Panipuri, or Pani puri, is a snack synonymous with the beaches of Mumbai. However, it is also very popular in all other parts of India. It is a part of the chaat family along with Bhelpuri. It is also known by many names like golgappa (plural golguppe) in North India, Foochka (Puchka) in West Bengal, Gupchup in some central parts of India like Hyderabad.

It is made from small, round, puffed, hard puris which form the 'container' or shell, and mashed potatoes and cooked chick-peas along with some finely cut onions, with salt and pepper added, and the chutneys are the stuffing. Normally, there are two chutneys, the hot and the sweet, each in a large round mud (or, nowadays, metal) vessel; although sometimes there is only one. The Chutneys are what is referred to by Pani, which means water in Hindi (the main ingredient of the Chutney), and they contain tamarind and fresh mint, as well as spices including cumin and black salt. The serving person will lightly crush open the puris on one side, put into it the stuffing, and then dunk it into both the chutneys and serve you the puri, which is now full. You have to put the entire puri into your mouth at one go and bite into it. This will release the barrage of different tastes into your mouth.

Panjab : The Punjab or Panjab province of Pakistan is the country's most populous region and is home to the Punjabis and various other groups. Neighbouring areas are Sindh to the south, Balochistan and Federally Administered Tribal Areas to the west, the North West Frontier Province, Azad Kashmir, Indian controlled Jammu and Kashmir and Islamabad to the north, and Indian Punjab and Rajasthan to the east. The main languages are Punjabi, Seraiki, and Urdu and the provincial capital is Lahore. The name Punjab literally translates from Persian into the words 'Panj' five, and 'Aab' water respectively, which can be translated as "five water" (hence the poetic name land of the five rivers), referring to the Beas, Ravi, Sutlej, Chenab and Jhelum rivers. Part of Indus river also lies in Punjab, but it is not considered one of the "five" rivers.

Panjgur : Panjgur is a district in the west of Balochistan province of Pakistan. Panjgur was notified as a district on July 1, 1977 when Makran district was given the status of a division and was divided into three districts. Previously it was one of the 3 tehsils of Makran district. For administrative purposes, the whole district is one sub-division, i.e., Panjgur, and further divided into one tehsil (Panjgur) and two sub-tehsils, named Gichk and Parome.

Panjnad River : Panjnad River (*panj* = five, *nadi* = river) is a river in Punjab, Pakistan. Panjnad River is formed by successive confluence of the five rivers of Punjab, namely Jhelum, Chenab, Ravi, Beas and Sutlej. Jhelum and Ravi join Chenab, Beas joins Sutlej, and then Sutlej and Chenab join to form Panjnad near Uch Sharif. The combined stream runs southwest for approximately 45 miles and joins Indus River at Mithankot. The Indus continues into the Arabian Sea. A dam on Panjnad has been erected; it provides irrigation channels for Punjab and Sind provinces south of the Sutlej and east of the Indus rivers.

Pankaj Udhas : Pankaj Udhas is a pre-eminent Ghazal singer from India. He is credited with bringing this unique singing style where Urdu verses of poets are set to music to the mass audience across the country along with other musicians like Jagjit Singh and Talat Aziz. Pankaj Udhas was born on 17 April 1951 in Jetpur in the Gujarat State in India. His older brother Manhar Udhas achieved some success as a Hindi playback singer in Bollywood movies.

His family movied to Bombay and Pankaj attended St. Xavier's College in Bombay, graduating with a degree in Arts. Pankaj was first noticed as a professional singer in the film Naam in 1986, in which his song Chitthi Aayee Hai became an instant hit. He recorded several albums since then and toured the world as an accomplished Ghazal singer. He has also composed music for many films and performed as a playback singer for others. He recieved the Padma Shri, a Government of India civilian award in 2006.

Pankho : Pankho is a tribe of chittagong hill tracts and considered a sub-branch of the Mongoloid race. In language and social lifestyle they have a lot of similarities with another tribe called Banajogi. Pankhos are short in height, have brown complexion, flat nose and small eyes. They live in the bandarban district of Chittagong Hills Tracts, but their original home was probably Burma (Myanmar). Having been driven out from there for some reason or the other several hundred years ago, they settled in this region. Pankhos and Banajogis are farmers. The jhum system of farming is still widely practised by them. Pankhos produce rice and other crops. But they also do the work of procuring timber by felling trees in the forest. In all these works women take part equally with men. Women also do the marketing. Like Burmese and Assamese tribal women, Pankho women are hardworking and enjoy a special place in the family.

Panna : Panna is a town in western Madhya Pradesh state of central India. It is famous for its diamond mines. It is the administrative center of Panna District. Panna was the capital of Chhatar Sal, the Bundela Rajput leader who led a revolt against the Mughal Empire. Upon his death in 1732, his kingdom was divided among his sons, with one-third of the kingdom going to his ally, the Maratha Peshwa Baji Rao I.

The kingdom of Panna went to Harde Sah, the eldest son of Chhatar Sal. In the early 19th century, Panna became a princely state of British India, and gained control states of the states of Sohawal and Nagod. Raja Nirpat Singh assisted the British in the Revolt of 1857, and the British rewarded him with the title maharaja. Maharaja Mahendra Yadvendra Singh acceded to the Government of India on January 1, 1950, and the kingdom became Panna District of the new Indian state of Vindhya Pradesh. Vindhya Pradesh was merged into Madhya Pradesh on November 1, 1950.

Panna National Park : Spread over an area of 543sq.km in the districts of Panna and Chhatarpur, this park was established in 1981. The nearest town from the park is Panna 20 km away and the rail head is at Satna which is at a distance of 95 km. The nearest airport is Khajuraho 20 km away. The forests of the park are tropical dry deciduous. The fauna found are leopard, panther, tiger, chinkara, sloth bear, wolf, wild pig, nilgai, gharial,mugger, crocodile, and peafowl.

Paonta Sahib : Paonta Sahib is a small town in the south of Sirmour district in the Indian state of Himachal Pradesh. It is an important religious spot for Sikhs and a bustling industrial town. It has a large Gurudwara on the banks of the river Yamuna, the reiver being the boundary between the states of Himachal Pradesh and Uttar Pradesh. The Gurudwara has linkages to the Sikh Guru Gobind Singh and the Sikh leader Banda Bahadur. It is near to the town of Nahan in Himachal Pradesh, Yamunanagar in Haryana and Dehradun in Uttaranchal. It is on the eastern extreme of the Doon valley.

Papad : Papad (also papadam, poppadom, papadum, and appalam) is an Indian and Sri Lankan flatbread. Typically, it is prepared using black gram bean flour, rice flour, or lentil flour with salt and peanut oil added. The ingredients are made into a dough and formed into a thin, round shape similar to a tortilla. As the dough is prepared, the papadum can be seasoned with a variety of different ingredients such as chilies, cumin, garlic, black pepper, or other spices.

Papadums are cooked by deep-frying in oil, which causes them to expand and crispen. They may also be cooked by roasting them over an open flame, in a toaster oven, or in a microwave oven. Depending on the cooking method they may be either soft and moist or crisp in texture. Most often served as a complement to a main dish, they are also eaten as a snack or as an appetizer to be topped with chutney, various dips or salsas. Commonly made in different sizes, the smaller ones are for snacks and the larger variety may be used as a food wrap.

Papi Kondalu Perantalapalli : As the mighty Godavari river races past the hills taking the course that resembles a narrow gorge, it appears to be in hurry. It is in Andhra Pradesh.

Papikonda Wild Life Sanctuary : Papikonda wildlife sanctuary is spread in three districts, Viz: Khammam, East Godavari and West Godavari. It is 50-km from Rajahmundry and extends over 591 sq km.

Papri Chaat : Papri Chaat or Paapri Chaat is a north Indian fast food. Chaat, an Indic word which literally means lick, is used to describe a range of snacks and fast food dishes; papri refers to crispy fried dough wafers made from flour and ghee. In Papri Chaat the papris are served with potatoes, chilis, yoghurt and tamarind chutney. The popular dish is often eaten from travelling food vendor stalls.

Paradas : The Paradas are a people mentionned in ancient Indian texts like the Manu Smriti, various Puranas,

Ramayana, and Mahabharata etc. They are referenced in the Puranic literature as Paradas as well as Paritas. Paradas and Paritas are sometimes equated to the Paladas and Palidas of king Ashoka's inscriptions. Numerous Puranic texts associates the Paradas with the Kambojas, Sakas, Yavanas and Pahlavas and brands them together as Panca-ganah (fiver-hordes). These five hordes were military allies of the Haihaya and Taljunga Kshatriyas of Yadava line and were chiefly responsible for dethroning king Bahu of Kosala. Later, king Sagara, son of king Bahu, was able to defeat the Haihayas and Taljungas together with these five-hordes. According to Puranic accounts, king Sagara had divested the Paradas and other members of the well-known Panca-gana (i.e. the Sakas, Yavanas, Kambojas and Pahlavas) of their Kshatriyahood and turned them into the Mlechchas. Before their defeat at the hands of king Sagara, these five-hordes were called Kshatriya-pungava (i.e. foremost among the Kshatriyas).

Paradesi Synagogue : The Paradesi Synagogue is the oldest synagogue in the Commonwealth of Nations, located in Kochi, Kerala, in South India. It was built in the year 1568 by the Malabar Yehudan people or Cochin Jewish community in the Kingdom of Cochin. Paradesi is a word used in several Indian languages, and its literal meaning is a "foreigner". Accordingly, the Paradesi Synagogue literally means a synagogue of foreigners. It is also referred to as the Cochin Jewish synagogue or the Mattancherry synagogue.

The synagogue is in what is known as Jew Street, in Jew Town, in Old Cochin. The complex has four buildings. It was built adjacent to the Mattancherry Palace temple on the land gifted to the Malabari Yehuden community by the king of Kochi, Rama Varma. In fact, the Mattancherry Palace temple and the Mattancherry synagogue have a common wall.

Param Vir Chakra : The Param Vir Chakra is an Indian military decoration given for valour in combat operations. It is India's highest military honor. The name is sometimes abbreviated as PVC. It literally means 'Wheel (or Cross) of the Ultimate Brave' (Sanskrit: Param, Ultimate; Vir (Pronounced veer), Brave; Chakra, Wheel, or its western equivalent, Cross). Equivalent awards in the United States are the Medal of Honor and the Victoria Cross in the United Kingdom.

The Param Vir Chakra (PVC) is the highest gallantry award for officers and other enlisted personnel of all military branches of India for the highest degree of valour or self-sacrifice in the presence of the enemy. It may be awarded posthumously and, indeed, most of the awards have been posthumous. Provision was made for the award of a bar for second (or subsequent) awards of the Param Vir Chakra. To date, there have been no such awards. Award of the decoration carries with it the right to use P.V.C. as a postnominal abbreviation.

The award also carries a cash allowance for those under the rank of second lieutenant (or the appropriate service equivalent) and, in some cases, a cash award. On the death of the recipient, the pension is transferred to the widow until her death or remarriage. The paltry amount of the pension has been a rather controversial issue throughout the life of the decoration. By March 1999, the stipend stood at Rs. 1500 per month. In addition, many states have established individual pension rewards that far exceeds the central government's stipend for the recipients of the decoration.

The PVC was established on 26 January 1950, by the President of India, with effect from 15 August 1947, and presently it is the second highest award of the government of India after Bharat Ratna (amendment in the statute on 26 January 1980 resulted in this order of wearing).

Parasgad Fort : Parasgad Fort is located about two kilometres south of Saundatti village, and stands on the south-west edge of a range of hills immediately overlooking the black soil plain down below. The hill which measures about 500 metres from north to south and about 300 metres from east to west, is irregular, and a good deal is covered with prickly pear and brushwood. Its sides are rocky and almost perpendicular. A deep gorge runs through it. Atop the hill-fort is a small ruined shrine to the Hindu deity Maruthi. The fort itself is uninhabited, and the remains of old houses are located in it.

A descent of several hundred steps leads to Yadravi village. This passes by a natural spring with a water tank measuring thirty by six metres called the Ramatheertha, and a cave housing statues of Hindu deities and mythological figures including Jamadagni, Parashurama, Rama, and Sita, a Shivalinga with a Nandi. The village of Yadravi is referred to as "Elarame" in an inscription found on a platform near the Bharamappa temple of the village. The inscription is dated Shaka 901 in the Hindu calendar.

Parashuram Kund : Tezu is the district headquarters of the Lohit district of Arunachal Pradesh. There is a famous pilgrimage centre Parasuram Kund some 21km north east of Tezu. It is a shrine of all-India importance located in the lower reaches of the river Lohit. Thousands of pilgrims, visit the place in winter every year, especially on the Makara Sankranti day for a holy dip in the sacred kund which is believed to wash away one's sins. The legend behind the belief recorded in the Kalika Purna, is that the great sage Parasuram washed away the sin of killing his mother in the waters of Brahma kund. A great fair is held to which wild cows, rare fur-rugs and other curios are brought down by the mountain tribes. There are also facilities for trekking from Tezu to glow lake which takes one day, hiking and river rafting and angling on the river Lohit. The nearest railway station is Tinsukia (120km) from where you can take buses via Namsai. There are also buses available from Sadia. The nearest airports are Tezu and Dibrugarh (Assam).

Parassinkkadavu : Parassinkkadavu is a small village about 16 km from Kannur town in the Kannur district of north Kerala state, south India. Parassinikkadavu is noted for the famous Muthappan temple where people go for worshipping Sree Muthappan. This is the only Hindu Temple in Kerala where a Theyyam performance is a daily ritual offering. Parassinkkadavu is also noted for the Parassinikkadavu Snake Park which is committed to the preservation and conservation of snakes as most species of the reptile are on the verge of extinction. There are about 150 varieties of snakes including the spectacled cobra, King cobra, Russell Viper, Krait and Pit Viper living in the park.

Parasuramesvera Temple : A 7th century Shiva Temple, classical in style,one of the oldest in Bhubaneswar. Located close to the main Bhubaneswar to Puri Road, on the same side as the Lingaraj Temple, the Grove of the Perfect Beings is a cluster of about 20 smaller temples. It's the best preserved of all Bhubaneswar's ancient temples and has finely detailed bas-reliefs of elephant and horse processions and Siva images.

Paratha : Paratha is an Indian or Pakistani flatbread, usually made with whole-wheat flour, fried in ghee, and sometimes stuffed with vegetables, especially boiled potatoes or radish or cauliflower and Paneer (Indian cheese). Indian immigrants brought this dish to Malaysia and Singapore, resulting in variations such as roti canai and roti prata. Parathas are enjoyed with vegetables, particularly gobi (cauliflower). Paratha in Trinidad and Tobago differs from Indian paratha in that it is generally thinner and larger. In Trinidad and Tobago it is commonly called "buss up shut" ("burst-up shirt"), especially by non-Indo-Trinidadians.

Parbattya Chattagram Jana Sanghati Samiti (PCJSS) : PCJSS is a political party in Chittagong Hill Tracts, Bangladesh. It was formed in the early 1970s to preserve the rights of the tribal people south-eastern Bangladesh.

Parchmarhi Biosphere Reserve : The Parchmarhi Biosphere Reserve is a conservation area in the Satpura Range of Madhya Pradesh state, India. It was created on March 3, 1999 by the Indian Government, and covers parts of Hoshangabad, Betul, and Chhindwara districts. The Biosphere reserve's total area is 4926.28 km². It includes three wildlife conservation units, the Bori Sanctuary (518.00 km²), Satpura National Park (524.37 km²), and Pachmarhi Sanctuary (461.37 km²). Satpura National Park is designated as the core zone, and the remaining area of 4501.91 km², including the Bori and Pachmarhi sanctuaries, constitutes the buffer zone.

The preserve is mostly covered in forest, part of the Eastern highlands moist deciduous forests ecoregion. It is an important transition zone between the forests of western and eastern India; the forests are dominated by Teak (Tectona grandis), but include the westernmost groves of Sal (Shorea robusta), which is the dominant tree of eastern India's forests. Large mammal species include tiger, leopard, wild boar, muntjac deer, gaur (Bos gaurus), chital deer (Axis axis), sambar (Cervus unicolor), and Rhesus Macaques.

Pargana : A pargana is a former administrative unit of the Indian Subcontinent, used primarily, but not exclusively, by the Muslim kingdoms. Parganas were introduced by the Delhi Sultanate, and the word is of Persian origin. As a revenue unit, a pargana consists of several mouzas, which are the smallest revenue units, consisting of one or more villages and the surrounding countryside. Under the reign of Sher Shah Suri, administration of parganas was strengthened by the addition of other officers, including a shiqdar (police chief), an amin or munsif (a civil arbitrator and revenue official who assessed and collected revenue) and a karkun. The pargana system persisted in several princely states, including Tonk and Gwalior. Parganas disappeared almost completely after the independence of India and Pakistan in 1947, although the term lives on in place names, like the districts of North 24 Parganas and South 24 Parganas in India's West Bengal state.

Pari Mahal (Palace) : Pari Mahal (Palace) was built by Sufi Muslims as mentioned in the Rajtarangni, Kashmir. There is a road leading from Chashma Shahi to Pari Mahal.

Parimarjan Negi : Parimarjan Negi (b. 9 February 1993) is a 12-year-old chess prodigy from India. In July 2005, he became the youngest International Master, when he earned his third and final IM norm at the Sort International open chess tournament in Sort, Spain.

He is set to be the youngest International Grandmaster, after he scored 6/10, a performance of 2568 at the Hastings Chess Congress. This tournament took place from December 28th, 2005, to January 6th, 2006, with 106 players at the start. Negi finished 16th when he was 12 years 10 months and 29 days old.

Parliament of India : The Parliament of India (or Sansad) is bicameral. It is located in New Delhi at Sansad Marg. This is the supreme legislative body of the Republic of India. The Indian Parliament consists of two houses—the Lok Sabha and the Rajya Sabha—and the President of India. Any bill can become an act only after it is passed by both the houses of the Parliament and assented by the President.

Parliamentary System of Pakistan : At the national level, Pakistan elects a bicameral legislature, the Parliament of Pakistan, which consists of a directly-elected National Assembly of Pakistan and a Senate whose members are chosen by elected provincial legislators. The Prime Minister of Pakistan is elected by the National Assembly. The President of Pakistan is elected by the Electoral College of Pakistan, which consists of both houses of Parliament together with the provincial assemblies.

In addition to the National Parliament and the provincial assemblies, Pakistan also has more than five thousand elected local governments. Pakistan has a multi-party system, with numerous parties. Frequently, no single party has a majority, and parties must ally with each other during elections, and then negotiate with other parties to form coalition governments. The bicameral federal legislature consists of the Senate (upper house) and National Assembly (lower house). According to Article 50 of the Constitution, the National Assembly, the Senate and the President together make up a body known as the Majlis-i-Shoora (Council of Advisers).

Pakistan's democracy has no recall method. However, past governments have been dismissed for corruption by the President's invocation of Article 58 of the Constitution. The President's power to dismiss the Prime Minister and dissolve the National Assembly was removed by the Thirteenth Amendment and partially restored by the Seventeenth Amendment.

Partition of Bengal (1905) : The Partition of Bengal in 1905, was made on 16 October by then Viceroy of India, Lord Curzon. The province of Bengal had an area of 189,000 sq miles and a population of 78.5 million. Eastern Bengal was almost isolated from the western part by geography and poor communications. In 1836, the upper provinces were placed under a lieutenant governor, and in 1854 the Governor-General-In-Council was relieved of the direct administration of Bengal. In 1874 Assam, including Sylhet, was severed from Bengal to form a Chief-Commissionership, and the Lushai Hills were added to it in 1898.

Partitioning Bengal were first considered in 1903. There were also additional proposals to separate Chittagong and the districts of Dhaka and Mymensingh from Bengal and attaching them to the province of Assam. Similarly incorporating Chhota Nagpur with the central provinces. Government officially published the idea in January 1904, and in February, Lord Curzon made an official tour to eastern districts of Bengal to assess public opinion on the partition. He consulted with leading personalities and delivered speeches at Dhaka, Chittagong and Mymensigh explaining the government's stand on partition.

The new province would consist of the state of Hill Tripura, the Divisions of Chittagong, Dhaka and Rajshahi (excluding Darjeeling) and the district of Malda incorporate with Assam province. Bengal was to surrender not only these eastern large territories but also to cede to the Central Provinces the five Hindi-speaking states. On the west side it was offered Sambalpur and a minor five Uriya-speaking states from the Central Provinces. Bengal would be left with an area of 141,580 sq. miles and population of 54 million, where 42 million would be hindus and 9 million muslims.

The new province was named Eastern Bengal and Assam with Dhaka as its capital and subsidiary headquarters at Chittagong. Its area would be 106,540 sq. miles with a population of 31 million, where 18 million would be muslims and 12 million hindus. Administration would consist a Legislative Council, a Board of Revenue of two members, and the jurisdiction of the Calcutta High Court would be left undisturbed. Government pointed out that Eastern Bengal and Assam would have a clearly demarcated western boundary and well defined geographical, ethnological, linguistic and social characteristics. The government of India promulgated their final decision in a resolution dated July 19, 1905 and the partition of Bengal was effected on October 16 of same year.

This created a huge political crisis. The Muslim's in the East Bengal had this impression that a separate region would give them more opportunity for education, employment etc. But the partition was not liked by the people in West Bengal and a huge amount of nationalist literature was created during this period in the West Bengal. Rabindranath Tagore wrote the national anthem of Bangladesh Amar Shonar Bangla during this period (in 1906). Amidst political protests, the two parts of Bengal were reunited in 1911.

Partition of Bengal (1905) : The Partition of Bengal in 1905, was made on 16 October by then Viceroy of India, Lord Curzon. The province of Bengal had an area of 189,000 sq miles and a population of 78.5 million. Eastern Bengal was almost isolated from the western part by geography and poor communications. In 1836, the upper provinces were placed under a lieutenant governor, and in 1854 the Governor-General-In-Council was relieved of the direct administration of Bengal. In 1874 Assam, including Sylhet, was severed from Bengal to form a Chief-Commissionership, and the Lushai Hills were added to it in 1898.

Partitioning Bengal were first considered in 1903. There were also additional proposals to separate

Chittagong and the districts of Dhaka and Mymensingh from Bengal and attaching them to the province of Assam. Similarly incorporating Chhota Nagpur with the central provinces. Government officially published the idea in January 1904, and in February, Lord Curzon made an official tour to eastern districts of Bengal to assess public opinion on the partition. He consulted with leading personalities and delivered speeches at Dhaka, Chittagong and Mymensigh explaining the government's stand on partition.

The new province would consist of the state of Hill Tripura, the Divisions of Chittagong, Dhaka and Rajshahi (excluding Darjeeling) and the district of Malda incorporate with Assam province. Bengal was to surrender not only these eastern large territories but also to cede to the Central Provinces the five Hindi-speaking states. On the west side it was offered Sambalpur and a minor five Uriya-speaking states from the Central Provinces. Bengal would be left with an area of 141,580 sq. miles and population of 54 million, where 42 million would be hindus and 9 million muslims.

The new province was named Eastern Bengal and Assam with Dhaka as its capital and subsidiary headquarters at Chittagong. Its area would be 106,540 sq. miles with a population of 31 million, where 18 million would be muslims and 12 million hindus. Administration would consist a Legislative Council, a Board of Revenue of two members, and the jurisdiction of the Calcutta High Court would be left undisturbed. Government pointed out that Eastern Bengal and Assam would have a clearly demarcated western boundary and well defined geographical, ethnological, linguistic and social characteristics. The government of India promulgated their final decision in a resolution dated July 19, 1905 and the partition of Bengal was effected on October 16 of same year.

This created a huge political crisis. The Muslim's in the East Bengal had this impression that a separate region would give them more opportunity for education, employment etc. But the partition was not liked by the people in West Bengal and a huge amount of nationalist literature was created during this period in the West Bengal. Rabindranath Tagore wrote the national anthem of Bangladesh Amar Shonar Bangla during this period (in 1906). Amidst political protests, the two parts of Bengal were reunited in 1911.

Partition of Bengal (1947) : The Partition of Bengal in 1947 divided Bengal into the two separate entities of West Bengal belonging to India, and East Bengal belonging to Pakistan. East Bengal was later renamed East Pakistan and is today the independent nation of Bangladesh.

Partition of India : The partition of India refers to the creation in August 1947 of two sovereign states of India and Pakistan when Britain granted independence to the former British Raj including treaty states. The later division of Pakistan, when its eastern wing separated into Bangladesh, is not covered by the term Partition of India, nor is the term used in reference to earlier separation of Ceylon (now Sri Lanka) and Burma (now Myanmar) from British administration of India. Ceylon was part of Madras Presidency from 1795 until it was made a separate Crown Colony in 1798. Burma was annexed by the British gradually during 1826-1886 and was governed as a part of British Indian administration until 1937, when it was established as a Crown Colony separate from India. Burma was granted independence on January 4, 1948 and Ceylon was granted independence on February 4, 1948. As for the rest of South Asia, Nepal and Bhutan had treaties with the British that designated them as independent states unlike the 'treaty states' (or princely states) which are covered under "Partion of India". Burma (or Myanmar) is generally not considered part of South Asia, irrespective of the fact that it was administered as part of British India for a century or so, since it otherwise shares very little terms of history and geography with South Asia.

Parvati : Parvati is the power and consort of Siva, the god of disintegration and destruction. A majority of goddesses of Hinduism are aspects and variations of Parvati. She is known by different names like Uma, Gauri, Kali, Durga, Haimavati etc.

Like her consort Siva, she also has two aspects: the mild and the terrible. When shown along with Siva she has only two hands, the right one holding a blue lotus and the left hanging loosely by the side. When represented independently she is shown with four hands, two hands holding red and blue lotuses and the other two exhibiting the varada and Abhaya mudras.

Her vehicle is Lion. According to the Pauranic accounts, in her first incarnation, Parvati was Daksayani, the daughter of Daksa. She was married to Lord Siva. When Daksa undertook the performance of a great sacrifice, he insulted Siva by not inviting him or his wife. However, Daksayani went to the sacrifice uninvited and being insulted she ended her life by igniting herself through the fire of yaga. Hence she came to be known as Sati, the chaste one.

She was next reborn as Parvati, the daughter of Himavan and Mena. After performing intense austerities she succeeded in pleasing Siva and making him accept her again as his consort. As the mother of the universe, Parvati is known as Amba and Ambika which means 'mother'.

Pasanda : Pasanda is a popular North Indian meat dish, derived from a meal served in the Court of the Moghul Emperors. The word is a variation on the Hindi word "pasande," or "the favorite one," which refers to the prime cut of meat traditionally used within.

Pasanda was originally made with leg of lamb, flattened into strips, marinated, and fried in a dish with multiple seasonings. In the present day, pasanda is also made using beef, mutton, chicken and turkey; in each case, the process and ingredients remain generally the same.

Although pasanda is usually served as a meat dish, it may also be prepared in kebab form. Reflecting the dish's flavor and its connection with the almond, pasanda also refers to a mild curry sauce made with cream, coconut milk, and almonds. Pasanda is spicy and heavily seasoned, but to a lesser extent than for most Indian dishes. As such, it is considered a relatively accessible dish for Westerners, appropriate for use as an introduction to Indian cooking in general.

Pasban : Pasban (The Defenders), is a Pakistani socio-political movement that aims to uproot what it sees as the current oppressive system and to establish a welfare state in Pakistan. Pasban's president is Altaf Shakoor.He was born in Karachi in 1959. An engineer by education and trader by profession, Shakoor was president of the students' union at NED University of Engineering and Technology in 1981–1982. Pasban was founded during 1991 and its focus of activities was to raise the voice against injustice. It gained popularity when in 1993 a poor electrician Ayub and his wife Asia Ayub were kept unlawfully and were severely manhandled by the well-known Pakistani police (for it's cruel methods of torture and humiliation of the common men) in a police station at Rawalpindi. Pasban stood against the brutality and started a movement. People, especially the youth joined the movement and followed the ray of hope lead by Pasban.

Pascoal Spice Village : It is located near the village of Khandepar, 8 kms northeast of Ponda National Highway

(NH) 4A. the lower end of the property is bounded by tributary of the Mandovi River and rises in elevation towards the hills of the interior. Spices are the indispensable ingredients of Goa's well known "chillie hot cussine". They are still grown in Goa on large income plantations along with other income producing crops of areca nuts, cashew nuts, coconuts, tropical fruit, etc. These plantations have manage to combine spices and tourism in a unique and favourable way one of the first plantations to realize this potential was Pascoal Spice Village. This idyllic screnc setting coupled with a wide variety of spice plants and cash crops is interspersed with a restaurant, cottages, open-air party half, boating, nursery, a wide variety of flowering plants, shrubs, fountains and farm animals.

Pashto : Pashto is the language spoken by the Pashtun people who inhabit Afghanistan and the western provinces of Pakistan. Pashto is classified within the Eastern Iranian branch of the Indo-European languages. Other notable related tongues include Ossetic, spoken in the Caucasus.

Pashtunistan : Pashtunistan or Pakhtunistan is what many Pashtun nationalists call the Pashtun-dominated areas of Pakistan. The Pashtuns in Afghanistan are the largest ethnic group in the country and are concentrated in the south and east, but nationalists have often included all of the western part of Pakistan as part of Pashtunistan. The Pakistani part of Pashtunistan comprises an area that runs from Chitral (where Pashtuns are a minority in the north of Pakistan, with Khowar people being the majority) to Sibi (in the southwest) and intentionally includes the ethnically mixed region of Balochistan. The Pashtun majority areas in western Pakistan include the North-West Frontier Province (NWFP), Federally Administered Tribal Areas (FATA) and the northern portion of Balochistan. The main language spoken in the Pashtunistan region is Pashto, but substantial numbers of Afghans Persian speakers can also be found throughout the Pashtun regions of western Pakistan where many Afghan refugees have established permanent roots. Thus, Pashtunistan can be defined in various ways depending upon the point of view of the political group involved.

Pashtuns : The Pashtuns are an ethno-linguistic group consisting mainly of eastern Iranian stock living primarily in eastern and southern Afghanistan, and the North West Frontier Province, Federally Administered Tribal Areas and Baluchistan provinces of Pakistan. Large additional colonies can be found in the Northern Areas, Azad Kashmir, and there are thought to be about 3 million in the city of Karachi, 1 million in Islamabad/Rawalpindi and an additional million in Lahore, as well as being scattered throughout other parts of Afghanistan. There are smaller communities in Iran and India, and a large migrant worker community in the countries of the Arabian Peninsula. The Pashtuns are typically characterized by their language, their pre-Islamic indigenous code of honor and culture Pashtunwali, and adherence to Islam.

The Pashtuns are the world's largest segmentary lineage (patriarchal) tribal group in existence. The total population of the group is estimated to be over 40 million, but an accurate count remains difficult to verify as there has not been an official census in Afghanistan since the 1970s, while in Pakistan, due to the migratory nature of many Pashtun tribes as well as the practice of secluding women, exact figures are to hard to attain.

Pashtuns : The Pashtuns are an ethno-linguistic group living primarily in the North West Frontier Province and Federally Administered Tribal Areas of Pakistan, and the eastern and southern parts of Afghanistan. They also constitute almost half of the total population of the Baluchistan province of Pakistan. Additionally, smaller colonies can be found in the Northern Areas of Pakistan as well as Azad Kashmir. There are thought to be about 3 million in the city of Karachi, 1 million in twin cities of Islamabad and Rawalpindi and an additional million in Lahore. There are twice the number of Pashtuns living in Pakistan compared to Afghanistan. There are smaller communities in Iran and India, and a large migrant worker community in the countries of the Arabian Peninsula.

The Pashtuns are typically characterized by their language, their pre-Islamic indigenous code of honor and culture Pashtunwali, and adherence to Islam. The Pashtuns are the world's largest segmentary lineage (patriarchal) tribal group in existence. The total population of the group is estimated to be over 40 million, but an accurate count remains difficult to verify as there has not been an official census in Afghanistan since the 1970s, while in Pakistan, due to the migratory nature of many Pashtun tribes as well as the practice of secluding women, exact figures are to hard to attain.

Pasni : Pasni is a fishing port and major town in Balochistan, Pakistan. It is located on the Makran coast on Arabian Sea about 300 Km from Karachi. Pasni is also sub-division of Gwadar district.

Pasur River : Pasur river is a big river in the Sundarbans area as an extension of the Rupsa river. South of Khulna, the Bhairab or the Rupsa flows further south and is renamed as Pasur near Chalna and falls into the Bay of Bengal flowing to the right of Trikona and Dubla islands. South of mongla upazila the river flows into the Sundarbans. The maximum flow of the Gorai-madhumati passes into this river through the Nabaganga. The Pasur is placed after the Meghna in size in the deltaic region. The river is joined by Mongla canal at about 32 km south from Chalna. Flowing further south the river meets the

Shibsa at about 32 km north from its mouth and debouches into the sea keeping its original name Pasur.

Patan : Patan is a city in Gujarat state of western India. It is the administrative seat of Patan District Patan is an ancient fortified town, founded in 746 by Vanraj Chavda, the most prominent king of the Chavda Kingdom. He named the city Anhilpur Patan after his close friend and Prime Minister Anhil. The city was also known as Anhilwara in the Middle Ages. Patan enjoyed a privileged status of capital of Gujarat, for about 600 years from 746 to 1411. The major Rajput clans of Chavdas (746-942), Solankis (942-1244) and Vaghelas (1244-1304) ruled the Hindu Kingdom of Gujarat from Patan.

Muhammad of Ghor attacked the city in the 1180s, but was rebuffed by the Solankis; Muhammed's general (and later Sultan of Delhi) Qutb-ud-din Aybak sacked the city between 1200 and 1210, and it was destroyed by the sultans in 1298. After the collapse of the Delhi Sultanate at the end of the 14th century Gujarat became an independent Sultanate, and Sultan Ahmed Shah moved the capital to Ahmedabad.

The modern town of Patan later sprung up near the ruins of Anhilwara, and contains many Jain temples. Patan was part of the Maratha state of Baroda from the mid-eighteenth century until India's independence in 1947, when Baroda became part of Bombay state, which in 1960 was separated into Gujarat and Maharashtra.

Patanjali : Patanjali is the compiler of the Yoga Sutra, a major work containing aphorisms on the practical and philosophical wisdom regarding practice of Raja Yoga. ("Yoga" in traditional Hinduism involves inner contemplation, a rigorous system of meditation practice, ethics, metaphysics, and devotion to the one common soul, God, or Brahma/Atman.) Virtually nothing is known about the life of Patañjali, and some scholars believe he is entirely mythical. Various references suggest he lived between 200 BC and 400 AD. Ancient texts often refer to Patañjali as an incarnation of the serpent god Ananta, and he is sometimes depicted as half human and half serpent.

Patañjali is the reputed author of the Yoga Sutra, as well as commentary on Panini's Sanskrit. There are also many ayurvedic texts attributed to him. Nearly all scholars believe these texts were actually written by different people in different eras.

Desiring to teach yoga to the world, he is said to have fallen (pat) from heaven into the open palms (anjali) of a woman, hence the name Patanjali. The Yoga Sutra probably dates around AD 200. Patañjali has often been called the founder of Yoga because of this work, although in reality is more a major figure. The Yoga Sutra is a treatise on Raja Yoga, built on the Samkhya school and the Hindu scripture of the Bhagavad Gita. Yoga is also found in the Puranas, Vedas and Upanishads. Still, this work is certainly a major work among the great Hindu scriptures and certainly is the basis of Raja Yoga. Patañjali's Yoga is one of the six schools of Hindu Philosophy. They give us the earliest reference to the popular term Ashtanga Yoga which translates literally as the eight limbs of yoga. They are yama, niyama, asana, pranayama, pratyahara, dharana, dhyana and samadhi.

Patenga : Patenga is a sea beach located 14 kilometres south of the port city of Chittagong, Bangladesh. It is near the mouth of the Karnaphuli River. Patenga is a popular tourist spot. The beach is very close to BNS Isha Khan Naval Base of Bangladesh Navy, and Shah Amanat International Airport.

Pathanamthitta : Pathanamthitta is one of the fourteen districts of Kerala state in South India. It was formed on

1 November 1982 with headquarters at Pathanamthitta town. Pathanamthitta is a landlocked district situated in the southern part of the state, and is bordered by Kottayam and Idukki districts in the north, Alappuzha in the west, Kollam in the south and has a border with Tamil Nadu in the east. The district was made up from combining areas from the Alappuzha, Idukki and Kollam districts. Major towns in the district are Pathanmthitta, Tiruvalla, Adoor, Ranni, Konni, Mallappally and Kozhencherry. More than 50% of the geographical area is covered by forests.

The district's name is a combination of two Malayalam words pathanam and thitta, which together mean "houses by the riverside". Pathanamthitta is a pre-dominantly agricultural district with cultivation of coconut, rubber, paddy, pepper and tea. The hilly terrain coupled with high humidity make it suitable for rubber and tea plantations.

Patharghata : Patharghata an archaeological site, rather a complex of sites, located in Panchbibi upazila under Joypurhat district of Bangladesh, extends over an area of approximately 9 sq km on both sides of the Tulsi Ganga river. The remains apparently comprise some mounds—Mission mound, Uchai mound, Baharampur mound, Majar of Nimai Shah, Bader dhap, Santal para mound, Kasiabari mound, Kusumba group of mounds, Gangria group of mounds, Bridhigram group of mounds and Bharampur mound. The mounds, located on the lateritic Barind tract, show traces of architectural remains. The whole area is strewn with ancient potsherds, glazed wares, bricks, brickbats, fragments of terracotta plaques and stone sculptures and other minor artifacts.

Pathari : Pathari is a formerly princely state of India, administratively under the Bhopal Agency subdivision of the Central India Agency. The state covered an area of 78 square kilometers and had a population of 6,293 in 1892.

Pathari's Muslim royal house was founded in 1794 by a Pathan of the Barakzai faction from Afghanistan, who rose through the ranks of the Mughal Empire. The rulers of Pathari were styled "Nawab": After Indian independence in 1947, the rulers of Pathari acceded to the Union of India, and the former state was incorporated into the new state of Madhya Bharat, which subsequently became Madhya Pradesh state on November 1, 1956.

Pather Panchali : Pather Panchali, released in 1955, is the first film of director Satyajit Ray's Apu trilogy. The film is a serene and beautiful depiction of a little boy's childhood in the Indian countryside in the 1950s.

The film was made on a shoestring budget by a hitherto unknown director, Ray. Apart from a seventy-year-old woman who made her name in the 1930s on the stage, none of the cast had ever acted before, and many had been plucked from the Indian countryside. After obtaining a grant from the government of West Bengal, Ray completed the trilogy at the behest of the Prime Minister of India, indicating the extent of the first film's cultural impact.

Pathiramanal : Pathiramanal is a small island located on the border of Kottayam—Alapuzha Districts in Kerala, India. The name 'Pathiramanal' means 'Sands of night'. The island is located in the Vembanad Lake. The island is an easily reachable location in the Kumarakom—Muhamma water route. It takes around 40 minutes from Kumarakom to reach Pathiramanal from Kumarakom. The journey through backwaters of Kottayam District is a marvellous experience. The scenic beauty of both sides of the lake as well as that of the island is mind blowing.

Patiala : Patiala is a city in the Punjab state of India. Patiala district is one of the famous princely cities of erstwhile Punjab. Forming the south-eastern part of the state, it lies between 29°49′ and 30°47′ north latitude, 75°58′ and 76°54' east longitude.It is the administrative headquarters of Patiala District, and was the capital of the premier princely state in the former Punjab Province of British India.

The city of Patiala is a famous seat of learning. It houses the Punjabi University, Thapar Institute of Engineering and Technology, Mohindra College, Govt. Medical College, M M Modi College, Govt. College for Girls, Bikram College, Khalsa College, Govt. Ayurvedic College, Yadvindra Public School (most Famous Sports School of Punjab esp for cricket—ex students like, Navjot Singh Sidhu—PLayed for India A team Cricket) and above all Netaji Subhash National Institute of Sports. Patiala is also the sports hub of Punjab. It has a number of playgrounds (both indoor and outdoor) which facilitate practice by the aspirants. The biggest is POLO GROUND, which houses an indoor stadium and open ground enabling a number of track and field events taking place simultaneously.Then there is Yadavindra Stadium, Rink Hall, Swimming Pools at the NSNIS and Defence Club.Punjabi University has its own sprawling grounds. Besides this Patiala also houses very important administartive offices of Punjab state viz. Punjab State Electricity Board, Punjab Pollution Control Board, Commissioner Office, Bhasha Vibhag and also the Head Office of State Bank of Patiala.

Patiala and East Punjab States Union (PEPSU) : The Patiala and East Punjab States Union (PEPSU) was a former state of India. It was created out of the merger of several Punjabi princely states on July 15, 1948, formally becoming a state of India in 1950. The capital and principal city was Patiala, and the last Maharaja of Patiala, Yadvindra Singh, served as Rajpramukh of the state during its short existence. The rajpramukh was appointed by the President of India, but the residents of the state also elected a 60-member state assembly, first elected on January 6, 1952. The Congress Party won 26 seats and Akali Dal 19 seats.

On November 1, 1956, PEPSU was merged into Punjab state. Part of the former state of PEPSU, including the southeastern portion of the state around Jind and the Narnaul exclave, presently lie within the state of Haryana, which was separated from Punjab in 1966.

Patkai : The Patkai or the Purvachal are the hills on India's eastern border with Myanmar (Burma). They were created by the same tectonic processes that resulted in the formation of the Himalaya. They are not as rugged as the Himalayas and its peaks are much lower in height. Features of the range include conical peaks, steep slopes and deep valleys. Three hill ranges come under the Patkai. The Patkai-Bum, the Garo-Khasi-Jaintia, and the Lushai Hills. The Garo-Khasi range is in the Indian state of Meghalaya. Cherapunji, on the windward side of these hills has the distinction of being the world's wettest place, having the highest annual rainfall. Climate ranges from temperate to alpine due to altitude.

Patna : Patna is the capital of the Indian state of Bihar, and one of the oldest continuously inhabited places in the world. Patna lies on the southern bank of the Ganges, as it flows past with the combined waters of the rivers Ghagra, Son and Gandak. At the point where the city is located, the sacred Ganges looks more sea than river: mighty, wide and never-ending. A bustling city of 1,200,000 people, the city is approximately 15 km long and 5 km to 7 km wide. The Buddhist and Jain pilgrim centres of Vaishali, Rajgir or Rajgriha, Nalanda, Bodhgaya and Pawapuri are all nearby. Patna is a sacred city for Sikhs also. Their tenth and last "human" guru, Guru Gobind Singh, was born here. It is the ideal gateway for all the places on this circuit. The monuments in and around the city take one down the history to its glorious past.

Apart from being the administrative centre of the state and its historic importance, the city is also a major educational centre and medical centre. Sadly, because of the neglect by the Union government of India and the apathy of the state government, the educational institutions, some of the oldest and most prestigious in the country, have fallen behind over the last decade. The walled old area, called Patna City by the locals, is also a major trading centre.

Patna Rice : Patna rice, a variety of the species Oryza sativa, and one of the varieties of long-grain white rice, is extensively cultivated in the Indo-gangetic plains, in and around Patna, capital of Bihar state, India. Patna rice is known for its elongated kernel with grain length greater than 6mm, and has been used as staple food by the local people for thousands of years. Sometimes, Patna rice is also called Parimal rice locally.

This mildly flavoured rice comes from the Bihar region of the Ganges plains. It has a robust, long and narrow, opaque grain that keeps its shape well for curries. Basmati rice is closely related to the Patna rice but has a stronger aroma. Patna rice is the most esteemed in UK and USA and is the highest priced rice in the grocery stores.

Patna Sahib : Patna Sahib is located in Patna capital city of Bihar. Guru Tegh Baduhur Ji conducted missionary work here. During this time that Guru Gobind Singh Ji was Prakash (entered into existence, not born, because his soul was free from the circle of birth & death (immortal)) in 1666 and spent his early years before moving to Anandpur. Moreover, Patna was visited by Guru Nanak Ji.

Patola : Patolu and Patola are the terms normally used in Gujarat for art of silk weaving with design in double Ikat i.e. for fabrics where the wrap and weft threads are coloured in section by tie dying before weaving and are then woven to form intricate multi-coloured designs. Today, Patan Patola is one of the finest hand woven textiles produced. Besides, Patan the double Ikat is found only in Bali in Indonesia.

Patriata : Patriata is a hill station situated 10 km east of the town of Murree in northern Punjab, Pakistan. It is the highest point in the area and the hills stand 9,000 feet above sea level. There is a chair lift and cable car system for transportaion to the highest point. The area is heavily forested and there are many monkeys and leopards ir. the area.

Pattadakal : Pattadakal is a city in the Indian state of Karnataka famous for its group of monuments that comprise of initial experiments in Hindu temple architecture. The uniqueness of this place derives from the presence of both the Dravidian or the Southern and the Nagara or the Northern (Indo-Aryan) styles of temple architecture.

Pattadakal was the capital of the Chalukya dynasty of Southern India, who built the temples in the seventh and eighth centuries. There are nine temples as well as a Jain sanctuary. The best known is the Virupaksha temple, built by Queen Lokamahadevi c. 740 to commemorate her husband's victory over the Pallava kingdom. Other temples include Mallikarjuna and Papanatha. The group of mounuments in Pattadakal was designated a World Heritage Site in 1987.

Pattali Makkal Katchi : Pattali Makkal Katchi, a Tamil, caste based political party. PMK participated in the National Democratic Alliance until December 2003, and was thus part of the Indian central government 1999-2003. For the 2004 Lok Sabha elections PMK joined United Progressive Alliance. Now PMK is part of the broad Tamil political front Democratic Progressive Alliance where also Dravida Munnetra Kazhagam, Indian National Congress, Marumalarchi Dravida Munnetra Kazhagam, Communist Party of India, Communist Party of India (Marxist) and Indian Union Muslim League are members. The PMK founder president is Dr. S. Ramdoss. Ramdoss had earlier worked intensively with the Vanniyar Sangham (Vanniyar Union). PMK is dominated by the Vanniyar caste, an OBC community. PMK has advocated the bifurcation of the state of Tamil Nadu, a proposal that was seen as casteist. PMK is mainly based in the northern half of the state.

Lately, he started a movement to save Tamil. Dr. Ramadoss, who is a qualified medical doctor, is the founder of this party. PMK is strongly favouring caste based reservations in education and jobs. PMK could achieve many of their objectives by strong, sometimes violent protests. Statistically, despite reservations in India and in particualr in Tamilnadu, social, economical and education profile of all the backward communities did not improve equally. This is clearly visible in the Northern Districts of Tamilnadu, where the PMK party and their supporting caste is dominant. Traditionally, now the members of PMK party were supporting then Congress,DMK and AIADMK. However, the community could not achieve as much development as the other backward communities could achieve, which were having similar backgrounds. Dr Ramadoss realized that this was because, despite the votebank, the Political leaders who hailed from their community did not have the power to demand the requirements of their members.

After the formation of PMK, Under the leadership of Dr Ramadoss, PMK could manage to get strong share of power both in the Regional Government in Tamilnadu and the National Government. Though their share of MLAs / MPs were not large, they were forming the decisive minority, which were badly needed by large parties to form stable Governments. Dr Anbumani Ramadoss is currently is the Health Minister in the Government of India. Dr Anbumani, who is also a qualified Doctor, is the son of Dr Ramadoss. For a long time, the politics in Tamilnadu, like in all other states is dominated by caste affiliations. Most other parties and their leaders were not directly and openly supporting their castes though, it was PMK which has started this trend. The other communities are trying to emulate this model and are not very successful yet.

Patua : Patuas sing songs, composed by the village poets who pick up the subject matter from the Ramayana, the Mahabharata and the puranas and more recently from novels. Some of the songs are simple in thought and language, while others have a deeper meaning and are shrouded in a jumble of words. 'Patuas' are of four kinds though all of them worship the same deity under different names. The difference lies in religious rituals and not in the aims and objects of worship. The 'Ghata patua' dances, sings and performs physical exercises in different villages. The best of the devotees leads a party of Patuas to walk on a fire of burning charcoal.

Pauri : Pauri is one of the Seven Districts of Garhwal region in Uttaranchal. Known for its panoramic view and natural beauty, Pauri also hosts several places of religious and tourist interest. The prestigious HNB Garhwal University, Sirnagar also falls in Pauri District. Lansdowne, Dhari Devi, Srinagar, Khirsu, Kotdwar are few among the several tourist attractions.

Pav Bhaji : Pav bhaji or pao bhaji is a specialty Portugues/Indian dish created by a Gujarati man in

Mumbai, India. In Hindi pav means bread and bhaji means a curry and vegetable mix. As it's cheap and filling, the pav bhaji can sometimes be a Mumbaikar's breakfast, lunch and dinner.

The pav bhaji consists of the bhaji and the pav (bread) garnished with coriander and chopped onions. The bhaji is usually potato-based. Potatoes are mashed or diced on a flat pan called a tava, and made into a thick gravy after adding diced tomatoes, green peas, carrots or other vegetables. A special blend of spices called the pav bhaji masala is added to this thick gravy. The gravy is then allowed to simmer on the pan for a few minutes and is served hot in a flat dish with a tablespoon of butter on top. The pav (bread) is roasted on the same pan with an ample amount of butter and masala until golden brown, and garnished with diced onion and a slice of lemon and served with the bhaji.The pav bhaji is mostly available on hand carts popularly known as Pav bhaji ki Gaadi, on the streets of Mumbai. It is also available in almost all hotels and eateries in Mumbai. Pav bhaji is to Mumbai what pasta is to Italy or the hamburger is to America.

Pawapuri : Pawapuri in Bihar is a holy site for Jains, located 38 kilometers from Rajgir and 90 kilometers from Patna, India. Around 500 BC, Lord Mahavira, the last thirthankar and founder of Jainism, breathed his last here. He was cremated at Pawapuri, also known as Apapuri ("the sinless town"). There was a great rush to collect his ashes, with the result that so much soil was removed from the place of his cremation that a pond was created.

Payasam : Payasam (Hindi: kheer) is a traditional Indian and Pakistani dish, a rice pudding typically made by boiling rice with milk and sugar. It is often flavored with cardamom and pistachios. It is an essential dish in many Hindu and Muslim feasts and celebrations in South Asia. Payasam is served as an offering to the Gods in

Hindu temples during rituals and ceremonies. Kheer is eaten at Muslim weddings and prepared on the feasts of Eid ul-Fitr and Eid ul-Adha. In Southern India, payasam is an integral part of Hindu culture. In the southern Indian state of Kerala, people have a particular affinity towards this dish. The payasams served in the temples of Guruvayoor and Ambalappuzha are renowned all over the region. The dish is also a must-have in all wedding feasts.

While payasam is traditionally made with rice, it can also be made with other ingredients like Vermicelli (semiya), ada, coconut and such.

Pazhassi Raja : Kerala Varma Pazhassi Raja, known as the Lion of Kerala, was the king of the Kottayam royal family of Malabar in Kerala, India during the last decades of the 18th century. He achieved the title Veera (brave) when he organized a freedom fight against British rule in guerilla warfare model.

While the British were busy with the political settlement of the district, a serious revolt was headed by Kerala Varma Pazhassi Raja of the Padinjare Kovilakom of the Kottayam family. The potent cause of the revolt was the unpopular revenue policy followed by the British East India Company in Malabar. He stopped all collections of revenue in Kottayam. The Raja further threatened to cut down all the black pepper vines if the Company's officers persisted in revenue collection.

In April 1796, a determined effort was made by the British to capture the Raja in his own palace at Pazhassi. This was in vain. On December 18, the British Commissioner issued a proclamation forbidding the people to assemble or to assist the Pazhassi Raja and warning them that if they did so, they would be considered as irreconcilable enemies of the Company and that their property would be confiscated.

On December 30, a futile attempt was made to reconcile the differences between the Raja and the Company. On 8th January 1797, PazhassiRaja's men launched daring attack on the havildar's guard stationed at Pazhassi and the whole party except one man was killed. In the battles fought on three successive days, 9th, lOth and 2nd March 1797, the detachment made by the Company forces was overpowered by the swords, spears, bows and arrows of Pazhassi Raja's men. As the situation was full of perils, a reconciliation with the i Pazhassi Raja became a matter of political expediency.

While South Canara and other parts of South India were being Seringapatnam (1799), Pazhassi Raja raised the standard of revolt a second time and; shook for a while the very foundations of British power. Colonel Stevenson's efforts early in 1801 cut off the pazhassi Raja from his adherents in South Malabar and by May the British troops had made much headway and with every port both above and below the ghats in British hands and the whole country disarmed, the Pazhassi Raja became a wanderer in the jungles accnmpanied by his wife and immedia attendants.

On May 24, 1804, Colonel Macleod issued a proclamation waming the people that they would be treated as rebels if they failed to fumish information about rebel movements and if they helped the Pazhassi troops with arms, ammunition or provisions. Finally the proclamation of June 16 offered rewards for the apprehension of Pazhassi—Raja, tWO Other members of his family and his principal lieutenants and declared their estates and properties confiscated from that date.

On 1 st November, Baber took direct charge of the operations and on November 30, 1805 he surrounded and shot the Raja dead in an operation on the banks of a Nullah. The Raja's body was cremated with "customary honours". With the death of Pazhassi Raja, the resistance movement in north Kerala came to an end.

P Chidambaram : P. Chidambaram is the finance minister of India in the Congress-led UPA government (2004- present). He was elected to the Lok Sabha in 2004 from Sivaganga in Tamil Nadu, the constituency from which he was first elected to the Lok Sabha in 1984.

He was minister of state for commerce and also for personnel from 1985 to 89 in Rajiv Gandhi's ministry and was minister of state for commerce with independent charge from 1991 to 1996 in the Narasimha Rao government. He was Finance Minister from 1996 to 1998 in the United Front government.

Peacock Dance : The Khonds, also called Samanlas are the most backward hill men dwelling in the inaccessible hilly region of Visakhapatnam and Srikakulam districts. During weddings and festival which falls in the month of April, the Khonds perform the peacock dance. Pirodi, a kind of flute and the tinkling bells around the ankles are the only musical accompaniments.

All the dancers put on white dhotis, tie anklets called Muyyangam, wear turbans, made of locally growing grass and tugged with colourful rags and fasten bunches of peacock feathers behind at their waists which look like peacock tails whenever they bend forward.

All the dancers stand in two rows in the beginning and imitate the cry of peacock. They form a circle and bend forward from their knees so as to look like a dancing peacock. After paying obeisance to mother earth and the Sun god they commence dancing. Putting their palms to their right legs move their left legs rhythmically, the anklets produce jingling sounds. They step forward and backward while the pirodi produces sonorous motes sitting, circling, stepping, bending and waving kerchiefs in their right hands, they look like dozens of peacocks dancing joyously in a circle. This includes gestures of the bridegroom going to the bride's house.

Peacock Throne : The Peacock Throne also known as Takht-e-Tavous was made for the Mughal Emperor Shah Jahan in the 17th century. The Peacock Throne was yet another example of Shah Jahan's aesthetic sense and artistic character. It was used as the Mughal Imperial throne for a period of about one century. After the decline of the Mughal Empire the Peacock throne was taken from Delhi by Nadir Shah of Persia during his invasion of the Mughal Empire in 1739. In the civil war following Nadir's assassination in 1747, the throne was destroyed. Subsequent Persian thrones copied its style and were also called the Peacock Throne.

Pearl Mosque : The "Pearl Mosque" is a name given to certain structures in more than one country. There is one in Lahore, Pakistan, that was completed in 1991. The Pearl Mosque inside the Red Fort in Delhi, India, that was built by Aurangzeb in 1659-60 is known as the 'Moti Masjid'. Another Pearl Mosque in India is in Agra and was built around 1647-53.

Pehlwani : Pehlwani is a form of wrestling native to India.The name Pehlwani is a result of the relatively recent influence of countries like Turkey and Iran.Though,the Indian wrestling sport itself existed much earlier under the name of Mallayuddha.

A practitioner of this sport is referred to as a pehlwan. An expert or master of this art style of wrestling is called a Guru/"Ustad" (great teacher). In its modern form of pehlwani in India is heavily influenced by the traditional Indian art of Mallayuddha.

Pelling : Pelling is a town in the district of West Sikkim. Pelling is nestled at an altitude of 2150 m (7200 feet). The town is located at a distance of 10 km from the district headquarters of Geyzing. A regular bus service connects the two towns. The access road however is in a terrible condition and in many places it is a one way path. However with the influx of tourists, the region is undergoing a metamorphous, with the roads being repaired and hotels being set up.

The mighty Himalayas and the Kanchenjanga is viewed at close quarters from Pelling. Pelling also forms the base from where trekkers and other peripatetic adventurers undertake the strenuous and arduous treks in West Sikkim. The land around Pelling is still a virgin territory and is bathed with alpine vegetation, with numerous waterfalls lining the hillside. In the months of winter, Pelling is sometimes covered with a blanket of snow.

Pena Ishei : This song is accompanied with the music produced through Pena in Manipur. A Pena is a musical instrument, in which a slender bamboo rod is attached to the round dry shell of gourd of coconut. The shell is cut out to make a circular opening which is covered with a thin, hide covering, to make a drum. A string of the horse tail is fastened from the end of the bamboo rod over the drum. The adjusting pieces are attached to make the string loose or tight on the bamboo rod. Another string is fastened to the curved iron rod. To produce music, the bamboo rod is held in the left hand and the drum shell is pressed against the chest. The curved iron rod is held in the right hand. The string on the bamboo is rubbed with that on the curved iron rod. The theme of the song is the love story of Khamba-Thoibi.

Pench National Park : Pench National Park is situated in Seoni and Chhindwara districts of Madhya Pradesh in India. It derives its name from the Pench River that flows through the National park from north to south dividing the park into almost equal western and eastern halves- the well forested areas of Chhindwara and Seoni districts respectively. It was declared a sanctuary in 1977 but raised to the status of National park in 1983. Later it was established as Tiger Reserve area in 1992.

The area of the National park is 293 km^2. It is located at 21°38' -21°50' North, 79°08'- 79°22' East. The terrain of Pench is covered with small hills and well-stocked teak mixed forest in the southern reaches of Satpura Ranges. Altitude varies from 425 to 620 metres above msl. The temperature varies from 4 °C in December to 42 °C in May. Average rainfall is 1300 mm.

Penner : The Penner (also Pennar or Penneru) is a river of southern India. The Penner rises on the hill of Nandidrug in Kolar District of Karnataka state, and runs 560 km (350 miles) north and east through the state of Andhra Pradesh to empty into the Bay of Bengal. The watershed of the Penner and its tributaries covers part of the southern Deccan plateau, including most of the Rayalaseema region of Andhra Pradesh and part of Karnataka. The Kolar Plateau forms the divide between the Penner watershed and those of the Kaveri, Ponnaiyar, and Palar rivers to the south. The Penner drains the northern portion of the plateau, which includes parts of Kolar and Tumkur districts in Karnataka. The Krishna River and its tributaries drain the Deccan plateau to the west and north of the Penner's watershed, and the low Erramala hills forms the northern divide of the Penner basin. The upper watershed of the Penner includes Cuddapah District, central and eastern Anantapur District, the southern part of Kurnool District, northwestern Chittoor District. The main tributaries of the Penner are the Jayamangali, Kunderu and Sagileru from the north, and the Chitrabvati, Papaghni and Cheyyeru from the south. The Penner then flows east through a gap in the Eastern Ghats ranges onto the plain of Coastal Andhra, where it empties into the Bay of Bengal 15 km east of Nellore at a place called Ootukuru.

Penner River : The Penner (also Pennar or Penneru) is a river of southern India. The Penner rises on the hill of Nandidrug in Kolar District of Karnataka state, and runs 560 km (350 miles) north and east through the state of Andhra Pradesh to empty into the Bay of Bengal. The watershed of the Penner and its tributaries covers part of the southern Deccan plateau, including most of the Rayalaseema region of Andhra Pradesh and part of Karnataka. The Kolar Plateau forms the divide between the Penner watershed and those of the Kaveri, Ponnaiyar, and Palar rivers to the south. The Penner drains the northern portion of the plateau, which includes parts of Kolar and Tumkur districts in Karnataka. The Krishna River and its tributaries drain the Deccan plateau to the west and north of the Penner's watershed, and the low Erramala hills forms the northern divide of the Penner basin.

The upper watershed of the Penner includes Cuddapah District, central and eastern Anantapur District, the southern part of Kurnool District, northwestern Chittoor District. The main tributaries of the Penner are the Jayamangali, Kunderu and Sagileru from the north, and the Chitrabvati, Papaghni and Cheyyeru from the south. The Penner then flows east through a gap in the Eastern Ghats ranges onto the plain of Coastal Andhra, where it empties into the Bay of Bengal 15 km east of Nellore at a place called Ootukuru.

Pentala Harikrishna : Pentala Harikrishna (born May 10, 1986) is a chess player from Andhra Pradesh in India. He is rated second amongst the top Indian players ranking next to Viswanathan Anand. Harikrishna became the youngest grandmaster from India in 2001.

Wipro was the sponsor of Harikrishna, although his contract with Wipro ended in 2004. In November 2004, he won the World Junior Chess Championship.

Perini : The Perini Thandavam is a war dance performed by males and is dedicated to Lord Shiva. It gained popularity under the rule of the Kakatiyas. Dr Nataraja Ramakrishna is responsible for the renaissance of Perini.

Periyar : The Periyar is one of the major rivers of Kerala state in southern India. It is the longest river in Kerala, with a length of 225 km.

It originates in the Western Ghats range near the border with Tamil Nadu state. It flows north through Periyar National Park into Periyar Lake, an artificial reservoir created in 1895 by the construction of a dam across the river. The lake has an area of 55 km^2. Water is diverted from the lake into the Vaigai River of Tamil Nadu via a tunnel through the Western Ghats. From the lake the river flows northwest to empty into Vembanad Lake on the Arabian Sea coast. Its largest tributaries are the Muthirapuzha, Mullayar, Cheruthoni, Perinjankutti and Edamala.

Periyar National Park : Periyar is a protected area, and a Project Tiger reserve in the South Indian State of Kerala in the mountains of the Western Ghats at the border to Tamil Nadu. It lies in the districts of Idukki and Pathanamthitta. The protected area covers an area of 777 km^2, out of which a 350 km^2 part of the core zone was made into the national park. The park is often called by the name thekkady also. Thekkady is approximately 100 km east of Alappuzha, 110 km west of Madurai and 120 km southeast from Kochi.

Periyar is also the name of a 26 km² of large artificial lake within the national park and also of the river flowing through this protected area.

Periyar National Park : Periyar National Park was established in the year 1950 and is named after the Periyar river. Situated in Idukki district, it is spread over 250sq km. The Periyar Wildlife Sanctuary at Thekkady surrounding the picturesque Periyar lake, near the Tamil Nadu border in Kerala, was designated a part of Project Tiger in 1973 and is one of the Project Tiger Reserves in India.

Periyar national park is famous for its scenic beauty. It is covered with dense evergreen, semi-evergreen and moist deciduous forests interspersed with grass lands on the upper slopes. Periyar is probably one of the few places, where one can observe the elephants in their natural surroundings. It is very much known for the tusk less elephants. The animals found in the park are elephant, gaur, sambar, bison, barking deer, Nilgiri languor, pig, tiger, panther, leopard, sloth, bear, jungle cat, small Indian civet and Malabar squirrel macaque.

Permanent Settlement of Bengal : The Permanent Settlement of Bengal—was an agreement between the East India Company and Bengali landlords with far-reaching consequences for both agricultural methods and productivity in the Empire and the political realities of the Indian countryside. It was concluded in 1793, by the Company administration headed by Lord Cornwallis.

Pernem : Pernem is a northmost administrative region or district in north Goa. It is also the name of the town of Pernem, which is its headquarters. It has a Municipal Council. Geographically, Pernem is surrounded by Bicholim taluka on East, Arabian Sea on West, Bardez taluka on south and Sawantwadi taluka (Maharashtra State) on north.

Pernem is counted as belonging to one of the two Goan sub-regions, the Novas Conquistas, or New Conquests. It was taken over, lost and finally regained from the Rajas of Sawantwadi, a state on Goa's northern border that allied sometimes with the Portuguese and sometimes with the Marathas. (The Kingdom of Sawantwadi was integrated into the district of Ratnagiri after 1947 and is now part of the district of Sindhudurg). Later, it was largely belonged to Deshprabhu family as an estate. After Liberation of Goa by Indian Armed Forces from Portuguese, it became part of Union Teritory of Goa.

Pervez Musharraf : General Pervez Musharraf ; born August 11, 1943 (Delhi, India) is the President of Pakistan. He became Head of State on June 20, 2001

Musharraf's parents came from a middle class background and both were college-educated. His mother, Begum Zehra Musharraf, majored in English Literature. She worked for the International Labour Organisation (ILO) and retired in 1986. Syed Musharraf-ud-Din, Musharraf's father, was a graduate of Aligarh University in India.

He joined Pakistan's Foreign Service in a clerical position and progressed in his career, retiring as a Section Officer in the Foreign Ministry. He spent several years in the capacity of support staff in the Pakistan Embassy in Ankara, Turkey where Musharraf spent part of his childhood and learned to speak fluent Turkish. Musharraf was born in Daryaganj in Delhi, India and after the independence of Pakistan, in 1947, his family settled in Karachi, Sindh, Pakistan.

In 1961, he joined the Pakistan Military Academy at Kakul. hE participated in the Indo-Pakistani War of 1971 as a Company Commander in the SSG Commando Battalion. In September 1987, heading a newly formed SSG Mountain warfare unit at Khapalu base (Kashmir) he launched an assault to capture the Indian held posts of Bilafond La pass in the Siachen Glacierbut was eventually beaten back. On promotion to the rank of Major General on January 15, 1991, he was given the command of an Infantry Division and later of a prestigious Strike Corps as Lieutenant General on October 21, 1995.

Musharraf became de facto Head of Government (using the title Chief Executive and assuming extensive powers) of Pakistan on October 12, 1999 following a bloodless coup d'état. On 12 October 1999, Sharif attempted to dismiss Musharraf and install ISI director Khwaja Ziauddin in his place. Musharraf, who was out of the country, boarded a commercial airliner to return to Pakistan. Senior Army generals refused to accept Musharraf's dismissal. Sharif ordered the Karachi airport to prevent the landing of the airliner, which then circled the skies over Karachi. In a coup, the generals ousted Sharif's administration and took over the airport. The plane landed with only a few minutes of fuel to spare, and Musharraf assumed control of the government. Prime Minister Nawaz Sharif was put under house arrest and later exiled. The existing President of Pakistan, Rafiq Tarar, remained in office until June 2001. Musharraf formally made himself President on June 20, 2001, just days before his scheduled visit to Agra for talks with India.

On September 15, 2004, Musharraf backed down from his commitment to step down as Army Chief, citing circumstances of national necessity that he felt required him to keep both offices. This was thus the second time since he took power that he refused to abide by a promise to step down and restore democracy. Musharraf is considered a moderate leader by Western governments. Many believe that Musharraf is sincere in his desire to bridge the Islamic and Western worlds and has previously spoken strongly against the idea of the inevitability of a 'clash of civilisations' between them. Furthermore, he has coined the phrase of "Enlightened Moderation" and is believed to be an ardent promulgator of the same.

Peshawar : Peshawar literally means City on the Frontier in Persian and is known as Pai-khawar in Pashto. It is the provincial capital of Pakistan's North-West Frontier Province. In ancient times the city was known as Purushapura when it was officially founded by the Kushans. Peshawar is situated near the eastern end of the Khyber Pass and sits mainly on the Iranian plateau along with the rest of the NWFP. Peshawar is literally a frontier city of South-Central Asia and was historically part of the Silk Road.

The Peshawar valley is covered with consolidated deposits of silt, sands and gravel of recent geological times. The flood Plains/Zones are the areas between Kabul River and Budni Nala. The meander flood plain extends from Warsak in the Northwest towards Southeast in the upper Northern half of the district. The Kabul river enters the district in the Northwest. On entering the Peshawar Plain, the Kabul River is divided into several channels. Its two main channels are the Adizai River Eastward flows along the boundary with Charsadda District. Another channel branching from the right bank of the Naguman River is the Shah Alam, which again merges with Naguman River further in the East.In general the sub-soil strata is composed of gravels, boulders, and sands overlain by silts and clays. Sand, gravel and boulders are important aquifer extends to a depth of about 200 feet. As further confined water bearing aquifer occurs at depths greater than 400 feet.

Peshwa : The Peshwa (also known in Marathi as Peshwe) were Brahmin Prime Ministers to the Maratha Chattrapatis (Kings), who began commanding Maratha armies and later became the hereditary rulers of the

Maratha empire of central India from 1749 AD to 1818 AD. They oversaw the greatest expansion of the Maratha Empire around 1760, and also its eventual annexation by the British East India Company in 1818.

Petrobangla : Petrobangla is the successor of Bangladesh Mineral Oil and Gas Corporation (BOGMC) which was created through the Presidential Order No 27 on 26 March 1972. The mineral operation of the corporation was segregated and vested with a new organisation, Bangladesh Mineral Exploration and Development Corporation (BMEDC), in 27 September 1972 through the Presidential Order No. 120. The reconstituted Bangladesh Oil and Gas Corporation (BOGC) was short named as Petrobangla through the Ordinance No. 15 of 22 August 1974. In 13 November, 1976, through the Ordinance No. 88, the importation, refining and marketing of crude and petroleum products were separated and vested with the newly formed Bangladesh Petroleum Corporation (BPC). BOGC and BMEDC were merged into a single entity called Bangladesh Oil, Gas and Minerals Corporation (BOGMC) by the Ordinance of the government No. 21 of 11 April 1985. In a partial modification of the Ordinance by the law No.11 of 28 February 1989 and the corporation was short named as Petrobangla and was given the authority to hold the shares of the companies dealing in oil, gas and mineral exploration and their development.

P Gopichand : Pullela Gopi Chand is the brightest star to emerge on the Indian badminton scene in a long time, after Prakash Padukone He was born on November 16th 1973, in Nagaland, India to parents Pullela Subhash Chandra Bose and Subbaravamma who were both interested in sports. Gopichand is indeed a story of sheer hard work, dedication and pure determination for the game of Badminton.

Though Gopichand nicknamed Gops, favoured cricket earlier, his elder brother made him switchover to Badminton. Gopi's skill at Badminton was the talk at St.Pauls where he had his schooling, when he was hardly around 10 years old. He suffered a setback in 1986, when he suffered a multiple ligament rupture. But this young fighter came back to the field with sheer determination and reached the finals of Andhra Pradesh State Junior Badminton ship in 1987, even though he lost the title to his elder brother Rajashekar. By the time he passed out of school in 1988, he had already made a mark in the Badminton field. He did his graduation in Economics from AV College, Hyderabad. In 1989 he won his first single title at the National Championship at Goa and then went on to win the doubles championship also.

By 1999, Gopichand achieved a world ranking of 26 winning the Indian international, Scottish, Toulouse, French championships etc. He received the SAARC gold medal the same year. Always a fighter, he refused to be crushed by his defeat in the 2000 Sydney Olympics and true to his recognition out played the Olympics champions to reach the finals of the All England Badminton ship, finally arriving at the forefront of international badminton. He defeated Olympic Gold medallist Anders Boeson in the Quarterfinals of this tournament. In the Semifinals he defeated world No.1 ceded player Peter Gade of Denmark, and in the finals he defeated Chen Hong of China. He achieved his career best world ranking of 5 in April 2001.

Gopichand was awarded the 'Arjuna Award' India's highest recognition for sportspersons, in 2000 for his excellent performance in the sport. He has tremendous respect for the rich Indian culture and tradition. He is the follower of 'The Art of Living' Guru Sri Sri Ravishankar. He is proficient in yoga and practices it in his spare time which help him to relax and focus better. Gopichand is also interested in music. A disciple of Prakash, this gentleman is considered a good defensive player, precise in his net play. He is employed by the Indian Oil Corporation in Hyderabad, but the IOC has permitted him to spend most of his time training at the Sports Authority facilities in Bangalore. This great player, with the vital combination of mental strength and concentration is sure to take the sport of badminton in India to new heights..

Phall : A Phall is a form of curry. It is widely reputed to be the hottest form of curry available, even hotter than the Vindaloo, with at least 10 or 12 ground chillies included in a standard portion. It is popular in Britain but is often not listed on the menu because of its level of spiciness. Cases have occurred where customers have vomited or passed out as a result of the extreme level of chili contained in a Phall. It is not clear if the Phall is actually an authentic indian dish at all; it may, like the Chicken Tikka Masala, have been created purely to satisfy curry restaurant diners who wanted to eat the strongest curry possible.

Phanishwar Nath 'Renu : Phanishwar Nath 'Renu' (1921-1977) is one of the great Hindi novelists of the post-Premchand era. His masterpiece is Maila Anchal (The Soiled Border, 1954), a social novel that depicts the life of a region and its people, the backward and the deprived. His short story Maare Gaye Gulfam has been made into a film. Another of his short story Panchlight (Petromax)is beautiful in its depiction of human behaviour. One can find many parallels between his and Premchand's writings only that if Premchand is a sea than he is a pond, talking in context of depth and expanse.

Phirnee : Phirnee (or firnee) is a North Indian/ Pakistani/Afghani dessert made from ground rice and milk and is very similar to kheer. The origin of phirnee can probably be traced back to the Mughals in India, but it is not uncommon to hear North Indians say "We've been making phirnee at home since I remember, just cause it has the "ph" sound doesn't mean it is Afghani/Persian".

Phoolan Devi : Phoolan Devi, popularly known as "The Bandit Queen", was an Indian dacoit-turned-politician. She was born into a family of the shudra sub-caste of boatmen called mallahs in the small village of Gorha Ka Purwa, Uttar Pradesh, India. She was married at eleven, but abandoned by her husband and family. Having suffered vicious abuse from many assailants, she was finally driven to take up the life of a dacoit, or bandit. In short order, she had accumulated her own gang, with herself as the leader.

She became known as the "Bandit Queen" who fought authority with knife and gun, and was often popularly regarded as champion of the downtrodden, after the fashion of Robin Hood. She first came to national and international attention in 1981 as the leader of a gang who allegedly killed 22 high-caste Thakur men in a village of Uttar Pradesh, in what was later dubbed the Behmai Massacre. She denied any involvement in the massacre. Pursued by the government and by various rivals, she nonetheless proved difficult to capture. The government of Indira Gandhi and the police finally made a deal with her that she and members of her gang would not face the death penalty. As a part of this arrangement, in 1983 she surrendered on a stage before a crowd of 10,000 people.

Imprisoned without trial for eleven years, she was released in 1994, after Mulayam Singh Yadav, the newly elected chief minister of the state of Uttar Pradesh, directed lawyers for the state to withdraw all charges against her. This occurred at a time when many lower-caste Indians were organizing among themselves and becoming more politically active; Devi was thus tremendously symbolic to this group. After her release,

Devi converted to Buddhism as part of the Indian Buddhist revivalist movement.

Still a popular hero, in 1996 she was elected to Parliament as a member of the Samajwadi Party. On July 25, 2001, she was gunned down by four men in front of her house in New Delhi. She is survived by her husband, Ummed Singh.

Phulbani : Phulbani is a town, which is also the district headquarters of Kandhamal district of Orissa state, India. It is located 211 km from Bhubaneshwar, the capital of Orissa. The region around Phulbani has a variety of flora and fauna.

Phulpati Dance : The Phulpati is another dance, exclusively for unmarried girls. It is a dance of the semi-rural womenfolk in MP. The agriculturist class of Malwa is not very much inclined to any dance by nature. During the Holi festival the revelers cannot restrain themselves from coming out with some sort of dance movements to the uneven manipulation of drums.

Pillars of Ashoka : The pillars of Ashoka are a series of columns dispersed throughout the northern Indian subcontinent, and erected by the Mauryan king Ashoka during his reign in the 3rd century BCE. The pillar is a column surmounted by a capital, which consists of a canopy representing an inverted bell-shaped lotus flower, a short cylindrical abacus where alternate four 24-spoked Dharma wheels with four animals (an elephant, a bull, a horse, a lion in this order), a four lions facing the four cardinal directions.

The four animals are believed to symbolize different steps of the Gautama Buddha's life:

—The Elephant represents the Buddha's conception in reference to the dream of Queen Maya of a white elephant entere her womb.

—The Bull represents desire during the life of the Buddha as a prince.

—The Horse represents—Kanthaka, the horse the Buddha rode for his Great Departure from palatial life.

—The Lion represents the attainment of Buddhahood. The four lions surmounting the capital symbolize the kingship of the Buddha and his roar over the four directions.

There are also non-religious interpretations to the symbolism of the pillars, describing the four lions as the symbol of Ashoka's rule over the four directions, the wheels as symbols of enlightened rule (Chakravartin), and the four animals as symbols of four surrounding territories of India:

—the Lion of the north.

—the Elephant of the east.

—the Bull of the south.

—the Horse of the west.

This secular interpretation is rather contradicted by the presence of the Edicts, which tend to make Ashoka's pillars a vehicle of religious proselytism rather that just a symbol of royal power.

Pin Valley National Park : Spread over an area of 675sq.km, this park is located in the Pin valley of the Spiti region of Lahaul and Spiti district. It was declared a National Park on 9th January 1987. The area has a mountainous track with elevation from 3,700 to 6,600mts from the mean sea level. The park is perpetually covered with snow above 5,000mts.

Pindaris : The Pindaris were the irregular horsemen who accompanied the Maratha armies in central India during the 18th century when the Mughal Empire was breaking up. The origin of their name is uncertain. The Pindaris were loosely organized under self-chosen leaders, and each band was usually attached to one or other of the great Maratha leaders. Their special characteristic was that they received no pay, but rather purchased the privilege of plundering on their own account.'They were men,' writes a chronicler of the period, 'of all lands and religions.They generally avoided pitched battles and plunder was their principal object, for which they perpetrated horrible cruelties on all whom they could get hold of.'

Pinjore Gardens : Pinjore Gardens, also called Yadavindra Gardens are 20 km from *Chandigarh,* 15 km from *Panchkula,* on the Chandigarh Shimla road. Taxis and buses ply regularly between Pinjore, Kalka, Panchkula and Chandigarh. Pinjore lies on the foothills of the lower Shivalik ranges. The fascinating Mughal Gardens one of the most popular picnic spots. A mini zoo, plants nursery, a Japanese garden, historic palaces and picnic lawns await tourists. Especially at weekends, fountains are switched on and after dusk, lights pick up the beauty of the palaces by night.

Special programs are arranged at the Yadavindra Gardens for the Baisakhi (spring) festival in April and for the Mango Festival in June and July. A range of accommodation is available at *Chandigarh,* but a taste of royalty can be savored at Pinjore itself by a stay at the Yadavindra Gardens Budgerigar Motel, run by *Haryana Tourism.* A Bhima Devi Temple and an old baoli in the Pinjore town have legendary connection with Pandavs and *Mahabharat.*

Pippala Cave : Above the hot springs on the Vaibhava Hill in Bihar, is a rectangular stone sculpted by the forces of nature which appears to have been used as a watch tower. Since it later became the resort of Pious hermits, it is also called Pippala Cave and popularly known as "Jarasandh Ki Baithak" after the name of the king Jarasandh, a contemporary of Lord Krishna described in the epic Mahabharata.

Pir Panjal Range : The Pir Panjal Range is a range of mountains that form a part of the Middle Himalayas or the Himachal in India. The well known hill-stations of Gulmarg and Pahalgam are present in this range.

Pir Shah Jurio : Pir Shah Jurio is a archaeological site located in Sindh, Pakistan. Pir Shah Jurio is a mature Indus Civilization village along the left bank of the Hub River. It consists of a small mound, which is nowadays partly covered by a cemetery. From its surface, typical potsherds and other finds were collected. This site is strictly connected with the sea, which is a few kilometers south of it. It was radiocarbon-dated to the third millennium BP, from a sample of Terebralia palustris shells.

Pir Sohawa : Pir Sohawa is an upland scenic rural location, popular for recreational walking and picnics, in the Margalla Hills near Islamabad, Pakistan. Reached by a 10km scenic drive, the summit peak, Mount Happiness, offers views south to Islamabad and north to natural scenery. Pir Sowaha is also visited in winter, as the elevation is sufficient for snowfall.

Pishin : Pishin is a district in the north west of Balochistan province of Pakistan. Prior to 1975, Pishin was a part of Quetta Pishin district. For administrative reasons Pishin was separated from Quetta and was made a new district on 18th January 1975. The district consists of one tehsil, Pishin, and three sub-tehsils : Huramzai, Barshore and Karazat. Over 99% of the people of the area are Muslims. The population of Pishin district is estimated to be over 400,000 in 2005.

Pithoragarh : Pithoragarh is the easternmost Himalayan district in the state of Uttaranchal, India. It is naturally landscaped with high Himalayan mountains, snow capped peaks, passes, valleys, alpine meadows, forests, waterfalls, perennial rivers, glaciers and springs. The flora and fauna of this area has rich ecologocal diversity. The geographical area of the district is 7169 km^2. As per the 2001 census, the total population of the district is 4,62,149. The total literacy rate is 76.48 percent. Pithoragarh town, which is located in Sour or Saur valley, is also its headquarter. The district is the part of Kumaon region of Uttaranchal state and which is also one of its administrative division.

Pithoragarh has many temples and ruined forts reminiscent of the once flourising reign of Chand Kings. There is Tibet plateau situated to the north of the district. Nepal lies on the eastern borders. The River Kali originates from Kalapaani, forms its continuous eastern boundary with Nepal. It is an Indian border district with China. The Hindu pilgrimage route for Mount Kailash-Lake Mansarovar passes through this district via Lipu-Lekh pass in the greater Himalayas. Previously, it was the part of Almora district of Uttaranchal, but, in 1960, Pithoragarh, as a separate district, was created. In 1997 a new district of Champawat was formed out of it, by reorganizing its boundaries. The district is administratively divided into five tehsils, namely Munsiyari, Dharchula, Didihat, Gangolihat, and Pithoragarh. Naini Saini is the nearest civil airport.The mineral deposits present in the district are magnesium ore, copper ore, limestones and slate stone.

Pitru Amavasya : This is celebrated on the Amavasya day in the month of Bhadrapada. When the sun is in the zodiacal sign of Kanya or Virgo and in conjunction with the moon. It is a very auspicious day for offering oblations to the Pitris that is names of the departed ancestors. The whole fortnight called Pitri Pakshas i.e. the fortnight preceding Amavasya is sacred for propitiating departed souls. People go to sacred rivers like Ganga in North India, Godavari and Krishna in Andhra and Kaveri in South India to offer oblations and pindas to their ancestors.

All Hindus take it to be an auspicious day, the twice born that is Dwijas and particularly Brahmins perform the rituals on an elaborate scale according to the rules laid down in religious manuals. The lower castes and particularly the poor people remain content with the offer of a day's ration called Sahityam or Swayampakam (food cooked one self) to their family priest in the name of their departed ancestors. The eatables and special dishes are prepared according to the means of the family. Non vegetarians drink liquor and eat meat for the satisfaction of the departed ancestor.

Piyain River : Piyain river is a tributary of the Surma river, originates from the Umgat river of Assam. The Umgat originates from the hilly areas of Assam. Flowing southward, the river enters Bangladesh through Sylhet district and branches out into two: the Piyain and the Dauki or Jaflong. After entering into Bangladesh, the Piyain follows a 7km-route westward along the international boundary and slighty turns southwest to meet the Surma river at Chhatak. At Pratappur border outpost, the Piyain branches out into three courses: the Old Piyain, the Pabitradhala and the Naiyadala. Currently the original flow of the Piyain follows the course of the Naiyadala and meets the Shari-goyain river at downreach. The Old Piyain and the Pabitradhala receives life during the rainy season.

P K Garg : Commander Pushpendra Kumar Garg (b.22 November 1963) is an Indian sportsperson in Yachting. He formed a team with Homi Motivala and won the bronze medal in the enterprise class at the 1990 and 1994 Asian

Games held at Beijing and Hiroshima respectively. They were also the world champions in the same class in 1993.

P. K. Garg received the Arjuna award for best performance in Yachting for the year 1990 and the Rajiv Gandhi Khel Ratna award jointly with Homi Motivala for overall best performance in sports for the year 1994-95 from the Government of India. He was a Lt. Commander at that time. He is with the Indian Navy.

Pocharam Forest & Wild Life Sanctuary : Located 15 Kms from Medak and 115 Kms from Hyderabad, this sanctuary can be reached by private transport from Medak. Pocharam Forest was the favourite hunting ground of the Nizam.

Pohela Boishakh : Pohela Boishakh is the first day of the Bangla Calendar. Pôhela Boishakh is celebrated in a festive manner in both Bangladesh and West Bengal. In Bangladesh, Pôhela Boishakh is a national holiday. It falls on April 14 or April 15 of the Gregorian calendar depending on the use of the new amended or the old Bangla calendar respectively. In Bangladesh, it is celebrated on April 14 according to the official amended calendar designed by the Bangla Academy.

Pôhela Boishakh is also known as Nôbo Bôrsho, Bangla (Bengali) for New Year, as it is the first day of the first month of Bôngabdo (Bangla Calendar). This day is a very festive time for Bengalis. Baishakhi fairs are arranged in many parts of the country. Various agricultural products, traditional handicrafts, toys, cosmetics, as well as various kinds of food and sweets are sold at these fairs. The fairs also provide entertainment, with singers and dancers staging jatra (traditional plays), pala gan, kobigan, jarigan, gambhira gan, gazir gan and alkap gan. They present folk songs as well as baul, marfati, murshidi and bhatiali songs. Narrative plays like Laily-Majnu, Yusuf-

Zulekha and Radha-Krishna are staged. Among other attractions of these fairs are puppet shows and merry-go-rounds.

Poikkal Kuthirai : This dance involves false-legged dummy horse.

Point Calimere : Point Calimere, also called Cape Calimere and Kodikkarai, is a low headland on the Coromandel Coast, in Nagapattinam district, in the state of Tamil Nadu, India. It is the apex of the Cauvery River delta, and marks a nearly right-angle turn in the coastline. A historic landmark here was the Chola lighthouse, however this was destroyed in the tsunami of 2004. There is a Wildlife and Bird Sanctuary here, which includes the cape and its three natural habitat types: dry evergreen forests, Mangrove forests, and wetlands. The forests of Point Calimere, also known the Vedaranyam forests, are one of the last refuges of the dry evergreen forests that were once typical of the East Deccan dry evergreen forests ecoregion. The Point Calimere Wildlife Sanctuary was created on June 13, 1967 to protect the forests, with an area of 24.17 sq. km. In 1988, the sanctuary was enlarged to include the Great Vedaranyam Swamp and the Talaignayar Reserve Forest, and renamed the Point Calimere Wildlife and Bird Sanctuary, with a total area of 377 sq. km.

Point Calimere is also associated with the Hindu epic Ramayana. The highest point of the cape, at an elevation of 4m, is Ramarpatham, meaning, "Rama's feet" in Tamil. A stone slab which bears the impressions of two feet, and is presumed to be the place where Lord Rama stood and reconnoitered Ravana's kingdom in Sri Lanka, which lies 48 km. to the south.

Pokharan-II : Pokharan-II refers to test explosions of five nuclear devices, three on 11 May and two on 13 May

1998, by India at Pokhran. These nuclear tests resulted in a variety of sanctions against India by a number of major states. On 18th May 1974 India's first nuclear explosion, code named Smiling Buddha, was conducted. After about a quarter century, on Buddha Jayanti, 11 May 1998, the Shakti was demonstrated: Shakti is a Sanskrit word which literally means strength, and Shakti is also the name of the Hindu Goddess of strength. Shakti was the codename for Pokharan-II.

Pokhran : Pokhran is a remote location in Thar Desert region in the Indian state of Rajasthan. Pokhran is the test site for India's nuclear program. The Atomic Energy Commission of India detonated its first underground nuclear weapon there on May 18, 1974. The Indian government, however, declared that it was not going to make nuclear weapons even though it had acquired the capacity to do so. It claimed that the Pokhran explosion was an effort to harness atomic energy for peaceful purposes and to make India self-reliant in nuclear technology, but subsequently, India conducted five nuclear tests on May 11 and May 13, 1998. Since then, India has declared a moratorium on nuclear testing.

Pola Festival : Children play 'GEDI' (walking on bamboo) from the festival of Hareli to Pola. They display various feats on GEDI and participate in GEDI race. Hareli is also beginning of festivals for Chhattisgarhi people. Pola and Teeja follow Hareli. People celebrate POLA by worshipping Bullocks. Bull race is also a major event of the festival. Children play with Nandia-Bail (Nandi the Vahan of Lord Shiva) idols made of clay and fitted with clay wheels.

Polar Satellite Launch Vehicle : Polar Satellite Launch Vehicle or PSLV is an expendable launch system operated by the Indian Space Research Organisation (ISRO). It was developed to allow India to launch its Indian Remote

Sensing (IRS) satellites into Sun synchronous orbits, a service that was, until the advent of the PSLV, commercially viable only from Russia. PSLV can also launch small size satellites into Geo Transfer Orbits. After some delays, the first launch of the PSLV occurred on 20 September 1993. Although all main engines performed as expected, an altitude control problem was reported in the second and third stages. After this initial setback, ISRO met complete success with the third developmental launch in 1996. Further successful launches followed in 1997, 1999, and 2001.

Poleramma Festival : This festival is celebrated for three days in Andhra. A big kumbham is offered and after, it is mixed with the blood of sacrificial buffalo. It is placed on the head of a person who scatters it around the village. At that time no outsider is allowed to stay there as it is believed that if an outsider carries away the Bali, his village would receive the blessings of the gods and not the village that worship the goddess. So the person carrying the bali is watched carefully and swords are waved over to him.

Pollywood : Pollywood, the colloquial name given to the Pashtu language movie industry in Peshawar, Pakistan. The "P" stands for Peshawar and the "ollywood" comes from Hollywood, the American movie industry.

Polo Park : Situated on a small ridge, this park is in Naharlagun and has interesting botanical specimens. There is also a small zoo housed in the park. Handicrafts Centre run by the Industries Department offers a good range of shawls, carpets, carved caskets and the beautiful cane & bamboo work.

Ponda : Ponda is located in the central part of Goa. It's right on top of the Panjim-Bangalore highway. Safa Masjid, a well-preserved mosque, built in 1560 by the Bijapuri ruler Ibrahim Adil Shah, is here. It is a remarkable temple because it is one of two Islamic shrines that escaped the Portuguese Inquisition in Goa. There are also many Hindu temples in the area, the most famous being the Mahalsa, Shantadurga, Mangesh and Navadurga temples. It is very close to the town of Farmagudi.

Pondicherry : Pondicherry is a Union Territory of India. It is a former French colony. It consists of four non-contiguous districts or enclaves and is named for the largest, Pondicherry.

The territory is currently undergoing a name change to the original name of the city, Puduchery meaning "new village" in the official Tamil language. The French spelt it "Poudichéry", which is the closest French approximation to the Tamil pronunciation. At some point, the hand-written 'u' was mistaken for an 'n', and the misspelling stuck.

Pondicherry consists of four small unconnected districts: Pondicherry, Karaikal, and Yanam on the Bay of Bengal and Mahé on the Arabian Sea. Pondicherry and Karaikal are by far the larger ones, and are both enclaves of Tamil Nadu. Yanam and Mahé are enclaves of Andhra Pradesh, and Kerala respectively. The territory has a total area of 492 km^2: Pondicherry (city) 293 km^2, Karaikal 160 km^2, Mahé 9 km^2 and Yanam 30 km^2. It has 900 000 inhabitants (2001).

Pongal : Pongal is an Indian festival to give thanks for the harvest. Pongal in Tamil literally means boiling over. It is traditionally celebrated at the time of harvest of crops and hence is a celebration of the prosperity associated with the event. Pongal is historically a secular festival independent of religion. It is celebrated by all people in the South Indian state of Tamil Nadu. While Pongal is predominantly a Tamil festival, the same period also marks similar festivals celebrated in several other places under different names. In Andhra Pradesh and

Karnataka, the harvest festival Sankranthi is celebrated. In northern India, it is called Makar Sankranti. In Maharashtra and Gujarat, it is the date of the annual kite-flying day, Uttarayan. It also coincides with the harvest festival in Punjab and Haryana, known as Lohri.

Ponmudi : Ponmudi (The Golden Peak) is a hillstation in Trivandrum district of Kerala south India. Its located 61 km north-east of Trivandrum city at an altitude of 610 m. Its is a part of the Western Ghats mountain range that runs parallel to the Arabian Sea. The climate is always pleasant, and the stay here can be arranged by the [General Administration Deaprtment of Kerala Government]]. It is connected to Trivandrum city by a narrow winding road which offers a very scenic view even on the way to the Ponmudi. The tea-gardens here are also very famous. The tourist resort is developed almost half a kilometer before the actual peak, which is often called the Echo Point. Ponmudi serves as a base for trekking and hiking.

Ponmudi : Ponmudi (The Golden Peak) is a hillstation in Trivandrum district of Kerala south India. Its located 61 km north-east of Trivandrum city at an altitude of 610 m. Its is a part of the Western Ghats mountain range that runs parallel to the Arabian Sea. The climate is always pleasant, and the stay here can be arranged by the [General Administration Deaprtment of Kerala Government]]. It is connected to Trivandrum city by a narrow winding road which offers a very scenic view even on the way to the Ponmudi. The tea-gardens here are also very famous. The tourist resort is developed almost half a kilometer before the actual peak, which is often called the Echo Point. Ponmudi serves as a base for trekking and hiking.

Other attractions near Ponmudi include Golden Valley and a number of rivulets and rapids, some even across the road. Located in a rich forest area, this whole place may be of great interest to those who are interested in tropical vegitation. There is also a rich wildlife around these hills. Golden Valley is a sneak-peak offered to the beauty of the hills. It is an access-point to the River Kallar. Well-rounded pebbles, lush green trees, the cool water, fishes and the sheer wilderness of the park enthralls the visitor.

Ponung Dance (Adis) : Adi village in Arunachal has a rich cultural life. The tribal people are famous for their Ponung that is dancing with the accompaniment of songs. A group of girls dance in a circle holding each other by stretching their hands over each others shoulders while the leader-usually a man called the Miri-dances and sings in the centre-holding aloft and shaking a sword like musical instrument called 'Yoksha'. First he sings a line and then it is repeated in chorus by the maidens rhythmically in circle at a low pace. On all important occasions ponung is arranged.

Ponwar : The Ponwar (also Panwar or Pawar) are a Maratha clan of kurmis that ruled the states of Chhatarpur, Dewas, Dhar, and Rajgarh in central India. They claimed descent from the Paramara clan of Rajputs, who ruled Malwa from the 9th to the 14th centuries. Over time, the Rajput ancestors had become almost entirely Maratha in their way of life and outlook. By the beginning of the 18th century, the family had served in the Maratha armies for several generations.Lot of villages of Jats in Delhi and western UP also have Panwar/Puar gotras. The state of Rajgarh came under Ponwar rule in the 16th century. The Ponwar Rawats, later Rajas, became tributaries of Sindhia in the 18th century.

Poonch : District Poonch, popularly known as mini Kashmir, is the smallest in area and the remotest district of Jammu and Kashmir, India. It is bounded by the Actual Line of Control (ALC) from three sides. The 1947-48 war between India and Pakistan divided it into two parts. One went to Pakistan and the other remained with India.

Porbandar : Porbandar is a coastal city in the Indian state of Gujarat, perhaps best known for being the birthplace of Mahatma Gandhi. It is the administrative center of Porbandar District.

The name "Porbandar" came from the combination of two words: "Porai", the name of a local goddess, and "Bandar" means port or harbour. Thus, 'Porbandar' translates to 'Porai's harbour'. Several sources refer to the area as 'Pauravelakul', a name known to have been in use during the 10th century; this ancient name may possibly translate to 'land of Porai's clan' or to that effect. The town finds mention in the Hindu epics as the hometown of Sudama, a beloved friend and class-fellow of lord Krishna; the town has also often been referred to as 'Sudamapuri' on that account.

Located in the extreme west of India, Porbandar is an important all-weather port on the Arabian sea. It supports a population (c.2001 CE) of over 150,000. Given its association with Mahatma Gandhi, Porbandar is today something of a tourist centre and is served by an airport and train line. Its deep sea port was built during the last quarter of the 20th century.

Port Blair : Port Blair (coordinates: 11°40′N 92°45′E) is the largest town in the Andaman Islands and the capital of the Andaman and Nicobar Islands union territory of India. It lies on the east coast of South Andaman Island and is the main entry point to the islands. It is also the headquarters for the Indian district of Andaman, and the local administrative sub-division (tehsil), which is also called Port Blair.

Port Blair : Port Blair (coordinates: 11°40′N 92°45′E) is the largest town in the Andaman Islands and the capital of the Andaman and Nicobar Islands union territory of India. It lies on the east coast of South Andaman Island and is the main entry point to the islands. It is also the headquarters for the Indian district of Andaman, and the local administrative sub-division (tehsil), which is also called Port Blair. The town's population as per the latest (2001) Census of India figures was 99,984.

The town is named for Archibald Blair of the British East India Company, who founded a nearby penal colony in 1789. Port Blair was founded by the British in 1858, the Cellular Jail surviving from this period. For a time during 1943 and 1944, Port Blair was the headquarters of the Indian National Army government under Subhash Chandra Bose. The town is a port, with ferries sailing to mainland India. Vir Savarkar Airport is situated in the city and is serviced by Indian and Jet Airways. It is also home to several museums and a major base for the Indian Coast Guard. Although damaged by the 2004 Indian Ocean earthquake, Port Blair survived sufficiently to act as a base for relief efforts in the islands.

Port Muhammad Bin Qasim : Port Muhammad Bin Qasim is a port in Karachi. It was constructed in the late 1970s to relieve congestion at Karachi Port. Port Qasim was named after the Muslim general Muhammad bin Qasim who captured the area around 712 CE. The port was developed close to the Pakistan Steel Mills complex near the Indus River delta. Port Qasim's residential area is a neighbourhood of Bin Qasim Town of Karachi.

Port Qasim is Pakistan's second busiest port, handling about 35% of the nation's cargo (17 million tons per annum). It is located in an old channel of the Indus River at a distance of 35 kilometres east of Karachi city centre. The total are of the port comprises 1,000 acres with an adjacent 11,000 acre industrial estate.

Port of Karachi : The Port of Karachi is Pakistan's largest and busiest seaport, handling about 60% of the nation's cargo (25 million tons per annum). The port is located between the Karachi towns of Kiamari and Saddar, close to the heart of old Karachi. The port is located close to the main business district of Karachi and several industrial areas. The geographic position of Karachi places the port in close proximity to major shipping routes such as the Straits of Hormuz. The administration of the port is carried out by the Karachi Port Trust which was established in the nineteenth century.

Port of Paradip : Port of Paradip is the primary seaport in the Indian state of Orissa. Located at latitude 20° 55.44' N and longitude 86°34.62' E, it is an artificial harbour which accepts sea traffic via man made lagoons. Former Chief Minister of Orissa Biju Patnaik, who was also a famed aviator and freedom fighter, spearheaded the port's establishment.

Porvorim : Porvorim is the legislative capital of the state of Goa, India. It the situated on the right bank (north bank) of the river Mandovi. The administrative capital Panaji (Panjim) is located on the opposite bank. Porvorim is considered an upmarket residental area as it lies on the prime Mumbai-Goa highway NH-17. There are many institutions in Porvorim, most notable is the catering college.

Posadigumpe : Posadigumpe is a small mountain in Kasargod district of Kerala state, south India. It is an ideal picnic centre and tourist resort located on a hillock 487.68 metres above sea level in Dharmathadka 30 km north-east of Kasargod. From the hill top one can see the Arabian Sea, Manglore, Kudremukh, etc.

Pothohari Language : The Pothohari language otherwise known as Mirpuri or Potwari is an Indo-

European language spoken from the Potwar district around Rawalpindi, Pakistan to the Indian-Kashmiri border in the Mirpur district in Azad Jammu Kashmir. It is closely related to Panjabi and Romani (Gypsy), but is distinct from these languages. There is some dialect continuum with Hindko and the Jhelumi dialect of Panjabi. Pothohari speakers may understand Panjabis both from India and Pakistan, but these groups may not understand Pothohari. Pothohari displays some characteristics which indicate that it is in fact older than Panjabi, disputing the idea that it is a dialect of Panjabi. The Romani language first developed prior to Panjabi, and this shares many characteristics unique only to Pothohari and Romani, and not shared with Panjabi.

Potohar : Potohar (or Potwar or Pothohar) Plateau is a plateau in Pakistan. The area was the home of the Soan civilization, which is evidenced by the discovery of fossils, tools, coins, and remains of ancient archaeological sites. The people, colorful landscape, lakes, hill ranges, flora and fauna are sufficient reasons to explore the land that is largely off the beaten track. But you do not see many backpackers in the area. The local people, Pothoharis, speak a distinctive dialect or language. Gujar Khan is called the heart of this region.

Potohar : Potohar Plateau is a plateau in Pakistan. The area was the home of the Soan civilization, which is evidenced by the discovery of fossils, tools, coins, and remains of ancient archaeological sites. The people, colorful landscape, lakes, hill ranges, flora and fauna are sufficient reasons to explore the land that is largely off the beaten track. But you do not see many backpackers in the area. The local people, Pothoharis, speak a distinctive dialect or language. Gujar Khan is called the heart of this region.

Potwar : Potwar in northern Pakistan is the country of the war-like Gakhar clan, later confirmed by the first

Mughal Emperor Babur; "Sultan Sarang was now of age, and finding that he could not oust his cousin (Hati Khan) by force of arms, he procured his death by posion and assumed the chiefship in 1525. He and his brother made their submission to Babur, and Adam Khan, with a Gakhar force, attended him to Delhi, and for this the Potwar country was confirmed to them by the Emperor. " Rawalpindi Gazetteer 1894.

The Potwar Plateau lies between the Indus river on the west and the Jhelum river on the east. Its northern boundary is formed by the Margalla Hills and the Kala Chitta Range. The Kala Chitta Range rises to an average height of 450 - 900 m and extends for about 72 km. The southern boundary is the Salt Ranges. The ruins of the Shahi destroyed by Mahmud of Ghazni in 11th Century and of ancient Gandhara destroyed in the 6th Century by the Hunas (Indo-Hephthalites) litter the countyside.

Pous Mela : The Pous Mela at Shantiniketan is held evey year around December 22 the date on which the Adi Brahmo shrine at the seat of Tagore was dedicated in 1891. The Mela has developed at Santiniketan and Sriniketan., providing a meeting ground for tribal , rural and elite cultural elements.

Pous-Sankranti (or Makar Sankranti) Mela : Pous-Sankranti (or Makar Sankranti) mela at Tirthamukh in Amarpur sub-division attracts a large number of devotees from all parts of the state. The mela is held at the source of the Gomati river popularly known as Tirthamukh. The devotees take a holy dip in the river on the day which marks the commencement of the Sun's northern course- the last day of the month of Pousa (mid—Jan). Pous-Sankranti mela is also held in other parts of the state of which mention may be made of Burbaria fair (in Amarpur sub-division), Mahamanipara fair at Belonia, Muhuripur fair,

Radhamadhabipura fair at Kanchanpur in Larmanagar sub-division.

Powa—Mecca : Side by side with the Madhav temple in Assam there is a celebrated Muslim shrine at Hajo, called Powa- Mecca i.e. 1/4th Mecca. According to the inscription on the wall of the mosque situated there, it was built by Mir Lutufullah-i- Shiraji, in 1657 during the reign of the Mughal emperor Shajahan. In front of the mosque lies the tomb of Gyasuddin Aulia who made the first attempts to propagate Islam in this part of the world. It is said that the foundation of the mosque partly consists of some earth brought from Mecca.

Prabhas Patan : Prabhas Patan, is situated in Gujarat(Saurashtra) and is a pilgrim place or Tirtha. Here Krishna is supposed to have left his mortal body at the end of Krishna avatar (Avatars), having been killed by a hunter by mistaking Krishna for a deer. As per the writing in Ramayana, Rama, i.e. Krishna in his earlier Rama Avatar (Avatars) is supposed to have given a boon to a monkey king Vali (Hindu mythology) whom he killed indirectly in hiding and not directly fighting with him in front. The above action of the hunter in Krishna avatar (Avatars) is supposed to be in compliance to the boon of Rama i.e. Krishna in his earlier Avatar.

The adjacent photo of 1957 shows the place where there is a board (not clear in photo) mentioning Krishnadehavisargana. This is also confirmed by the local people there at that time as per the piligrim. This pilgrim also remembers the place as Prabhas Paten near Veraval. There is also another board on the tree (not clear in photo) which as far as the memory of the said pilgrim goes, indicates that the sampling was planted by Late C. Rajagopalachari(Ex Governor-general of India).

Prabhat Rainjan Sarkar : Prabhat Rainjan Sarkar (1921-1990) was an Indian philosopher, social revolutionary, poet and linguist. Above all this, however, he is usually remembered for his role as one of the foremost spiritual teachers of Tantra and Yoga of the twentieth century; the founding figure behind Ananda Marga, he is often known by his spiritual name, Shrii Shrii Anandamurti.

Prafulla Kumar Mahanta : Prafulla Kumar Mahanta is a former president of the Asom Gana Parishad (AGP), a major political party in the Indian state of Assam. He had been a chief minister of the state for two terms, and was one of the youngest chief minister's in the country's history.

He is a former president of the All Assam Students Union, a student organization that led the Assam Movement between 1979 and 1985. In August 2005, his membership in the AGP was terminated and he floated a new political party, Asom Gana Parishad (Progressive), on September 15, 2005.

Pragati Green Meadows & Resorts : Spread over 26 acres and an hour drive from Hyderabad, Pragati Resorts offers facilities like swimming, boating, children park, coffee and snack bar, restaurant, conference hall etc.

Praja : Praja Party isa a council party in Bangladesh wmade its debut in the beginning of July I929 as a loose parliamentary group. Evolving with the maiden name of the Bengal Praja Party (Bengal Tenant Party) it transformed itself by the end of the year into a public platform with the name of the Nikhil Banga Praja Samiti (All Bengal Tenant Association) and was renamed the Krishak (Krsak) Praja Party (Peasant Tenant Party) in April 1936 mainly for the purpose of fighting the first provincial elections under the Government of India Act, 1935 thus turning it more or less into an electioneering machinery. It went into oblivion almost immediately after the I937 elections, notwithstanding its electoral success.

The Bengal Praja Party was formed by a coterie of eighteen (of the total of thirty) Muslim members of the Bengal Legislative Council following a snap election held in June I929 with Ak Fazlul Huq as its leader, and Abdur Raheem, a Delhi-born Urdu-speaking Calcutta merchant (not to be confused with Sir Abdur Rahim) as the deputy leader. Other office bearers of the Council Praja Party were Tamizuddin Khan (Secretary), Khan Bahadur (later knighted) Mohammad Azizul Huque and Shah Abdul Hamid (Joint Secretaries), and Fazlullah and Mohammad Hussain (Party whips). The Bengal (Council) Praja Party committed itself to adhere to the majority decision in all matters in the Council. Among other things it declared to champion the cause of tenants and working class people and support the dyarchy and appointment of ministers if their selection was as per the choice of the party.

The Nikhil Banga Praja Samiti, forming the second phase of the Praja Party, sought a broader political base extended actually to the rural hinterland with the slogan of 'land to the tillers'. The Nikhil Banga Praja Samiti was a mixed bag accomodating Muslim leaders of differing political strands, many of whom were Calcutta-based, on its top heavy Executive Committee. Its President Sir Abdur Rahim was flanked by five Vice-Presidents in the persons of AK Fazlul Huq, Abdullah Al-mamun Suhrawardi, Khan Bahadur Abdul Momin, Abdul Karim and Mujibur Rahman. The Secretary of the Samiti, Mohammad Akram Khan, was similarly flanked by two joint secretaries—Shamsuddin Ahmed and Tamizuddin Khan. Though formed late in 1929, the Samiti did not start functioning as an affiliating body till I932, and when it did, a few mofussil tenant bodies, like the Tippera Krishak Samiti, refused to come under its umbrella.

The Samiti's activity was confined to holding annual conferences and adopting pious resolutions airing grievances of the peasantry and demanding their redress. A split occured in the Samiti in 1934 when Abdur Rahim became the President of the Indian Legislative Assembly. Fazlul Huq—faction took control of the Samiti installing him to the Samiti Presidency in breach of a solemn pledge made earlier. With the approach of the Provincial elections under the 1935 Act, the Samiti adopted the new nomenclature of the Krishak Praja Party to win over the rural voters.

The Praja Party, to use the term as its generic name covering all its phases, had, doubtless added a new style and a new dimension to Bengal politics by activating the rural hinterland. Egalitarianism or a social revolution was not on its cards; the social composition of its leadership would not, rather could not, have wanted it. Its leadership, comprising a coterie of elitist Muslims belonging to lesser landowners and higher grades of peasants aspiring after social and political leadership, wanted to dislodge the incumbent Muslim leadership of the province, represented by the higher echelon of Muslim landlords and wealthy urdu-speaking merchants of Calcutta. It found in the Bengal Tenancy (Amendment) Act, 1928 a handy issue to attack the landlords and to win over the peasantry. The Krishak Praja Party made full use of the issue of the abolition of the permanent settlement without compensation to landlords.

Prakasam Barrage : Prakasam Barrage in Vijayawada completed in 1957, the Prakasam Barrage is an impressive 1223.5m long, modern regulator and road bridge that stretches across the river Krishna.

Prakasam District : Prakasam District is an administrative district in the state of Andhra Pradesh,India. The district headquarters are located at Ongole. The district occupies an area of 17,626 km^2 and has a population of 3,054,941 (as of 2001).

Some of the main towns in Prakasam district are Markapur, Chirala, Addanki, Kandukur, Giddalur, Podili, Dornala, Cumbum, Kanigiri and Chimakurthi. Markapur is India's main slates manufacturing town and is where the historic temple of god Chennakesava is situated. Chimakurthi is famous for granite. Dornala is also known as diguva Srisailam, since it is very near the historic pilgrimage of Srisailam. The district was established in 1972 and was named after Tanguturi Prakasam, a famous leader.

Prakash Karat : Prakash Karat, a communist politician from India. The 56-year old Prakash Karat was elected as the General Secretary of the Communist Party of India (Marxist) on the 11th of April, 2005. Karat ushers in a new generational change within the CPI(M) and as a behind the scenes politician, analysts say, he will have a major role to play in shaping up the coalition relationship with the Congress-led United Progressive Alliance government.

Married to social activist and party colleague Brinda, Karat was drawn into the Left movement in the 1960s, as a student in the Madras Christian College. He later went to the University of Edinburgh. He was rusticated there for anti-apartheid protests but taken back on good behaviour. At Jawaharlal Nehru University, in New Delhi, he founded the Students Federation of India and joined the CPI(M) in 1970.

Karat worked underground for one-and-a-half-years during the Emergency rule of 1975-76 imposed by then prime minister Indira Gandhi and was arrested twice. Over the years Karat has kept a low profile but emerged as a key leader of the party. He was elected to the party Central Committee in 1985 and the politburo in 1992.

Prakash Padukone : Prakash Padukone is one of the noted Badminton player of India. He was born on 10th June 1955, in Bangalore. At the age of 14, he became the

National Junior Badminton Champion and at 15, the National Champion.

He was the National Badminton Champion for nine consecutive years during 1970-78. When he was only 15, he made a record by winning junior boys and men's singles badminton titles in 1971. In 1980, he won the Badminton Grand Slam by winning three major international badminton tournaments including All England Badminton Championship. He also represented India in Thomas Cup Matches. In the 7th Asian Games, held at Tehran in 1974, he won a bronze medal.

In the Common Wealth Games held at Edmonton (Canada) in 1978, Prakash won the final of men's single's event by beating Ray Talbot of Britain in straight sets and won a gold medal. In the First World Games held in USA (1981), he was awarded a bronze medal. He also won the Alba World Cup in the same year defeating Han Jain of China.

He received 'Arjuna' award in 1972. He is estimated to have won about 15 International titles in the first half of 1980's. He was ranked number one in 1980 and 1981 in the world rankers. After his career he served as a chief of Badminton Association of India for a few years. Later he resigned. Now he is concentrating on conducting high standard tournaments, camps and workshops specially for juniors through his academy based at Bangalore.

Pran Kishore Kaul : Pran Kishore Kaul is a famous Kashmiri stage personality. In addition to acting, he has directed and written screenplays. He was bestowed an award from the Sahitya Natak Academy for his novel Sheen Tu Watu Pod. He was one of the founders of the Miltsar Kashmir Music & Dance Group, a group that travels widely with the goal of supporting Kashmiri and Indian arts.

Prasar Bharati : Prasar Bharati (Broadcasting Corporation of India) is India's national public broadcaster. It comprises Doordarshan television and All India Radio. Prasar Bharati was established on November 23, 1997 following a demand that the government owned broadcasters in India should be given autonomy like those in many other countires. The Parliament of India passed an Act to grant this autonomy in 1990, but it was not enacted until September 15, 1997.

Pratapsinh Rane : Pratapsinh Rane (also known as Pratapsing Rane or Prataphsin Rane), (born 1939) is an Indian politician from the state of Goa. He is the current chief minister of Goa, having taken office on June 7, 2005. He served as the Chief Minister of Goa five times previously—from 1980 to 1985, 1985 to 1989, for three months in 1990, from 1994 to 1999 and from February 3, 2005 to March 4, 2005, when he was dismissed and the state was put under president's rule. The state was under president's rule for three months and then Rane became chief minister again. Rane has been a member of the Indian National Congress for his entire political career.

Prathamashtami : In Orissa, this festival is celebrated for the well being of the first born in the family, whether boy or girl. The celebration falls on the eighth day of the dark fortnight of the lunar month of Margashira. Oblations are offered to God Ganapathi to protect the child against all hurdles in life. The child is given a new dress, feasted and blessed by the parents and other elders and friends.

Pratiharas : The Pratiharas (Pariharas in Hindi), were an Indian dynasty who ruled kingdoms in Gurjar region of Rajasthan and northern India from the 6th to the 11th centuries. They are called Gurjara-Pratiharas in one late inscriptions that indicates the region of their origin. The Arab chronicles mention they were the rulers of the Jurz (i.e. Gurajara) region. A widely helf belief among the historians was that they were connected with the Khazars and descendants of the Gurjara tribe that arrived with the Hunas the end of the 5th century. Most historians now believe that they were of indegenous origin. The Pratiharas were one of the Agnikula clans of Rajputs, according to a legend given in later manuscripts of Prithviraj Raso. The legend is not mentioned in the 1585 CE Udaipur manuscript.

Preamble : The preamble is not a part of the Constitution of India as it is not enforceable in a court of law. However, the Supreme Court has, in the case of 'Kesavananda Bharati v. State of Kerala', recognized that the Preamble is a part of the Constitution and may be used to interpret ambiguous areas of the Constitution where differing interpretations present themselves. However, the Preamble is useful as an interpretive tool only if there is an ambiguity in the article itself and should not be treated as a rights bestowing part of the Constitution.

An interesting side note concerns the words "SOCIALIST" and "SECULAR" in the preamble. The original drafting used the words "SOVEREIGN DEMOCRATIC REPUBLIC". The two additional words "SOCIALIST" and "SECULAR" were introduced by the controversial 42nd amendment. The amendment was pushed through by Indira Gandhi in 1976, when she had dictatorial powers. A committee under the chairmanship of Sardar Swaran Singh recommended that this amendment be enacted after being constituted to study the question of amending the constitution in the light of past experience.

The wording of the Preamble highlights some of the fundamental values and guiding principles on which the Constitution of India is based. The Preamble serves as a guiding light for the Constitution and judges interpret the Constitution in its light. In a majority of decisions, the

Supreme Court of India has held that the objectives specified in the preamble constitute the basic structure of the Indian Constitution, which cannot be amended.

The first words of the Preamble—"We, the people"—signifies that power is ultimately vested in the hands of the people of India. The Preamble lays down the most important national goals which every citizen and the government must try to achieve, such as socialism, secularism and national integration. Lastly, it lays down the date for the adoption of the Constitution—26 November 1949.

Premchand : Munshi Premchand (July 31, 1880-October 8, 1936) ("Premchand") was one of the greatest literary figures of modern Hindi and Urdu literature. Premchand has written about 300 short stories, several novels as well as many essays and letters. He has also written some plays. He also did some translations. Many of Premchand's stories have been translated into English and Russian.

President of Pakistan : The President of Pakistan Sadr-e-Mamlikat is Pakistan's Head of State. At various times in history, changes in the Constitution of Pakistan have altered the powers and privileges associated with the office of the President. At present, Pakistan has a semi-presidential system of government.

According to the Constitution, the President is chosen by an electoral college consisting of the Senate, National Assembly, and the provincial assemblies.

The Constitution gives the President the reserve powers—subject to Supreme Court approval or veto—to dissolve the National Assembly of Pakistan (triggering new elections) and thereby to dismiss the Prime Minister. The President also chairs the National Security Council and appoints the heads of the Army, Navy and Air Force.

In 1947 Pakistan became a dominion within the British Commonwealth with the British Monarch as head of state (reiging as "King / Queen of Pakistan"). The monarch was represented in Pakistan by a Governor-General of Pakistan. In 1956, dominion ended when Pakistan established its first constitution, and the positions of Queen and Governor-General were merged into the President.

Pakistan's first president was Iskander Mirza, who was also the last Governor General. In 1958, he abrogated the constitution and declared martial law. A few weeks later, he was overthrown in a bloodless Coup d'état by General Ayub Khan who had himself declared President. The constitution was revised, and the President became the ruler of Pakistan. The constitution also stipulated that the President be elected by the people. Elections were held in 1963, and Khan defeated the sister of Muhammad Ali Jinnah, Fatima.

Ayub Khan continued as president until March 25, 1969, and he passed the Presidency onto Yahya Khan. Yahya Khan stepped down after the (Indo-Pakistani War of 1971), and Zulfiqar Ali Bhutto became the new president and presided over the formation of a new Constitution. This constitution was completed in 1973, and reduced the presidency to a figurehead position, giving power to the Prime Minister. Bhutto stepped down as President and became Prime Minister, symbolizing the transition. The President was henceforth elected by legislative assembly members, not by popular vote. Popular vote would be used to directly elect the members of the National Assembly, including the Prime Minister.

In 1978, Prime Minister Bhutto was toppled by General Muhammad Zia-ul-Haq who declared himself President. The presidency again became the premier position in the Pakistani government. Zia introduced the Eighth

Amendment which gave reserve powers to the President's office. Zia died in 1988, and the Prime Minister's office regained leadership of the country. The Presidency retained its reserve powers until 1997, when the Thirteenth Amendment was passed.

However, the 1999 coup of General Pervez Musharraf brought executive powers back to the President's office. National and provincial elections were held in 2002. In December 2003, the Seventeenth Amendment partially restored the President's reserve powers—but made the exercise of those powers subject to Supreme Court approval or veto within 30 days. In January 2004, the Electoral College gave Musharraf a vote of confidence, as result of which he was (according to the Constitution) "deemed to be elected." Musharraf's term of office as president ends in 2007.

Press Trust of India : Press Trust of India is a nonprofit cooperative among the Indian newspapers. It overtook over the operations of the Associated Press of India and the Indian operations of Reuters soon after India's independence on August 27, 1947.

Prince Abdul Karim Khan : Prince Abdul Karim Khan was the younger brother of Khan of Kalat, Mir Ahmadyar Khan, the last ruler of Balochistan. After the British left Balochistan in August 1947.The Khan declared to join Pakistan. However, protests broke out and people demanded provincial autonomy. The refusal to grant autonomy to Balochistan and the continued existence of the Sandeman system re-sulted in civil unrest. On the night of May 16, 1948 Prince Abdul Karim Khan, decided to lead a national liberation movement.

The Prince invited the leading members of nationalist political parties—the Kalat State National Party, the Baloch League, and the Baloch National Workers Party—to join him in the struggle for the creation of an independent "Greater Balochistan." Apart from his political motives, the Prince was a member of the royal family and the former governor of the Makran province; he was upset by Pakistan's recognition of Sardar Bay Khan Gichki as Makran's ruler.

Prithviraj Chauhan : Prithviraj Chauhan (c. 1168-1192) was a king of the Rajput Chauhan (Chahamana) dynasty, who ruled a kingdom in northern India during the latter half of the 12th century. He succeeded to the throne c. 1179, while still a minor, and ruled from the twin capitals of Ajmer and Delhi. Prithviraj reconsolidated control of the Chauhan kingdom and conquered several neighboring kingdoms, which made his state the leading Hindu kingdom in northern India. He campaigned against the Chandela Rajputs of Bundelkhand. His kingdom included much of the present-day Indian states of Rajasthan and Haryana, and parts of Uttar Pradesh and Punjab. To this day, Prithviraj is considered to be a legendary hero and martyr by Hindus.

The Muslim Ghaznavid Empire, which bordered Prithviraj's kingdom to the north, was conquered by the Afghan Muhammad of Ghor towards the end of the 12th century. A dispute over a fortress on the border of the two kingdoms brought the armies of the two kingdoms into conflict at the First Battle of Taraori in 1191. Prithviraj allowed him to go despite his generals asking him not to do so. Following year Ghori came again and the Second Battle of Taraori started. Ghori knew that Rajputs did not fight in the night and only started fighting after sun had come up. He attacked in the early morning hours when Prithviraj and his army were sleeping and was able to win. Nearly 100,000 Rajput soldiers are said to have died in the battle, and Prithviraj was taken captive and imprisoned in Ghazni, where he was tortured and ultimately murdered.The battle may have been the most decisive in Indian history.

Prithviraj Raso : The Prithviraj Raso or Prithvirajaraso is an epic about the life of Rajput king Prithviraj III Chauhan, who ruled Ajmer and Delhi from 1165 to 1192. It was composed by Chand Bardai, Prithviraj's court poet and adviser to the king who accompanied him in all his battles. Chand Bardai belonged to the community of record keepers, poets and scribes called Charans who accompanied Hindu Rajput armies to encourage and exhort the warriors to bravery in battle by reciting the great deeds of their illustrious clan forebears.

Over time, Prithviraj Raso has been embellished with the interpolations and additions of many authors. Only a part of the existing texts are likely to have been the original text. There are many versions of the Raso, but scholars agree that a small 1300 stanza manuscript in Bikaner is closest to the the original "Prithivraj Raso". In its longest form, in the Udaipur manuscript, the epic comprises 16,306 stanzas. The language of the texts available today largely appears to be post-15th century. Prithviraj Raso is a source of information on the social and clan structure of the Kshattriya communities of northern India.

Priya Nath Karar : Priya Nath Karar, known by his monastic name Sri Yukteswar Giri (May 10, 1855-March 9, 1936), was the guru of Paramahansa Yogananda. He was a Vedic astrologer, or jyotishi, a yogi, and an exponent of the Bhagavad Gita.

He was a member of the Giri branch of the swami order. His guru was Lahiri Mahasaya of Benares. Yogananda later styled Sri Yukteswar Jnanavatar, or "Incarnation of Wisdom".

Priyanka Chopra : Miss World 2000 Priyanka Chopra, the fifth Indian to win the coveted crown was born on 18th July 1982 in Mumbai to Capt. Dr. Ashok Chopra and Dr. Madhu Chopra.

Her upbringing in a family belonging to the army has made her travel widely all over the country and has exposed her to the multi cultural Indian society. Priyanka was a resident student of La Martiniere Girls College in Lucknow and studied for a short while at Maria Goretti College in Bareilly. Having completed class 10th from Boston USA her ambition was to become a software Engineer or a Criminal Psychologist.

Priyanka's interest in modeling implanted in her a desire to win the Miss World beauty pageant, a dream she claims to have held for six years. Back in India from US she participated in the Femina miss India contest and then the World pageant which changed her life drastically. Her family, especially her mother has been her sole inspiration.

Priyanka is a genuine, selfless, down to earth, warm and loving personality. She has a penchant for Indian music and dance, a flair for writing poetry and short stories, enjoys reading and theatre, and has worked for several social welfare programmes. Priyanka who believes that her power with words as one of her strongest personality traits, was a topper in English language and has won prizes for Extempore Speech and also for singing and dancing. Priyanka was the only Indian from her class in US to have been selected at state level for the National opus Honour choir.

Priyanka Chopra is the latest of beauty queens to join the Bollywood industry. She did a three month acting course in Mumbai and has signed up films in Hindi and Tamil. Her debut film in her film career is 'Andaaz' opposite Sunny Deol.. Her recent films are 'Waqt',

'Aitraaz', "Mujse Shaadi Karoge" has established her as one of bollywood's top actresses at the moment.

Priyanka Vadra : Priyanka Vadra (born January 12, 1972), a member of the Nehru-Gandhi political family, is the daughter, granddaughter, and great-granddaughter of Indian Prime Ministers. She was born in Delhi to Sonia and Rajiv Gandhi. She is married to Robert Vadra and they have two children.

She attended Modern School in Dehli. She holds a degree in psychology from Delhi University. In the 2004 parliamentary elections, she was her mother's campaign manager and helped supervise her brother Rahul Gandhi's campaign. Notwithstanding, she has said: "I have said it a thousand times, I am not interested in joining politics..."

But very lately (June 2004), she has indicated that she will bear responsibilities in the Congress Party in the state of Uttar Pradesh, and this has also been reported in the media. In a recent campaign speaking to the BBC she said: "I am very clear in my mind. Politics is not a strong pull, the people are. And I can do things for them without being in politics". She makes regular trips to her mother's and brother's constituencies of Amethi and Rae Bareilly and deals with constituents.

Professor Jagdish N. Bhagwati : Jagdish Bhagwati, renowned professor, member of UN Secretary General Kofi Annan's High-level Advisory Group and the External Advisor to the Director General World Trade Organisation (WTO), is regarded as one of the foremost international trade economists of his generation.

He was born in Mumbai, India in the year1934. He did his B.com from Mumbai in 1954 and post graduated in 1956 from Cambridge University with a first in Economics Tripos. He then did his Ph.D at MIT

(Massachusetts Institute of Technology) in 1967. After studying in England and the United States, Bhagwati returned to India in 1961 and served as Professor of Economics at the Indian Statistical Institute, and then as Professor of International Trade at the Delhi School of Economics. He returned to MIT in 1968, leaving it twelve years later to join Columbia, as the Ford International Professor of Economics. Bhagwati is one of the only 10 scholars who hold the title of University Professor at Columbia.

Professor Bhagwati has made major contributions to pure theory and is engaged with major practical policy problems as Economic Adviser to the Director-General of GATT(1991-1993) and Special Adviser to the United Nations on Globalisation. He is a Fellow of the Econometric Society and has been elected a member of the American Philosophical Society, and the American Academy of Arts and Sciences.

He also writes regularly for The New York Times, The Wall Street Journal and The Financial Times. He has written or edited 40 books, written hundreds of articles, and founded and edited two journals, 'Economics and Politics' (1989) and 'The Journal of International Economics' (1971), the premier journal in the field today. Among his famous books are 'In Defense of Globalization' (2004);'Free Trade Today' (2002);'The Wind of the Hundred Days' (2000);'A Stream of Windows' (1998);'India in Transition' (1993);'World Trading System at Risk' (1991);'Protectionism' (1988); 'Economics & Politics' (founder-editor); 'The Journal of International Economics' (founder-editor) etc.

He has been honored with Honorary D.Litt degrees from several universities they are, Erasmus (Netherlands) and Sussex (UK), South Gujarat University. Among the awards he has received are the Mahalanobis Memorial Medal (India), the Bernhard Harms Prize (Germany), the

Kenan Prize (USA), the John R. Commons Award (USA), the Freedom Prize (Switzerland), and the Frank E. Seidman Distinguished Award in Political Economy (USA). Professor Bhagwati has delivered many prestigious lectures, among them are the Frank Graham Lecture at Princeton, the Bertil Ohlin Lectures at the Stockholm School of Economics, the Harry Johnson Lecture in London, the Eyskens Lectures in Belgium, the Radhakrishnan Lectures in Oxford, and the Prebisch Lecture at UNCTAD IX in Johannesburg.

Bhagwati is currently Director of the Program on International Migration: Economics, Ethics and Law at the Columbia University Law School. He presents himself as the human face of global laissez-faire economics. On the personal front Bhagwati, is now living in America, with his wife Padma Desai, who is the Gladys and Ronald Harriman Professor Of Comparative Economic Systems at Columbia University and a scholar of Russian and other former socialist countries' transition problems. They have one daughter, Anuradha Kristina Bhagwati, a U.S. Marine officer. At 70, he is widely tipped as a future Nobel laureate, so respected among his fellow economists for his insights into the workings of foreign trade.

Professor Raj Reddy : Professor Raj Reddy, one of the prominent scientists in computer science in the US, is presently serving as the Director of the West Coast campus of Carnegie Mellon University, USA. Professor Reddy a native Indian, earned a bachelor's degree in civil engineering from Guindy Engineering college of the University of Madras, India, in 1958 and a Master's degree in technology from the University of New South Wales, Australia, in 1960. He received a doctor's degree in Computer science from Stanford University in 1966 and the same year began his academic career as an Assistant Professor in the same University.

Since 1969 for over three decades, the professor has been a member of the Carnegie Mellon University faculty. He served as the Founding Director of the Robotics Institute at the University from 1979 to 1991. For the next ten years, he served as the Dean and professor of Computer Science and Robotics, at the School of Computer Science and now as the Director of the West coast campus.

Dr. Reddy's research interests include the study of human-computer interaction and artificial intelligence. His main area of work is in artificial intelligence in particular with computers that can see, hear, walk, talk etc. His current research project include speech recognition and universal digital libraries, an Information Appliance for rural environments for use by illiterate people, where all creative works of the human race are available to anyone anywhere.

Professor Raj Reddy's achievements are many. He is a Fellow of the Institute of Electrical and Electronics Engineers, the Acoustical Society of America and the American Association of Artificial Intelligence (AAAI). He was elected a member of the National Academy of Engineering in 1984 and also awarded the Legion of Honor by President Mitterand of France. He is a member of the Computer Science and Telecommunications Board of the National Academy of Sciences and was Chairman of the DARPA Information Science and Technology Group from 1987 to 1990. He was president of AAAI from 1987 to 1989. He is on the Technology Advisory Board of Microsoft Corp. and received the IBM Research Ralph E. Gomory Visiting Scholar Award in 1991. He was the Co-Chair of the PITAC (President's Information Technology Advisory Committee) from 1999 to 2001under both Clinton and Bush.

In 1994, Professor Redy received jointly with Edward Peigenbaum, the Turing Award which is the most prestigious in the computer science "For pioneering the design and construction of large scale artificial intelligence systems, demonstrating the practical importance and potential commercial impact of artificial intelligence technology". He also received the prestigious Padma Bhushan Award for his outstanding contributions in computer science and information technology from President K.R. Narayanan of India in an award ceremony in New Delhi. He has been awarded honorary doctorates (Doctor of Science Honoris Causa) from SV University in India, Universite Henri-Poincare in France, University of New South Wales in Australia, Jawaharlal Nehru Technological University in India, University of Massachusetts in USA, University of Warwick in England, Anna University in India and the Indian Institute for Information Technology (Allahabad).

On the personal front, Dr. Reddy's hobbies include walking and mainly reading. He lives in Pittsburgh with his wife of 37 years and they have two daughters. His daughters live on the West Coast, in Silicon Valley, California. He visits his native country once a year, his seven brothers and sister live near Bangalore. Today, this brilliant scientist is among the most respected names in the US in the field of robotics and artificial intelligence.

Project Tiger : Project Tiger is a wildlife conservation project initiated in India in 1972 to protect the Royal Bengal Tigers. It was launched on April 1, 1973 and has become one the most successful conservation ventures in modern history. The project aims at tiger conservation in specially constituted 'tiger reserves' which are representative of various bio-geographical regions falling within India. It strives to maintain a viable tiger population in their natural environment. Today, there are 27 Project Tiger wildlife reserves in India covering an area of 37,761 km^2.

Prothom Alo : Prothom Alo is a major daily newspaper in Bangladesh, published from Dhaka. In Bangla, the phrase Prothom Alo means first light. Matiur Rahman is the current editor of the newspaper.

Protima Gowri (Bedi) : Protima Bedi was an accomplished Odissi dancer and an actress.

In 1990 she founded Nrityagram, India's first and only dance village set up exclusively for the preservation of the seven classical Indian dance styles and two martial art forms of India.

Proto-Indo-European Language : The Proto-Indo-European language (PIE) is the hypothetical common ancestor of the Indo-European languages. There is no direct evidence of PIE, because it was never written down. All PIE sounds and words are reconstructed using the comparative method. Many of the words in the modern Indo-European languages seem to have derived from such "protowords" via regular sound change (e.g., Grimm's law).

All Indo-European languages are inflected languages (although many modern Indo-European languages, including Modern English, have lost much of their inflection). By comparative reconstruction, it is quite likely that at least the latest stage of the common PIE mother languages (Late PIE) was an inflectional language, which was more suffixing than prefixing.

However, by means of internal reconstruction and morphological (re-)analysis of the reconstructed, seemingly most ancient PIE word forms, it has recently been shown to be very probable that at a more distant stage PIE (Early PIE) may have been a root-inflected language, as was Proto-Semitic. As a consequence, it seems to be highly probable that PIE once was of the root-and-pattern morphological type.

P C Sorcar : P.C. Sorcar (February 23, 1913 - January 6, 1971) was the stage name of Protul Chandra Sorcar, a famous Indian magician. He was an internationally active magician throughout the 1950s and 1960s, performing his Indrajal show before live audiences and on television.

Sorcar died of a heart attack at the age of 58 in Ashaikawa, Hokkaido, Japan, on January 6, 1971, where he was performing. He is the father of animator/director/laserist Manick Sorcar and magicians P.C. Sorcar, Jr. and P.C. Sorcar, Young.

Sorcar was born on February 23, 1913 in Ashekpur, Tangail District in Bengal (now in Bangladesh). He studied in Shibnath High School. His initial magic lessons were from the magician Ganapati Chakraborty. He became famous starting from the mid 1930s, when he performed shows in Kolkata and also in Japan and several other countries.

Pt. Jawaharlal Nehru : Pt. Jawaharlal Nehru was born in Allabahad on November 14, 1889. He received his early education at home under private tutors. At the age of fifteen, he went to England and after two years at Harrow, joined Cambridge University where he took his tripos in Natural Sciences. He was later called to the Bar from Inner Temple. He returned to India in 1912 and plunged straight into politics. Even as a student, he had been interested in the struggle of all nations who suffered under foreign domination. He took keen interest in the Sinn Fein Movement in Ireland. In India, he was inevitably drawn into the struggle for independence.

In 1912, he attended the Bankipore Congress as a delegate, and became Secretary of the Home Rule League, Allahabad in 1919. In 1916 he had his first meeting with Mahatma Gandhi and felt immensely inspired by him. He organised the first Kisan March in Pratapgarh District of

Uttar Pradesh in 1920. He was twice imprisoned in connection with the Non-Cooperation Movement of 1920-22.

Pt. Nehru became the General Secretary of the All India Congress Committee in September 1923. He toured Italy, Switzerland, England, Belgium, Germany and Russia in 1926. In Belgium, he attended the Congress of Oppressed Nationalities in Brussels as an official delegate of the Indian National Congress. He also attended the tenth anniversary celebrations of the October Socialist Revolution in Moscow in 1927. Earlier, in 1926, at the Madras Congress, Nehru had been instrumental in committing the Congress to the goal of Independence. While leading a procession against the Simon commission, he was lathi-charged in Lucknow in 1928. On August 29, 1928 he attended the All-Party Congress and was one of the signatories to the Nehru Report on Indian Constitutional Reform, named after his father Shri Motilal Nehru. The same year, he also founded the 'Independence for India League', which advocated complete severance of the British connection with India, and became its General Secretary.

In 1929, Pt. Nehru was elected President of the Lahore Session of the Indian National Congress, where complete independence for the country was adopted as the goal. He was imprisoned several times during 1930-35 in connection with the Salt Satyagraha and other movements launched by the Congress. He completed his 'Autobiography' in Almora Jail on February 14, 1935. After release, he flew to Switzerland to see his ailing wife and visited London in February-March, 1936. He also visited Spain in July 1938, when the country was in the throws of Civil War. Just before the court-break of the Second World War, he visited China too.

On October 31, 1940 Pt. Nehru was arrested for offering individual Satyagraha to protest against India's forced participation in war. He was released along with the other leaders in December 1941. On August 7, 1942 Pt. Nehru moved the historic 'Quit India' resolution at the A.I.C.C. session in Bombay. On August 8,1942 he was arrested along with other leaders and taken to Ahmednagar Fort. This was his longest and also his last detention. In all, he suffered imprisonment nine times. After his release in January 1945, he organized legal defence for those officers and men of the INA charged with treason. In March 1946, Pt. Nehru toured South East Asia. He was elected President of the Congress for the fourth time on July 6, 1946 and again for three more terms from 1951 to 1954.

P T Usha : The first Indian woman (and the fifth Indian) to reach the final of an Olympic event by winning her 400 m hurdles Semi-final. She was born in Kerala in 1964. When she was just 12, she joined a Sports school at Cannanore where she received guidance and training from O.P. Nambiar, the noted athlete coach. Her full name is Pilavulakandi Thekkeparambil Usha.

In the 10th Asian Games held at Seoul in 1986, P.T.Usha kept the flag of India flying high by winning 4 gold and 1 silver medal in the track and field events. Here she created new Asian Games records in all the events she participated. P.T.Usha also won the most medals at a single championship -six at Jakartha in 1985. Her five gold at the 6th Asian Track and Field Championship is also a record for the most number of gold medals by a single athlete in a single international meet.

Usha's success story begins from the 1982 Asiad in which she won two gold medals in 100 meters and 200 meters respectively. At the Los Angels Olympics held in 1984, Usha missed a medal and she had to remain content with 4th place. Yet, she was the first Indian woman runner to have the honour of coming at the 4th place in the history of Olympics missing a bronze medal by 1/100 of a second. She won 17 medals -13 gold, 3 silver and a bronze in four Asian Track and Field Championship during the period from 1983-89.

Usha has won 101 international medals so far. At present she is employed as an officer in the Southern Railway. In spite of her age, married status and motherhood she is still active in sports.

Public Gardens : Hyderabad has several beautiful gardens, one of the most popular being the Public Gardens, which also encloses the State Legislature, State Archaeological Museum, Jubilee Hall, Jawahar Bal Bhavan etc.

Pudukkottai : Pudukkottai District was carved out of Tiruchirappalli and Thanjavur districts in January 1974. The district has an area of 4663 Sq. Km. with a coast line of 39 km. The district lies between 78.25' and 79.15' of the Eastern Longitude and between 9.50' and 10.40' of the Northern Latitude. It is bounded by Tiruchirappalli district in the North and West, Sivaganga district in the South, Bay of Bengal in the East and Thanjavur district in the North East. Pudukkottai was organised as a separate district, on 14th January 1974, comprising the former Pudukkottai Division of Tiruchirappalli district with some additions from Thanjavur district. At present, this district is composed of two Revenue Divisions, namely, Pudukkottai and Aranthangi and nine Taluks, namely, Kulathur, Illuppur, Alangudi, Pudukkottai, Gandarvakottai, Thirumayam, Aranthangi, Avudaiyrakoil and Manamelkudi. There are 765 Revenue Villages. The area of the district is 4663 Sq. Kms. The population of the district is 14,52,269 (as per Census 2001 Provisional figures). The district depends a great deal on the monsoon for its water supply.

Pulao : Pulao is a South Asian dish made of rice. It is made with peas, potatoes, mutton, beef or chicken. Usually served on special occasions and weddings; very high in food energy and fat. Biryani is an Indian and Pakistani dish very similar to pilav. It is made from basmati or similar aromatic rice. This is an original mughal dish introduced to India during the mughal period.

Puli Vesham : This is a popular one-man dance performed during Dussehra and Muharram festivals. An able bodied man with a narrow strip of cloth around the waist, and the whole body painted with stripes like a tiger and elaborate make-up, sporting a long tail, dances vigorously in tiger like strides and wild jumps. A Dappu or Mridangam provides the rhythm. In some parts of Andhra a second man behind the dancer carries the artificial but heavy tail tied to the back of the dancer. The dancer lifts a brass pot full of water with his teeth depicting an unruly tiger's devouring nature and strength.

Pulicat : Pulicat is a town which lies in the Tiruvallur District, in the state of Tamil Nadu, India. It is approximately 40 km to the north of Chennai, on the seaward side of the barrier island of Sriharikote, which separates Pulicat Lake from the Bay of Bengal. Pulicat Lake is a shallow salt water lagoon which stretches for about 60 km along the coast and is today a nondescript fishing village.

The Dutch built a fort here as early as 1609, and it was for a long time their chief settlement on the Coromandel Coast. It repeatedly changed possession, until finally occupied by the British in 1825. It became part of the Madras Presidency, which later became Madras state in independent India, later renamed Tamil Nadu in 1968. The Dutch church has been built over several times and is rather dilapidated today, and the Dutch fort has fallen into ruin. The old lighthouse still stands at the opposite bank of the lake. The cemetry dating to 1600 has been taken under the wing of the Archeological Survey of India and so has survived the passage of time. The grand, Latin inscribed tombs and graves, carved with skeletons rather than the cross, have been quite well preserved. The cemetry lies behind the market and visitors often don't know that it is there.

Pulicat is also a bird sanctuary. Every year between the months of October and March, thousands of migratory birds land here. Though several varieties can be seen, the flamingos are the most, covering the swamps surrounding the lake, giving it a pink tinge.

Pulicat Lake : Pulicat Lake is a brackish-water lake on the Coromandel Coast of southeastern India. It lies at the border of Tamil Nadu and Andhra Pradesh states, 60 km north of Chennai. The barrier island of Sriharikote separates the lake from the Bay of Bengal. Sriharikote is home to the town of Pulicat. The lake is 60 km long and from 0.2 to 17.5 km wide, and is the second-largest brackish water ecosystem on India's east coast, after Orissa's Chilka Lake. The lake is shallow, and varies in area with the tides and seasonal rainfall, from 460 sq km in high water to 250 sq km in low water.

The shallow lake is known for its diversity of aquatic birds, and is an important stopover on migration routes. Approximately 15,000 flamingos visit the lake each year, along with pelicans, kingfishers, herons, painted storks, spoonbills and ducks. The beaches of Sriharikote are an important nesting spot for sea turtles. Although much of the lake is protected as a wildlife sanctuary, proposals for a petrochemical complex, power plant, and a satellite port on Ennore creek have raised concern about the continued ecological health of the lake.

Pulihora : Pulihora is a very common preparation in Andhra Pradesh Indian cuisine. Puli means sour taste.

Pulihora can also be referred as sour rice. It is also known as tamarind rice or lemon rice. In the North coastal part of Andhra Pradesh, viz., Srikakulam, Visakhapatnam and Vizianagaram districts, people used to call it Saddi but younger generations may not know this name.

Pumsavanam : It is a ritual for begetting a male child in Kerala. It is conducted in the third month of pregnancy. If it is the first pregnancy, it can be in the forth month also. The pregnant women consumes one head of barley and two beads of black grain along with a little curd accompanied by religious chanting. Among Nayars and Ezhavas the ceremony is known as 'Pulikuti' a customary rite of drinking the juice of sour fruits by women during the first pregnancy.

Punarbhaba River : Punarbhaba river originates from the depressed lowlands of Baliadangi upazila in Thakurgaon district and ultimately becomes a tributary of the ganges. The upper course of this river is just a few kilometres west of the Atrai. The main source of the Punarbhaba is the Brahmanpur Barind. After flowing south the Punarbhaba meets with the Dhepa river which is a distributary of the Karatoya. Just south of Dinajpur town it flows between the western and west-central Barind, and drains the west of the west-central part. Its valley is 3 to 8 km broad. It joins the Mahananda south of Rohanpur (Nawabganj district). Total length of the river is about 160 km. It has three tributaries—the Tangon, Kulik and Nagar. The Tangon has an entrenched valley, even in the Piedmont Plain. Along the Kulik the land is markedly undulating. The Nagar forms the western border of Dinajpur district for many kilometres. Flowing through India, it again forms the boundary of Bangladesh near Bholahat, then flows through Nawabganj district and joins the Ganges south of Nawabganj town. There are no tidal effects on this river.

Pundit Shriram Sharma Acharya : Pundit Shriram Sharma Acharya (September 20, 1911 – June 2, 1990) was a seer, sage and a visionary of the New Golden Era—Founder of All World Gayatri Pariwar. Pundit Shriram Sharma Acharya undoubtedly belongs to a category of divine rishis. His life and work represent a marvellous synthesis of the noble thoughts and deeds of great personalities like Swami Vivekananda, Sri Aurobindo, Mahatma Gandhi, Socrates and Confucius. Rev. Pt. Shriram Sharma was a rishi of the present age whose heart pulsated with compassion for all beings. Every moment of his life was devoted to the welfare of people and the refinement of the moral and cultural environment. He also pioneered the revival of spirituality, creative integration of the modern and ancient sciences and religion relevant in the challenging circumstances of the present times. His personality was a harmonious blend of a saint, spiritual scientist, yogi, philosopher, psychologist, writer, reformer, freedom fighter, researcher, eminent scholar and visionary.

Pune : Pune, formerly known as Punavadi and Poona by the British, is a city located in the western Indian state of Maharashtra. Referred to as the "Queen of the Deccan," Pune is the cultural capital of the Maharashtrians whose native language is Marathi. According to the 2001 census provisional results, it has a population of 4,485,000 in 2005. This figure includes the population of the city of Pimpri-Chinchwad, which is the industrial twin of Pune. The combined population of the metropolitan region would be close to 5 million in 2005. Marathi is the most popularly spoken language, though English and Hindi are also widely used. The city has witnessed a sizeable investment in the software and automobile sectors, resulting in an influx of skilled labour from all over the country. Several suburbs are now completely cosmopolitan and real-estate prices have boomed since 2003.

Pung Cholom : This dance form owes its origin to 'Kirtan' of Sri Chaitanya. It is performed as an invocatory number preceding the Sankirtana and Ras Lila. It is a highly refined classical dance number characterised by the modulation of sound from a soft whisper to a thunderous climax. There is the interplay of intricate rhythms and cross rhythms with varying markings of time from the slow to the quick with graceful and vigorous body movements.

Punjab : Punjab is a state in northwest India and forms apart of the larger Punjab region, which also includes the Punjab province of Pakistan and the Indian states of Haryana and Himachal Pradesh. The Punjab state borders the Punjab province of Pakistan to the west, Jammu and Kashmir to the north, Himachal Pradesh to the northeast, Haryana to the south and southeast, the Union Territory of Chandigarh to the southeast and Rajasthan to the southwest. The total area of the state is 50,362 square kilometres (19,445 square miles). The population is 24,289,296 in 2000. Punjab's capital is Chandigarh which is administered separately as a Union Territory since it is also the capital of neighbouring Haryana. Other major cities of Punjab include Amritsar, Ludhiana, Jalandhar and Patiala.

The word "Punjab" is a combination of the Persian words 'Panj' five, and 'Aab' water, giving the literal meaning of the Land of the Five Rivers. The five rivers which Punjab is named after are the Jhelum; the Chenab; the Ravi; the Beas and the Sutlej. In 1947, the Punjab was partitioned between newly-independent India and Pakistan along religious lines, with the mostly Sikh and Hindu eastern portion to India and the Muslim western portion of the region going to Pakistan. Punjab is a predominantly agricultural state. The largest grown crop is wheat. Other important crops are rice, cotton, sugarcane, millet, maize, barley and fruit. Textiles and flour milling are the major industries. Road, rail and river transport links are extensive throughout the region.

Punjab Agricultural University : The Punjab Agricultural University was established in 1962 at Ludhiana on the pattern of land grant colleges of USA with integrated teaching research and extension programme. It is committed to continue improvement in the productivity and profitability of agriculture and allied sectors.

Widely acclaimed as Best Agricultural University in Asia, the PAU has achieved distinguished status at the national and international level. It has played a unique role in ushering green revolution in India and has the distinction of winning the first Best Institution Award of the Indian Council of Agricultural Research for the year 1995. At present the university offers 5 bachelors, 51 Masters and 42 Doctorate programmes in 50 departments of 5 constituent colleges. It also offers Bachelor of Education programme and 5 Diploma programmes in its 5 constituent colleges viz. : College of Agriculture, College of Agricultural Engineering, College of Veterinary Science, College of Home Sciences, and College of Basic Science and Humanities. An Institute of Agricultural has been established at Gurdaspur. In 1988 the university shifted from trimester to semester system and in 1993 from letter grade system to evaluation to 10.00 credit point average scale.

Punjab Hill States Agency : The Punjab Hill States Agency was an administrative unit of British India. The agency was created in 1936, and was composed of a number of princely states the present-day Indian states of Himachal Pradesh and Uttaranchal. The Punjab Hill States Agency was created out of the Punjab States Agency, which was created in 1901. The states came under British suzerainty after the Anglo-Nepalese War of 1814-16, and were known as the Simla Hill States. They later came under the authority of the British province of Punjab, with the exception of Tehri-Garhwal, which was under the authority of the United Provinces. After Indian Independence in 1947, the states acceded to the Government of India, most of the states became the new state of Himachal Pradesh, with Tehri-Garhwal becoming part of Uttar Pradesh. In 2000, the northern portion of Uttar Pradesh, including the former state of Tehri-Garhwal, became the new Indian state of Uttaranchal.

Punjab Hill States Agency : The Punjab Hill States Agency was an administrative unit of British India. The agency was created in 1936, and was composed of a number of princely states in the present-day Indian states of Himachal Pradesh and Uttaranchal. The Punjab Hill States Agency was created out of the Punjab States Agency, which was created in 1901. The states came under British suzerainty after the Anglo-Nepalese War of 1814-16, and were known as the Simla Hill States. They later came under the authority of the British province of Punjab, with the exception of Tehri-Garhwal, which was under the authority of the United Provinces. After Indian Independence in 1947, the states acceded to the Government of India, most of the states became the new state of Himachal Pradesh, with Tehri-Garhwal becoming part of Uttar Pradesh. In 2000, the northern portion of Uttar Pradesh, including the former state of Tehri-Garhwal, became the new Indian state of Uttaranchal.

Punjab National Bank (PNB) : Punjab National Bank (PNB), established in 1895 in Lahore, then a part of undivided India is the second largest public sector commercial bank in India with about 4500 branches and offices throughout the country. The bank, along with 13 other major commercial banks of India, was nationalisd on 19th July, 1969, by the Government of India.

Punjab Province of Pakistan : The Punjab province of Pakistan is the country's most populous region and is home to the Punjabis and various other groups. Neighbouring areas are Sindh to the south, Balochistan and Federally Administered Tribal Areas to the west, the North West Frontier Province, Azad Kashmir, Indian controlled Jammu and Kashmir and Islamabad to the north, and Indian Punjab and Rajasthan to the east. The main languages are Punjabi, Seraiki, and Urdu and the provincial capital is Lahore. The name Punjab literally translates from Persian into the words 'Panj' five, and 'Aab' water respectively, which can be translated as "five water" (hence the poetic name land of the five rivers), referring to the Beas, Ravi, Sutlej, Chenab and Jhelum rivers. Part of Indus river also lies in Punjab, but it is not considered one of the "five" rivers.

Punjab is Pakistan's second largest province at 205,344 km²(79,284 square miles) and is located at the northwestern edge of the geologic Indian plate in South Asia. The capital and main city of Punjab is Lahore, which has been the historical capital of the region. Other important cities include Multan, Faisalabad, Gujranwala, and Rawalpindi. The province is home to six rivers: the Indus, Beas, Sutlej, Chenab, Jhelum, Ravi.

The province is a mainly a fertile region along the rivers valleys, while spare deserts can be found near the border with India and Balochistan. The region contains the Thar and Cholistan deserts. The Indus River and its many tributaries traverse the Punjab from north to south. The landscape is amongst the most heavily irrigated land on earth and canals can be found throughout the province. Weather extremes are notable from the hot and barren south to the cool hills of the north. The foothills of the Himalayas are found in the extreme north as well.

The population of the province is estimated to be 86,084,000 in 2005 and is home to over half the population of Pakistan. The major language spoken in the Punjab is Punjabi and Punjabis comprise the largest ethnic group. Punjabis themselves are a heterogenous group comprising different tribes and communities, although caste in Pakistani Punjab has more to do with traditional occupations such as blacksmiths or artisans as opposed to insurmountable social cleavages. The most important tribes within Punjab include the Gakhars, Jats, the Arain, the Gujjars and the Rajputs. Other smaller tribes are the :Awans, and Maliks.

In addition, there is a significant shift towards the usage of Urdu by the educated classes of the province as the Punjabis are the most ardent supporters of the nation-state of Pakistan and all of its national institutions. There is also a nationalist movement amongst the somewhat related Seraikis in the south of Punjab and many wish to see a separate the region into a new province of Seraikistan. Other smaller groups in the province include Hindko, Pakhtuns, Balochs, Kashmiris, Muhajirs and others. The population of Punjab is over 99% Muslim with a Sunni majority and Shia minority. There are small non-Muslims groups of Christians, Ahmadis and Sikhs.

Punjab Regiment : The British Indian Army had a number of Punjab regiments in its fold which was amalgamated to form two regiments, namely the 1st and the 2nd Punjab. At the onset of independence in 1947, the 1st Punjab Regiment being predominantly a Muslim regiment went over to the newly-raised Pakistan army, while the 2nd Punjab Regiment was retained in the Indian Army. The Punjab Regiment is known for its fighting spirit and put up a commendable defence in the Battle of Longewala in the Indo-Pakistani War of 1971.

Punjab Region : The Punjab is a region straddling the border between India and Pakistan. Punjab has a long history and rich cultural heritage. The people of the Punjab are called Punjabis and they speak a language called Punjabi. The three main religions in the area are Islam, Hinduism, and Sikhism.

Ancient Punjab (or the Greater Punjab) had comprised vast territories of Northern India, eastern Pakistan and parts of Afghanistan. It once extended as far as river Yamuna in the east. The Panjabis, i.e., the inhabitants of Panjab, in ancient times, were also known as Vahikas or Arattas. The name comprised such ethnic elements as the Gandharas, Madras, Prasthalas, Khasas, Vasatis, Trigartas, Pauravas, Malavas, Yaudheyas, Saindhavas, Sauviras; the Iranian and trans-frontier peoples such as the Kambojas, Pahlavas; and the persianised Ionians (Yavanas) as well as the nomadic Scythians or Shakas.

The region, populated by Indo-Aryans, has been invaded and ruled by many different empires and races, including the Persians, Turks, Mughals, Afghans and British. Around the time of the fifteenth Century, Guru Nanak founded the Sikh religion, which quickly came to prominence in the region, and shortly afterwards, Maharaja Ranjit Singh reformed the Punjab into a secular and powerful state. The nineteenth Century saw the beginning of British rule, which led to the emergence of several heroic Punjabi freedom fighters. In 1947, at the end of British rule, the Punjab was split between Pakistan and India.

A historical region of the northwest Indian subcontinent bounded by the Indus and Yamuna rivers. It was a center of the prehistoric Indus Valley civilization and after c. 1500 B.C. the site of early Aryan settlements. Muslims occupied the western part of the region by the eighth century, introducing Islam, and although they later conquered the eastern part, Hinduism remained entrenched there. The Mughals brought the region to cultural eminence until their empire declined in the eighteenth century. The

Punjab was controlled by Sikhs from 1799 to 1849, when it was annexed by Britain. It was partitioned between India and Pakistan in 1947.

Once a single entity, it is now split between two nations: Pakistan's Punjab Province and India's Punjab state. The Indian states of Haryana and Himachal Pradesh were also parts of the former undivided Punjab. Delhi had been apart of the British Punjab province. Punjab, India covers an area of 50,362 square kilometres (19,445 square miles). Punjab, Pakistan is 205,344 square kilometres, (79,284 square miles). Roughly half of Pakistan's population lives in Pakistani Punjab. Punjabi is spoken by (approx) 90% of population in Pakistani Punjab and 92.2% in Indian Punjab. The capital city of the Indian Punjab is Chandigarh. The capital city of the Pakistani Punjab is Lahore.

Punjabi : Punjabi is the language of the Punjabi people of the Punjab regions of India and Pakistan. It is an Indo-European language of the Indo-Iranian subfamily. It is an agglutinative and tonal language where words are ordered 'Subject Object Verb'. The Punjab people suffered a split between India and Pakistan during the Partition of 1947. However, Punjabi language and culture tend to be uniting factors in spite of national and religious affiliations.

Punjabi People : The Punjabi people (also Panjabi people) are an Indo-Aryan people and speakers of the Punjabi language, an Indo-Aryan tongue, and can be found primarily in the Punjab region of Pakistan and India. In Pakistan, Punjabis comprise the largest ethnic group at roughly 44% of the total population and reside predominantly in the province of Punjab. In India, ethnic Punjabis can be found across the greater Punjab region which now comprises the states of Punjab, Haryana and Himachal Pradesh and the Union Territories of Chandigarh and Delhi. Significant numbers of Punjabis are also found in a wide-ranging diaspora around the world. The name comes from the Persian words 'Punj' meaning five and 'aab' meaning water. Punjab means 'the land of five rivers.' The five rivers that run through Punjab, originating in the Himalayas, are the Beas, Satluj, Ravi, Chenab and Jhelum. Beas, and Satluj merge into one river retaining the name Satluj at Harike near Ferozepur in Punjab, just before crossing the border into West Punjab (Pakistan) and eventually merging into the river Indus.

Punnathur Kotta : Punnathur kotta (Annakotta) is a small place near Guruvayoor in Thrissur district of Kerala, south India. This place is famous for the Elephant Sanctuary. This place is only 3km from Guruvayoor temple where elephants are trained for temple purposes. Here right now more than 60 elephants are kept. All these elephants were offered by devotees of Lord Guruvayurappa. Gajapooja (Worshipping Elephants) & Anayoottu (Feeding Elephants) are conducted here, as an offering to Lord Ganesha.

Punya : Punya an extinct socio-economic festival, was a ceremony of annual settlement of the revenues of Bengal. It was a pre-British system associated with revenue settlement and revenue collection. Under this system the government invited all zamindars, taluqdars, ijaradars and all other revenue paying people to a function at which revenue demands of the previous year were cleared and settlement of the new made. On this occasion, the nawab held darbars and conferred khilats or robes of honour on the people who could please him. Similarly, the zamindars and other landholders also used to hold punya with his raiyats or tenantry. The raiyats cleared the preceding year's arrears and took the settlement for the new year. The raiyats assembled at the zamindari kachari and took pan or betel leaf from the zamindars or their naibs. Music, dance, jatra, mela, cattle race, cock-fight, boat race, and various other entertaining competitions marked the occasion.

Puppet Dance : It is not known how old the tradition of puppets dances is in Bengal. The first reference to puppets is, however, found in yusuf-zulekha, a 15th century epic. There are three forms of puppets in Bengal: rod puppets, string puppets and glove puppets. The puppeteer manipulates string puppets with strings so that the puppets appear to be dancing. As the musicians play their drums, cymbals and flutes, an artist sings a song and makes the puppets dance to reflect the mood of the song. Rod puppets and string puppets are used to present palagan or narrative plays, usually on the stories of Radha-Krishna and Rama-Sita. Such plays are also composed on contemporary social events. The primary purpose of these plays is didactic. However, they are also highly entertaining. In West Bengal, rod puppets are still popular in the 24 Parganas and string puppets in Nadia.

Puppet Play : This is one of the most ancient forms of folk art in Orissa. The skilful movement of the inanimate puppets in the hands of the artistes holds the audience's attention. Like actors and actresses of flesh and blood, the puppets look lively. In this play in order to hide the secrets and tricks of the play, only one curtain is hung up and another one is propped up from the ground. behind these two curtains the artists perform their manipulations. They send out the actors and actresses of the play through the dividing line.

Pupunki : In India, Pupunki is a village close to the Damodar River separating the Dhanbad and the Bokaro districts near the NH-32 highway. It has its own age old Ashram namely the Pupunki Ashram. Pupunki Ashram was the traditional age old home and educational hub for Gurus and their disciples. To this day the runts of the same remain.

Purana Qila : Literally translated, Purana Qila means "Old Fort". Recent archaeological excavations have exposed evidences such as pottery which throws a new light on the existence of the city of Indraprastha at this place in Delhi, as mentioned in the great epic of Mahabharata. The fort itself is believed to have belonged to the Pandavas. Sher Shah Suri renovated it in 1545. However, he soon lost it to the Mughal emperor Humayun, who made good use of the octagonal red sandstone tower known as Sher Mandal as his library and observatory. Today it houses the Delhi Zoo and a boat club. The historic structure of the Old Fort or Purana Qila has stood witness to the restoration of the city of Delhi, the periods of anarchy, and the rise & fall of empires, which bring alive history of Delhi.

Puranas : The Puranas (Sanskrit , pura?á "ancient", since they focus on ancient history of the universe) are part of Hindu Smriti; these religious scriptures discuss varied topics like devotion to God in his various aspects, traditional sciences like Ayurveda, Jyotish, cosmology, concepts like dharma, karma, reincarnation and many others.

Sage Vyasa is credited with compilation of Puranas from age Yuga to age, and for the current age, he has been identified and named Krishna Dvaipayana, the son of sage Parashara. According to tradition they were written by Vyasa at the end of Dvapara Yuga, while modern scholarship dates them to the latter half of the first millennium AD.

One of the main objectives of the Puranas was to make available the essence of the Vedas to the common man, and the Vedas were basically meant not for the scholars but for the ordinary man. They bring forth the Vedic knowledge and teachings by way of myths; parables, allegories and stories; legends; life stories of kings and other prominent persons; and chronologies of historical events. The Puranas unfolds the principles of Hinduism in a very simple way.

In all these Puranas the goddess Lakshmi is given a laudable place without any sectarian dispute. In the Vaishnavite Puranas, Shiva starts telling the efficacy of Vishnu to the Goddess Parvati. While Shaiva mythology places goddess Parvati, the consort of Shiva, as one half of His body (ardha naareeshvara tattva), Vaishnavites place the Goddess Lakshmi in the heart of Vishnu itself, as if it were a lotus (hridaya kamala). This is to depict the inseparable union of Universal purusha and prakriti, seed and field, or male and female.

Purandara Dasa : Sri Purandara Dasa (1494-1564) ("the follower (dasa) of Lord Purandara Vittala [Lord Vishnu in one of his many avatars.]") is known as the father (Pitamaha) of Carnatic music. The dasas, among them Sripadaraya, Sri Kanaka Dasa, Sri Jagannatha Dasa, Sri Vijaya Dasa, and Sri Kamalesha Vittala, propounded bhakti to the Lord through music over several years. Purandara Dasa is believed to be an avatar of Sage Narada. Sri Purandara Dasa always concluded his songs with a salute to Lord Purandara Vittala.

He is believed to have composed around 475,000 songs, although only a thousand or so of them are known today. All his musical compositions are in Kannada, the state language of Karnataka. He was part of the Bhakthi Movement in India and most of his compositions are designed to reach the common man allowing him to comprehend the glory of God. Today in Carnatic music, no artist's concert is complete without the rendering of a few of his compositions

Purdah : Purdah is the practice of requiring women to cover their bodies so as to cover their skin and conceal their form. This separates the two genders from each other in all aspects of Middle Eastern culture. Women are restrained from participating in many of the activities in which males are prevalent.

Purdah is evident in the Islamic world, but is also observed by other communities in the Indian subcontinent. The usual garment worn is a burqa, which may or may not include a yashmak, a veil to conceal the face. The eyes may or may not be exposed. Purdah was rigorously observed under the Taliban in Afghanistan, where women had to observe complete purdah at all times when they were in public. Only close male family members and other women were allowed to see them out of purdah. In other societies, purdah is often only practiced during certain times of religious significance.

In historically Islamic Arab countries, such as Saudi Arabia, purdah has more cultural than religious significance, being a custom. Even in the United Arab Emirates, where women can wear skirts and similar modest garments, Arab women often observe purdah. A form of purdah is also seen in other religions such as Christianity and Judaism. Certain Christian and Jewish denominations require women to be 'covered' whilst worshipping (if only by a hat or similar symbolic object).

Puri : A puri or poori is an Indian unleavened bread made from a dough of atta (whole grain durum wheat flour), water and salt by rolling it out into discs of approximately 12 cm diameter and deep frying it in ghee or vegetable oil. Traditionally served in South Asia (India, Pakistan, Bangladesh, Sri Lanka) it is best eaten if it is served immediately. This ensures maximum taste and also delights guests with a puffed up version which gradually sinks as it releases hot air. Torn off pieces are folded and used to pick up beans/rice/etc which are too small or messy to be eaten with fingers alone. Puri is usually served at special or ceremonial functions; they sometimes play a part in ceremonial rituals when various vegetarian foods are offered in prayer. Puri is often served with potato masala or with korma. A variant of the puri is the Chola puri which is thrice as big as a regular puri and thus a single chola puri often constitutes a full meal.

Puri : Puri is a city in the Indian state of Orissa. The city is famous for its Jagannath temple. Puri is situated on the coast of Bay of Bengal and is a popular beach resort. iT is the site of the Govardhana matha, one of the four cardinal institutions established by Sri Adi Shankaracharya, the others being those at Sringeri, Dwaraka and Jyotirmath. Puri is also famous for its annual Ratha Yatra, or "Festival of Chariots", when the deities Jagannath, Baladeva, and Subhadra, are brought out of the temple, and placed in a chariot procession. This festival occurs on various dates of the Gregorian calendar, typically in the June or July months.

Purple Frog : Nasikabatrachus sahyadrensis is a frog species from the Western Ghats, India. It was discovered in October 2003 and forms its own family, marking the first discovery of a new frog family since 1926. Common names for this species are Purple Frog or Pignose Frog.

Purulia District : Purulia district (also spelled Puruliya) is one of the 19 districts of West Bengal state, India. Purulia town is the district headquarters. Earlier, the district was a part of Bihar state, India. The District has no such industries to provide economic support to the common mass. Majority of the population are economically weak and need special support from the Government machinery to uphold their economic as well as social life. Purulia became famous in 1995 as the site of the famous Purulia arms drop.

Purusha Sukta : Purusha sukta is hymn 10.90 of the Rigveda, dedicated to Purusha, the "cosmic man". It is the only Rigvedic hymn dedicated to Purusha, and thus, even though appearing in a late book of the Rigveda, the oldest attestation of the Purusha myth. As a creation hymn, its archaic mythological setting is in striking contrast to the famous creation account of RV 10.129-130 with its monotheistic and philosophical speculation. Vaishnavite scholars such as Shukavak N. Dasa have commentated that Purusha sukta identifies Vishnu as the Supreme Being, and it is regularly chanted in Hindu worship. The Purusa-sukta is found in all the four Vedas and is therefore mentioned in the Pancaratras and the Puranas as the most important Vedic hymn (along with the Gayatri mantra).

Purushottam Das Tandon : Purushottam Das Tandon (August 1, 1882 – July 1, 1962), was a freedom fighter from Uttar Pradesh in India, of Punjabi Khatri descent. He is widely remembered for his efforts in achieving the Official Language of India status for Hindi. He was revered as Rajarshi.

Purushottam Das Tandon is one of the patriarchal figures of the Indian National Congress. He presided over the Congress session in Nasik in 1950. He was a staunch champion of Hindi as a national language. and believed in upholding Hindu ideals. He was deeply religious and had considerable influence over the religious sect called the Radhasoamis. He emphasized the essential oneness of Hindu-Muslim culture in spite of palpable differences.Born on August 1, 1882, Tandon had his education in Lahore. He entered the legal profession in 1906. He joined the Congress in 1899 even as a student. He was associated with the Congress committee which inquired into the Jallianwalla Bagh incident. He was imprisoned in 1928 for active participation in the non-cooperation movement. He was imprisoned again during the Civil Disobedience Movement in 1930.From 1932 onwards he was imprisoned a number of times for organizing peasant movements. In

1937-38 and again in 1945 he presided over the Utter Pradesh Legislature as Speaker with great distinction. He was elected to the Lok Sabha in 1952 and the Rajya Sabha in 1956. He retired from active politics in 1956. The Bharat Ratna was conferred upon him on 1961. He passed away in July 1, 1961

Purva Mimamsa : The main objective of the Purva ("earlier") Mimamsa school was to establish the authority of the Vedas. Consequently this school's most valuable contribution to Hinduism was its formulation of the rules of Vedic interpretation. Its adherents (Mimamsakas) believed one must have unquestionable faith in the Vedas and perform the fire-sacrifices or yajñas regularly. They believe in a magical power of the mantras and yajñas which sustains all the activity of the universe. In keeping with this belief, they laid great emphasis on dharma, which they understood as the performance of Vedic rituals. The Mimamsa accepted the logical and philosophical teachings of the other schools, but felt that these paid insufficient attention to right action. They believed that the other schools of thought, which pursued moksha (release) as their ultimate aim, were not completely free from desire and selfishness. In Hinduism, we are all illuminated under the light of god. When we have moksha, we believe that we become closer to god. According to the Mimamsa, the very striving for liberation stemmed from a selfish desire to be free. Only by acting in accordance with the prescriptions of the Vedas could one attain salvation (rather than liberation)—which includes a belief in the varna and ashrama system. At a later stage, however, the Mimamsa school changed its views in this regard and began to teach the doctrines of God and mukti (freedom). Its adherents then advocated the release or escape from the soul from its constraints through what was known as jnana (enlightened activity). While Mimamsa does not receive much scholarly attention these days, its influence can be felt in the life of the practising Hindu. All Hindu ritual, ceremony and religious law is influenced by it.

Purvanchal : Purvanchal is a geographic region of north-central India, which comprises the eastern end of Uttar Pradesh state. It is bounded by Nepal to the north, Bihar state to the east, Bagelkhand region of Madhya Pradesh state to the south, and the Awadh region of Uttar Pradesh to the west. It is one of the Aspirant states of India. The region lies on the Indo-Gangetic plain, and is densely populated. Most of the countryside is given to intensive agriculture. Bhojpuri is the predominant language or dialect in the region, in addition to Hindi. Like Bihar state just to the east, slow economic growth, agricultural mechanization, and the closure of sugar mills have led to increased unemployment, social and political discontent, and some unrest in the region. In 1991 the government of Uttar Pradesh established the Purvanchal Vikas Nidhi, to fund regional development projects that advance balanced development, meet local needs, and redress regional disparities.

Purvanchal : Purvanchal is a geographic region of north-central India, which comprises the eastern end of Uttar Pradesh state. It is bounded by Nepal to the north, Bihar state to the east, Bagelkhand region of Madhya Pradesh state to the south, and the Awadh region of Uttar Pradesh to the west. It is one of the Aspirant states of India. The region lies on the Indo-Gangetic plain, and is densely populated. Most of the countryside is given to intensive agriculture.

Bhojpuri is the predominant language or dialect in the region, in addition to Hindi. Like Bihar state just to the east, slow economic growth, agricultural mechanization, and the closure of sugar mills have led to increased unemployment, social and political discontent, and some unrest in the region. In 1991 the government of Uttar Pradesh established the Purvanchal Vikas Nidhi, to fund regional development projects that advance balanced development, meet local needs, and redress regional disparities.

Pushkalavati : Pushkalavati is an ancient site situated in Peshawar valley in Sarhad, Pakistan. It is located on the banks of Swat River, near its junction with Kabul River, now it is known as Charsadda. Puskalavati meaning Lotus City was the capital of ancient kingdom Gandhara from the 6th century BC to 2nd century AD. The ruins of Pushkalavati consist of many stupas and sites of two old cities.

Pushkar Fair : Of singular improtance is the annual fair held at Pushkar, near Ajmer. Thousands of pilgrims come to bathe in the holy waters of the Pushkar lake. Legend has it that the lake appeared miraculously on the spo, where petals of a lotus blossom fell from the hands of Lord Brahma, the creator. Pushkar has an atmosphere of an ancient religious town, peaceful and secluded. But, for twelve days in the month of Kartik, it is transformed into a spectacular fair ground. The fair is overwhelming in its magnitude and in its visual impact. Vendors peddle their dazzling range of wares in hundreds of roadside stalls. Beautiful camels raced and paraded are also bought and sold.

Gaily canopied booths selling snacks, sweetmeats, ice crushes, bangles, brassware, cloth and camel saddles and halters are a photographer's delight. In the evening, the entire amosphere reverberates with the ringing of bells. At night, hundreds of small oil lamps placed on green leaves, set the lake alight. Floated by worshippers after the arti puja, this act of worship is called 'deepdan'. A special tourist village complex is set up the Rajasthan Tourism development Corporation to cater to the rush. This not only offers tented accommodation, but also has a round-the-clock Coffee Shop, Dining Hall, Tourist Information Counter, Foreign Currency Exchage Counter, Post Office and Medical aid facilities.

Pushkar Lake : Pushkar Lake is an artificial lake in Rajasthan state of western India. It is located near the town of Pushkar in Ajmer District. The lake was created in the 12th century when a dam was built across the headwaters of the Luni River. Legend has it that the lake was created when a lotus blossom dropped from the hand of the god Brahma into the Pushkar valley. Thousands of pilgrims come to bathe in the waters of the lake during the festival of Kartik Poornima in November.

Puthandu : Puthandu (Tamil New Year) On the Tamil New Year's Day, a big Car Festival is held at Tiruvadamarudur near Kumbakonam. Festivals are also held at Tiruchirapalli, Kanchipuram and many other places. The Tamil New Year (variously called the Thamizh Puthaandu and Thamizh Varusha Pirappu) and Vishu are celebrated on the same day respectively in the Southern Indian states of Tamil Nadu and Kerala. They generally fall on 13 April or 14 April. The first month of the Tamil New Year is called Chithrai. Every year in the month of Chithrai, in the temple city of Madurai, the Chithrai Thiruvizha is celebrated in the Meenakshi Temple. A huge exhibition is also held, called Chithrai Porutkaatchi. In some parts of Southern Tamil Nadu, it is also called Chithrai Vishu. The day is marked with a feast in Hindu homes and the entrance to the houses is decorated elaborately with kolams.

Puttaparthi : Puttaparthi is the birth place and abode of Sathya Sai Baba. Situated in the Anantapur district of

Andhra Pradesh, Puttaparthi draws thousands of the guru's devotees from all over the world. Puttaparthi houses Prashanthi Nilayam, the ashram of the Baba. It is well connected by road, rail and air to the outer world. It used to be a small, isolated, backward village till the late 1960s when the presence of Sathya Sai Baba attracted devotees.

Puttaparthi also has a charitable hospital, the Anjaneya (Hanuman) Swamy Temple, the Village Mosque, the Sathyabhama Temple, and the Sri Sathya Sai Hill View Stadium. Puttaparthi ashram of Sai Baba also provides rooms for retirees for life. They can book a room at the ashram by paying a fixed amount of money upfront. Thereafter all expenses like medical, food etc, are borne by Baba's ashram. This has given a chance to old people to live in a peaceful, clean habitat where they are well taken care of.

Putu Mayam : Putu mayam is a sweet dish of rice noodles with coconut and jaggery as main ingredients. It is popular in southern India, Sri Lanka, Malaysia, and Singapore, as a snack or breakfast food. The process for making putu mayam (also known as string hoppers in English) consists of mixing rice flour or iddiyappam flour with water and/or coconut milk, and pressing the dough through a sieve to make vermicelli-like noodles. These are steamed, usually with the addition of juice from the aromatic pandan leaf (screwpine) as flavoring. The noodles are served with grated coconut and jaggery, or, preferably, gur (date palm sugar). In some areas, gula melaka (coconut palm sugar) is the favorite sweetener.

P V Narasimha Rao : Pamulaparthi Venkata Narasimha Rao was the ninth Prime Minister of the Republic of India, and led one of the most important administrations in India's modern history that oversaw major economic transformation and checked national security crises.

A polyglot, Rao could speak 17 languages, including Urdu, Marathi, Hindi, Telugu and English with fluency akin to a native speaker. His mothertongue was Telugu. Along with Devulapalli Ramanuja Rao and sri Kaloji Narayana Rao, a great human rights activist in India, P.V. edited a Telugu bi-weekly magazine called "Kakatiya" in his early 20's. His father's name was P. V. Ranga Rao. They belonged to a village called "Vangara" in Karimnagar District of Andhra Pradesh, India. He also learned several European languages that are typically not spoken in India, including French and Spanish. Rao studied at Osmania University and the Universities of Mumbai and Nagpur; he held a Bachelor's and Master's degrees in law.

Rao was an active freedom-fighter during India's indpendence movement, and after independence, he joined politics full time. Rao served brief stints in the cabinet (1962 - 1971) and chief ministries (1971 - 1973) for the state of Andhra Pradesh. When the Indian National Congress split in 1969, he remained loyal to Prime Minister Indira Gandhi, and stayed so during the national emergency (1974-1977). He then rose to the national level in 1972 by serving in several ministries, most significantly home, defence and foreign affairs (1980 - 1984), in the cabinets of Indira Gandhi and Rajiv Gandhi. He was the first PM from South India and Andhra Pradesh.

After the assassination of Rajiv Gandhi and the general elections of 1991, Rao was chosen to lead the Congress party, and when Congress won a plurality in parliament later that year Rao was invited to head a minority government. He was the first person outside the Nehru-Gandhi dynasty to serve as Prime Minister for five continuous years. He was also the first Prime Minister to lead a minority government for a full term (five years) and the first prime minister from southern India.

Narasimha Rao became Prime Minister in 1991. Many claimed that India's leftist economic policies had caused economic stagnation. In the early 1990's longtime leftist regimes such as USSR and China were in the process of liberalization. Rao believed India would benefit from undertaking such an economic transformation. He appointed Manmohan Singh (India's PM since 2004) as Finance Minister to accomplish his goals.

Rao provided the much needed political will and support to push economic reforms. India's economy grew by an average of 6.3% between 1991-2000, a growth rate that continues with a predicted rate of 6.7% for 2005. This growth has been claimed by some of Rao's supporters, such as the IMF, to be the result of spending cuts, deregulation, and good leadership.

Rao picked conservative BJP leader Atal Behari Vajpayee to represent India in the World Disarmament Conference. Although they were opponents, Vajpayee's hardline pro-nuclear stance was in accordance with Rao's own views. Vajpayee later became the Prime Minister. Rao suffered a heart attack on December 9, 2004 and was taken to the All India Institute of Medical Sciences, where he died 14 days later at the age of 83.